FIELD&
STREAM

THE TOTAL
FISHING
MANUAL

FIELD &
STREAM

THE TOTAL
FISHING
MANUAL

JOE CERMELE
and the Editors of
FIELD & STREAM

weldon**owen**

CONTENTS

TECHNIQUES

TACTICS

A GOOD FISHING BUDDY IS HARD TO FIND.

I don't mean a good friend you happen to take fishing now and then. Don't get me wrong: It's always great to introduce new pals to fishing, and they can be a lot of fun on the water—but a friend you take fishing is not quite the same as a fishing buddy. A fishing buddy is a special kind of friend.

A good fishing buddy is as serious a fisherman as you are, so you don't have to worry about him getting bored or stuck on the bank. It's even fine if he's more serious than you, just as long as he's not some know-it-all who questions every lure you rig. No one wants to fish with that guy.

A good fishing buddy is ready to hit the water at a moment's notice. He lends you his spare reel when you forget yours at home—again. He pitches in for gas.

A good fishing buddy can tell when you're frustrated on the water and knows when to shut up and leave you alone. He's quick to help you net a fish, even if it means leaving the pod of rising trout he had all to himself, and lets you get away with adding a couple inches when you tell a fish story.

My lifelong friends Joe and Andy are good fishing buddies. My oldest brother, Brian, is a good fishing buddy. And Joe Cermele—the author of this book—is most definitely a good fishing buddy.

I've known Cermele for as long as I've been a magazine editor. He and I first worked together at *Salt Water Sportsman* before we eventually joined *Field & Stream* right around the same time. We've fished for striped bass and bluefish in the New Jersey surf, fly-cast to wild browns on the Delaware River in upstate New York, and floated from dawn to dusk for summer smallies on Pennsylvania's Susquehanna. Every trip with Cermele is memorable: You always learn something new, you always have a blast, and you always end the day looking forward to your next day on the water with him.

But don't take my word for it. In this book, you can see just the kind of fishing buddy Cermele is. Every page contains his down-to-earth (yet unmatchable) fishing expertise, his easygoing wit, and, of course, his endless passion for everything that swims, from small pickerel to giant bluefin.

It would be a stretch to consider this book a fishing buddy, but there's no doubt that it's the perfect fishing companion.

COLIN KEARNS

Editor-in-Chief
Field & Stream

ONE OF MY FAVORITE ASPECTS OF FISHING

is that it's a constant learning process. No matter how good you are or confident you feel, fishing is a game of curveballs. Maybe a flood changes the bottom contour of your local lake, and suddenly the hole that has always held bass is now a shallow flat. It becomes your job to figure out how the fish have adapted to that change and, given this unexpected shake-up, where you need to cast a lure. What was oh so familiar is now an entirely new piece of water.

Of course, a plot twist doesn't have to come from Mother Nature. Perhaps you can do no wrong with 10- to 12-inch brown trout in your local stream, and you suddenly decide it would be really nice to catch one measuring 20 inches or better. Doing so is going to require you to examine what you already know about catching small fish—from where they live to what they eat to what time of day they bite best—and build off that knowledge when formulating a plan for targeting a true giant. You might have to trade your tried-and-true spinner for a 7-inch stickbait. You might need to be on the river just after dark instead of at noon. What it all boils down to is that being a successful angler is about your willingness to constantly evolve.

I've been blessed with the opportunity to fish all over the world with anglers from all walks of life, and while I'll never forget the fish we caught, more important to me is what I learned from them that has helped me hook up more often—or hook up to bigger fish—in my home waters. I absorb every trick, hack, or wisdom I can, because an angler's best weapon is not his rod, lure, or fly but the knowledge of how, when, and where to use them most effectively.

Since the first edition of this book hit shelves, I've traveled to many new bodies of water and fished with many new anglers. So have the other respected contributors that supply *Field & Stream* with its exceptional fishing coverage. We've evolved, and since we're in the business of making sure you're at the top fishing game at all times, we decided to update these pages with some fresh insight guaranteed to put more fish in the net, whether you prefer to cast a nightcrawler under a bobber for bluegills, work a Carolina rig for bass, strip streamers for trophy trout, or jig shoulder-crushing tuna in the deep blue sea.

JOE CERMELE

Fishing Editor

Field & Stream

TOOLS

I'VE NEVER BEEN MORE OVERWHELMED BY FISHING TACKLE

than on my friend Ross Robertson's boat. Ross is a walleye guide on Lake Erie, and I've fished with him numerous times when we have boated trophy walleye after trophy walleye while the rest of the fleet struggles. Ross's knowledge of the fishes' behavior certainly plays a role, but it's fair to say that his understanding of tackle is equally important.

Each time, there were dozens of lure boxes aboard, each meticulously labeled and organized by color and diving depth. He switched out different weights and lines as conditions changed. If he didn't like the way a lure was trolling, he could make just a few cranks of the precisely set line-counter reels or nudge the speed of the trolling motor half a mile an hour to tweak the action. The choreography made my head spin.

Conversely, Virginia catfish guide Chris Eberwien leaves the dock with hardly more than a few hooks, a handful of sinkers, and some fresh-cut shad. His technique boils down to casting and waiting, but while his approach is much simpler than walleye trolling, it doesn't mean his gear knowledge doesn't factor into his success. He once told me, "If you can't fit your thumb between the point and shank of your circle hooks, they're too small for big cats."

Whether your intention is to dunk some worms at the local lake and just see what bites or to gain a working knowledge of intricate seasonal patterns of a target species, step one is learning which gear you need to for the best chance at glory. This chapter has something for everyone with every mission, from collecting your own bait to modifying your lures to getting the best performance possible from your outboard.

1 USE THE 15 GREATEST LURES OF ALL TIME

Whether you target bass or walleyes, trout or stripers, salt- or freshwater fish, these are lures that actually work. Some are lures your granddad fished. Others have earned their reputation for productivity in more recent decades. In all cases, though, you'll find a lure that catches fish, time after time.

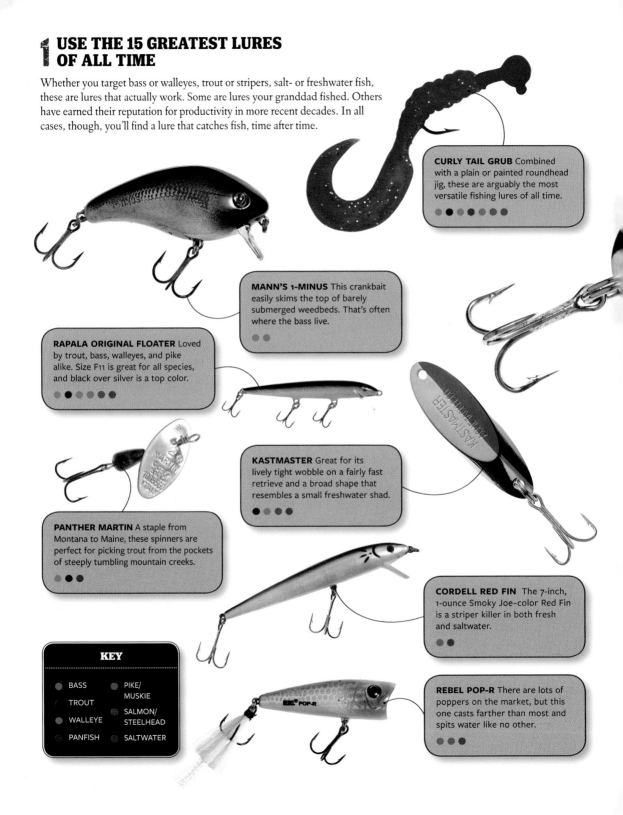

CURLY TAIL GRUB Combined with a plain or painted roundhead jig, these are arguably the most versatile fishing lures of all time.

MANN'S 1-MINUS This crankbait easily skims the top of barely submerged weedbeds. That's often where the bass live.

RAPALA ORIGINAL FLOATER Loved by trout, bass, walleyes, and pike alike. Size F11 is great for all species, and black over silver is a top color.

KASTMASTER Great for its lively tight wobble on a fairly fast retrieve and a broad shape that resembles a small freshwater shad.

PANTHER MARTIN A staple from Montana to Maine, these spinners are perfect for picking trout from the pockets of steeply tumbling mountain creeks.

CORDELL RED FIN The 7-inch, 1-ounce Smoky Joe–color Red Fin is a striper killer in both fresh and saltwater.

REBEL POP-R There are lots of poppers on the market, but this one casts farther than most and spits water like no other.

KEY

- BASS
- TROUT
- WALLEYE
- PANFISH
- PIKE/ MUSKIE
- SALMON/ STEELHEAD
- SALTWATER

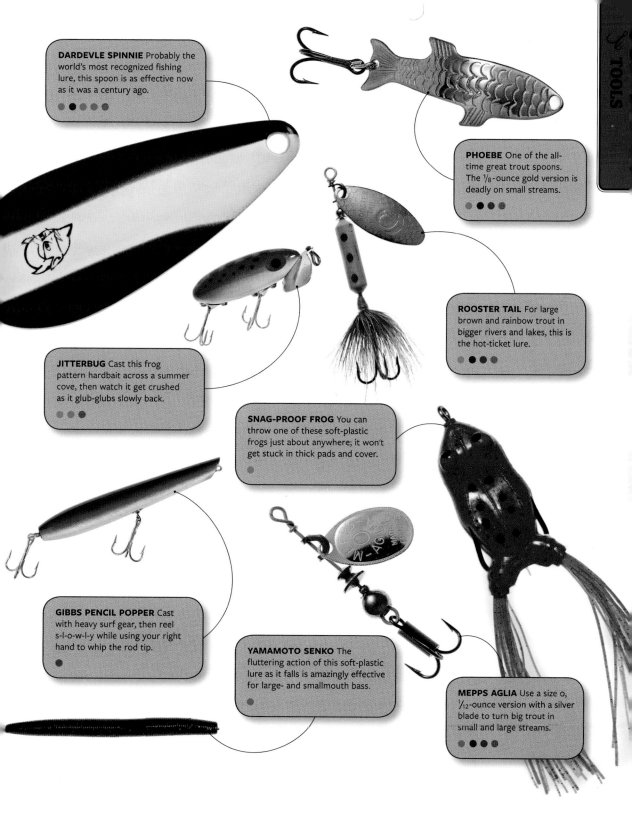

DARDEVLE SPINNIE Probably the world's most recognized fishing lure, this spoon is as effective now as it was a century ago.

PHOEBE One of the all-time great trout spoons. The 1/8-ounce gold version is deadly on small streams.

ROOSTER TAIL For large brown and rainbow trout in bigger rivers and lakes, this is the hot-ticket lure.

JITTERBUG Cast this frog pattern hardbait across a summer cove, then watch it get crushed as it glub-glubs slowly back.

SNAG-PROOF FROG You can throw one of these soft-plastic frogs just about anywhere; it won't get stuck in thick pads and cover.

GIBBS PENCIL POPPER Cast with heavy surf gear, then reel s-l-o-w-l-y while using your right hand to whip the rod tip.

YAMAMOTO SENKO The fluttering action of this soft-plastic lure as it falls is amazingly effective for large- and smallmouth bass.

MEPPS AGLIA Use a size 0, 1/12-ounce version with a silver blade to turn big trout in small and large streams.

2 BUILD A BUCKET LIST

Home waters will always be special, but I don't know many anglers that don't have a distant species or far-flung destination they dream of fishing someday. I've been lucky enough to travel far and wide in pursuit of many species, and I can say that a bucket list–worthy location or target doesn't have to require spending thousands of dollars or many hours in the air to reach. These eight locations—all varied in distance and cost—are the ones that have stuck

● TRINITY RIVER ALLIGATOR GAR
Location: *Athens, Texas*
Alligator gar get a bad rap as trash fish, but in my opinion, they're one of the most impressive gamefish in the country. Routinely breaking the 6-foot mark, and weighing in at over 100 pounds, these fish can be caught just as easily by a shore-bound angler as a boating angler. Grab a stout rod and reel, secure some carp or shad as bait, and you're in the gar game. Hold on tight after you set the hook.

● LAKE ERIE SMALLMOUTHS
Location: *Buffalo, New York*
I've fished for smallmouth bass across the country, but time and time again, eastern Lake Erie proves to be the most impressive bronzeback fishery. Though the presentations change throughout the season, what doesn't change is the size of the fish. Here, a 4-pounder is barely worth a photo, because it's only a matter of time before you hook a 6-plus-pounder. This is the only place I've ever caught a 7-pound smallmouth, and I've seen other anglers catch them multiple times.

● WHITE RIVER BROWN TROUT
Location: *Flippin, Arkansas*
The beauty of the White River is that the monster brown trout that make it so famous are as accessible to wading anglers as they are to those with boats. This makes a trip to the White easy on any budget. If your goal is to catch a brown you can measure in pounds instead of inches, you arguably have a better shot here year-round than any other place in the country.

● COLUMBIA RIVER WHITE STURGEON
Location: *The Dalles, Oregon*
When you see a 300-pound sturgeon jump completely out of the water at the end of your line, it'll stop your heart. Not only do you have to battle a fish that strong and heavy, you have to do it against the massive amount of current ripping down the Columbia. That's why sturgeon guides use tackle more commonly seen on boats chasing bluefin tuna. Your shoulders will ache, but you'll never experience another fight so powerful in freshwater.

with me most. Some are memorable for the fish themselves, but others make the list for the challenge, conditions, or potential for a great story. If you're still working on your bucket list, consider adding some of these spots in the mix.

MISSISSIPPI DELTA REDFISH
Location: *Venice, Louisiana*
Redfish live in many places throughout the country, but there's no place I'd rather chase them than in the Mississippi Delta. Not only is the southern end of Louisiana one of the most likely places to find truly giant bull reds year-round, the sheer vastness of the marsh is awe inspiring. You can fish here for a week and never see another boat.

CREE RIVER PIKE
Location: *Stony Rapids, Saskatchewan, Canada*
While there are near-countless trophy pike waters in northern Saskatchewan, the only one I've ever experienced is Cree River, and it's an experience I'll never forget. With hundreds of square miles of pristine, unpressured pike water, it's well within the realm of possibility to hook multiple 40 plus inch fish per day here. Fifty-inch fish are also not out of the questions. It's pure paradise for fly and conventional anglers alike.

MIRAMICHI RIVER ATLANTIC SALMON
Location: *Miramichi, New Brunswick, Canada*
The waters of the Miramichi are hallowed and steeped in fly-angling history. Unlike Atlantic salmon runs in the United States that have largely died off, the Miramichi plays host to healthy runs of these hard-fighting fish. They are incredibly challenging to get to eat a fly, but the work is all worth it when a fresh "bright" salmon takes to the air after the hook set.

RIO NEGRO PEACOCK BASS
Location: *Barcelos, Amazonas, Brazil*
Fishing the Amazon presents challenges. It's not the easiest place to reach, and it isn't exactly an inexpensive trip. However, watching a 15-plus-pound peacock blow up on a topwater lure just isn't a thrill you can experience in the States. I became addicted to peacocks in Florida, where a 10-pounder is considered huge. When the opportunity to chase the giants in their native waters arose, I took it, and I recommend you do the same. You won't regret it.

3 MAKE OVER LURES WITH TOOTHPASTE

An occasional cleaning with toothpaste can make your lures sparkle like new. It has a brightening agent and mild abrasives that restore lures to their original finish. Rinse them in warm water and then scrub gently with a soft-bristled toothbrush and toothpaste. This is particularly effective on spoons with a brass, copper, gold, or silver finish, which are much less attractive to fish when dull.

4 DO DIY CUSTOM LURE COLORS

Permanent-ink felt-tipped markers are great for making on-the-scene pattern repairs to plastic fishing lures and for increasing their visibility under specific light conditions. Use black or blue to draw distinct scale patterns or vivid dark-light contrasts. Red is good for adding bright gill slashes. Make glaring eyes with yellow and black. Carry a few colors in your tackle box.

5 SECURE YOUR LURE

Put a drop of superglue on your hook or jighead shank before threading on any soft-plastic lure. The instant bond prevents the lure from slipping back on the hook with repeated casting. Soft plastics that slip down on the hook quickly lose their enticing action and often must be discarded long before they are worn out.

6 TUNE A CRANKBAIT

The effectiveness of a crankbait depends primarily on how straight and deep it runs during a retrieve. Since anglers often bounce them off rocks, logs, or other bottom cover, these lures frequently get out of tune—which means they'll begin running to one side, rolling over, vibrating improperly, or simply staying too shallow. Here's how to get that crankbait into fish-catching shape:

STEP 1 With a pocketknife, scrape the paint away from each hook holder (and the hook if it's a sloppy paint job). This ensures that the trebles will swing freely from side to side, which allows maximum vibration and will prevent it rolling.

STEP 2 Replace the round split ring on the line-tie eye with an oblong one to prevent your line from sliding into the split, which can keep a crankbait from diving properly.

STEP 3 If the crankbait runs to one side, say to the right, hold the lure with the bill facing you and, with a pair of needle-nose pliers, gently rotate the line-tie eye clockwise, so that the bottom of it (the edge facing you) moves slightly to the left. Don't bend the eye; rotate it—and only a little bit. Make a short cast and retrieve quickly to see if you've corrected the problem. Repeat, if necessary, until the lure runs straight and true.

Replace

Rotate

Scrape

7 KEEP LURES FROM HANGING UP

When deep-diving lures hang up on the bottom, the front or belly treble hook is usually to blame. To avoid snags, simply remove the front treble. The remaining rear treble hook will still catch fish. For further protection, add a split shot or two 18 inches ahead of the lure. This will keep the lure in a slightly head-down position that lifts the rear hook away from snags.

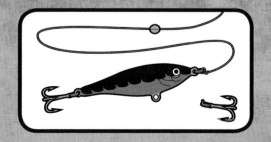

8 BUILD A BUDGET LURE

During the Great Depression, hard-up anglers crafted lures out of scrap wood and metal like this Copper Tube bait, which once filled tackle boxes across the nation and can be built on the cheap. These directions are for a bass lure, but you can make it in different sizes to catch everything from panfish to pike, and even muskies. For saltwater species, just substitute PVC pipe. Here's how to make your own.

1. Place a 2³/₄-inch section of ¹/₂-inch-diameter copper plumbing pipe in a vise. Cut the front end of the pipe at a 45-degree angle.

2. Sand each end to remove burrs that could nick fishing line.

3. Drill two ¹/₂-inch holes (top front and bottom rear), and again remove burrs.

4. At this point, the lure will sink slowly. If you you want it to sink faster, seal the back with caulk, let dry, drop in three No. 5 split shot, and caulk the front. Now it'll rattle, too.

5. Remove excess caulk and clean the lure, then mask the lower half of the body and spray black paint across the top.

6. Superglue an eye (available at hobby shops) on each side of the front. Once set, spray the lure with lacquer.

7. Add a split ring to the front and a sharp treble hook to the rear.

9 MAKE YOUR OWN TROUT SPINNERS

It's easy to make your own in-line spinners that look as good as the name brands. Here's how to do it—and save money in the process.

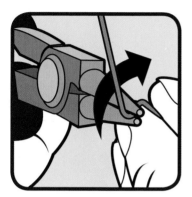

STEP 1 Start with a 6-inch length of .023-inch stainless-steel wire for a trout-size lure. (Larger spinners for pike or bass require thicker wire.) Use round-nose pliers to make a round, open loop with a tag end 2 inches long. Slide a dressed or plain treble hook into the loop.

STEP 2 Now add the extras. The components for one home-brewed spinner cost maybe 50 cents. Slip the first body component—a brass bead in this case—over both the tag end and the main wire. Then bend the tag end at a right angle above the bead and trim. This locks both the bead and hook in place.

STEP 3 Add remaining components and—in the case of a Mepps-style lure—a spinner blade mounted on a free-spinning clevis. Make sure no rough edges will impede the blade's motion. Use the pliers to form another round loop at the top of the lure. Finish with two or three wraps of wire at the base of that upper loop.

10 MOP 'EM UP

Want worm flies with max wiggle? Crappie baits with extra flutter? How about perch jigs that spring to life with the slightest twitch? Make your way to the cleaning aisle at the auto-parts or hardware store. Microfiber mop heads and washing pads cost little more than a quality bucktail at the fly shop, and you can find them in many colors. One pad provides enough soft, chunky worm tails to make more mop bugs than you could fish in a season. And the possibilities are nearly endless. I recently made some extra-thick steelhead worms, a batch of beadhead bugs for mudding carp, and some light jigs that pickerel and stocker trout have smashed with extreme prejudice. So get to making your own and go clean up on the water.

These four rigging methods will get any style of soft-plastic lure ready for action.

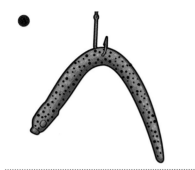

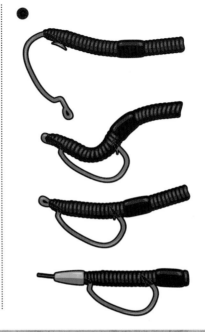

WACKY RIG (A) This killer setup for bass involves hooking slim soft-plastic bait through the middle. Both ends are left free to wiggle, and in most cases no weight is added. It's especially effective with Senkos.

TUBE RIG (B) There are several good ways to rig tubes such as the Gitzit. Most often I go with a small internal jighead. For a 3½-inch tube, use a 2/0 ⅜-ounce, insider-style jighead. Insert the hook in the tube's head and rotate it so it passes down inside the body without exiting. Continue by forcing the head of the jig into the tube, leaving only the hook eye exposed. Then work the hook point out and through the tube at the rear so the tube lies straight.

TEXAS RIG (C) Most often used with plastic worms and lizards, this rig is adaptable to other baits, like jerkbaits. Put a conical worm weight on the line first and then attach the hook. Thread the hook point about ½ inch into the worm's head and then through the worm's underside. Slide the worm up the hook shank so it just covers the hook eye. Rotate the hook until it faces upward toward the worm's body. Grab the worm right behind the hook bend, push its body slightly forward, and then bring it back down on the hook point until the point is almost but not quite all the way through the plastic. The bait should now lie straight. I use a 3/0 Gamakatsu offset-shank worm hook for a typical 6- or 7-inch worm, but any similar style is fine.

CAROLINA RIG (D) To make this common rig for bottom dredging, Texas-rig a worm or lizard but leave the hook eye exposed. Tie 18 inches of clear leader between the hook and a small barrel swivel. On your main line, thread a brass Carolina weight (or lead sinker), followed by a small red glass bead, and tie your main line to the other side of the swivel. The weight will click against the glass bead as you fish to help attract bass.

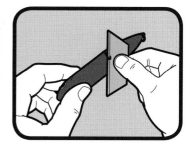

12 MAKE SPOOKS SPOOKIER

The Heddon Zara Spook, a stogie-shaped, dog-walking stickbait, has been duping bass for more than 70 years. Heddon offers several versions, but the 5-inch, ⅞-ounce Super Spook is the favorite of legendary pro bass angler Penny Berryman. Berryman performs several modifications that turn her Super Spook into a "Superb" Spook, and it would take a Brink's truck to haul all the money Berryman has won with this lure. Her tweaked lure is 4⅜ inches long and weighs about ¾ ounce—almost the size of the original Zara Spook. However, her Superb Spook is stouter, and it presents a better profile and splashes more when walked across the surface.

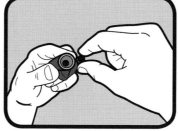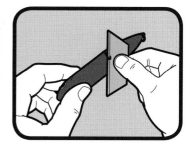

STEP 1 Remove the hooks. Mark off a ⅝-inch-wide section of the lure around the middle hook hanger. The mark on the nose side should be ¼ inch from the split-ring hanger. Saw off the marked section. Save the split ring and put it on the line eye to give the bait freedom to sashay.

STEP 2 Place two small ball bearings, six BBs, or two 8-mm glass beads inside the lure. They'll rattle and make the lure's tail sit deeper for better hookups. Apply a coat of 5-minute epoxy with a toothpick to the sawed openings on each half of the lure. Let the epoxy set.

STEP 3 Shave off the excess epoxy with a razor. Smooth the joint with 220-grit sandpaper and finish with a buffing compound. Replace the hooks with longer-shaft Gamakatsu hooks. A red front treble reduces short strikes by encouraging bass to attack the head of the bait.

13 MIX UP A CARP COCKTAIL

Fishermen over in Europe and devoted U.S. pay-lake anglers have been blending their own special carp baits and chum in the kitchen for decades. A veteran pay-lake pro handed down this secret recipe to me, and it's his go-to late-summer mix for everything from common carp to koi and buffalo carp. It's a salty-sweet cherry concoction these fish can't resist, with a little alcoholic kick on the back end.

INGREDIENTS

4 oz. Cheerwine cherry soda

1 lb. oats

1 tsp. kosher salt

3 oz. E&J Brandy

3 Tbsp. flour

STEP 1 Stir all the ingredients together in a large bowl or small bucket. If you can't find Cheerwine—a staple in the South—try Dr Pepper. To give the oats time to soak in all the flavors, blend 1 to 4 hours before fishing. I store the mix in a zip-seal bag and toss it in a cooler to keep it out of the sun.

STEP 2 When you get to your spot, throw a couple of small handfuls of the mix into the water where you'll be casting, but don't pitch it too far. Next, bait your hook with whole-kernel sweet corn, bread, dough, or a chickpea. Tightly pack the mix around the bait, forming a blob no bigger than a golf ball and no smaller than a grape. I mold a second ball around my slip sinker, too.

STEP 3 Cast gently so the bait mixture doesn't fly off. Once the rig touches down, don't move it. The oats will start to break down in the water, making a nice neat pile around your sinker and hook. This will help the carp zero in on your spread, where they will hopefully suck up your bait as the delicious aperitif loosens their inhibitions.

14 SOFT-SELL A MUSKIE

Traditional crankbaits and spinners are still the best search lures for locating widely dispersed, pressured muskies on still waters. But too often, even with the best lures, the fish only want to look. They'll follow, but then they are likely to turn away. The solution is to have a second rod rigged and handy. If you follow up with a big 8- to 10-inch soft-plastic bait, you'll often get them to take it.

SOFTEN UP Soft-plastic baits have several benefits. First, many muskies have not seen them before. Second, they can be fished vertically to already located fish. Third, muskies are more likely to hold on to these soft, squishy baits long enough for you to set the hook. Insider favorites include Reaper Tails, Monster Tubes, and giant Slug-Gos, each rigged on a ½- to 1-ounce jighead.

FLIP OUT If a muskie follows but doesn't take your search lure, quickly flip the soft bait to where you last saw the fish. Then let the lure plummet to the bottom. A lot of muskies will hit it on the fall. If not, yank it up and let it fall again.

BE VERSATILE Soft plastics are excellent baits for flat water with little structure, and they can also be used to search for muskies on bars and shoals known to hold fish, as well as on flowages with lots of likely cover.

15 GIVE NEW LIFE TO OLD BASS LURES

Every bass angler owns a magical plug or crankbait that catches fish when others can't. It's critical that you take extra care of these MVPs to keep them from losing their mojo. Tennessee bass pro Craig Powers has been duping bass for decades with his "antique" P70 Rebel Pop-Rs; his "bass body shop" restores about 2,000 lures a year. Here's how Powers says you can keep your lures from needing an overhaul.

STOP RUST BEFORE IT STARTS Corroded split rings are a major reason you end up with rusty hooks and discolored finishes. Powers replaces factory split rings with noncorrosive stainless-steel split rings. He also stores his prize baits in flat utility boxes to keep them from banging against one another, which chips the finish. Line the bottom of each slot with a piece of ½-inch-thick hard craft foam for added protection.

FRESHEN UP Remove rust stains and restore dull finishes by polishing baits with ketchup.

Not sure what to buy at the tackle shop? You can't go wrong with one of these top producers.

1. NIGHTCRAWLERS Whether you dig your own or pick up a container at the tackle shop, nightcrawlers are arguably the most universal bait used in freshwater.

2. CRAYFISH These freshwater crustaceans, best fished in rocky areas, are candy to bass, walleyes, and perch. You can use a whole live crayfish or just the tail meat.

3. FATHEAD MINNOWS These small, relatively inexpensive baitfish can be fished by themselves on a plain hook or on lead jighead for deeper presentations, as in ice fishing.

4. LEECHES Their dark color stands out in the water, and their wiggle is

hard for fish to resist. They'll catch everything from perch to smallmouths but are best known as the premier live bait for walleyes.

5. GIZZARD SHAD A live adult gizzard shad makes an excellent bait for trophy freshwater striped bass, pike, muskies, and even blue and flathead catfish.

6. SALMON EGGS Although these salmon eggs won't catch a wide variety of species, if you're after members of the trout family, they are quite tempting.

7. MEALWORMS Available in orange and red colorations, these beetle larvae have an armor-like exterior that makes

them hearty, and their bright color helps them stand out in the water.

8. WAXWORMS The caterpillar larvae of wax moths, waxworms are very tiny but very potent. They'll catch trout anywhere they live, but "waxies" shine as panfish baits.

9. CRICKETS Crickets are delicate and don't live long on the hook, but then it doesn't take long for a bluegill, trout, or crappie to slurp one up. Find them at a bait or pet shop.

10. SHINERS "Shiner" is used to refer to any silver- or gold-scaled baitfish species. Use large golden shiners for largemouth bass or pike, smaller ones for trout, crappies, and smallies.

17 HARVEST NATURE'S BAIT BOUNTY

If you have a shovel and a lawn, you've got all the worms you need. But that's not the only productive bait around. The creek you fish can supply its own—for free. (Just be sure to check bait-collection regulations in your area before heading out.)

Good bait shops carry some of these critters, but expect to pay at least $17 for a dozen hellgrammites, $5 for 12 shiners, and $3 a pound for crayfish.

HELLGRAMMITES Most fish love these nasty aquatic larvae. Pick them off the bottom of submerged rocks by hand, or stretch a seine across a fast-water section of the creek and flip rocks upstream. The current will flush the bugs into the net.

MINNOWS They're easier to catch off the main current, so approach from midstream with a seine and corral the school against the bank as the net closes. If the bait is thick and the water fairly shallow, a quick swipe with a long-handled dip net will work too.

CRAYFISH Find a stretch of slow-to-moderate current, then flip rocks and scoop up crayfish with a dip net. You can also stretch a seine across the creek and walk downstream to it while splashing and kicking rocks to spook crayfish into the mesh.

SALAMANDERS Often overlooked, this bait is like catnip to bass and big trout. Look for them under larger rocks near the water's edge. Good rocks are often dry on top but cool and moist underneath. Moss-covered rocks farther up the bank are also good.

GRUBS Find rotten logs or wood near a creek bed. Peel away the bark to expose the soft, dead wood, or dig in the dirt underneath, and you'll likely find some fat white grubs. Finding a trout or crappie that won't eat them? Impossible!

GRASSHOPPERS The best way to catch hoppers is to walk through the tall grass that often flanks a stream with a cheap butterfly net. Just skim the net across the tips of the blades; you'll have a dozen or more hoppers in a flash.

18 BUZZ A WORM

With two conductive rods, jumper cables, and a car battery, you can make nightcrawlers come crawling to you in no time. An entomologist we asked about this trick figured that the electricity hyperstimulates the worm's nervous system, causing its muscles to become hyperexcited and send the worm fleeing to the surface. Here's how to jump-start your day of fishing.

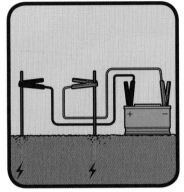

STEP 1 Find a patch of soft earth and hammer rebar or copper rods about 8 to 10 inches into the ground and 2½ to 3 feet apart. Then clamp one end of the jumper cables to each rod.

STEP 2 Wearing rubber gloves, extend the cables as far from the rods as they'll go. Attach the cables to the battery. Do not go near the rods while they're hot.

STEP 3 The payoff comes fast—in a minute or even less. Once you see worms surfacing, disconnect the cables from the battery and then from the rods. Gather bait and get fishing.

19 BECOME A WORM FARMER

Worms catch more fish than any other bait, but they are often difficult to find just when you need them most. If you plan on doing a lot of plunking this season, you may want to consider propagating your own steady supply of wigglers by setting up a worm farm. All it takes is a little know-how and a proper storage container.

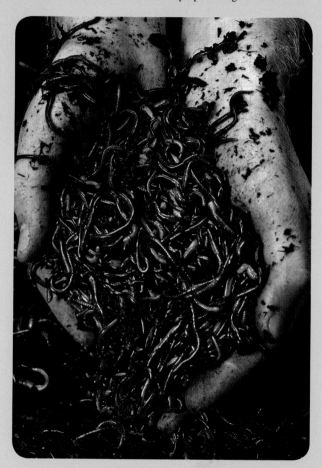

STEP 1 Drill two parallel rows of $^1/_8$-inch holes lengthwise across the lid and one row around the sides of the box a few inches below the top to allow air to circulate and moisture to disperse. Holes should be spaced 1 inch apart.

STEP 2 Install the plastic spigot alongside a bottom corner of the tub per the manufacturer's instructions. Or drill or cut a $^3/_4$-inch hole and plug it with a cork. This will be used to periodically drain the fluid that accumulates as a result of the worms' composting activity.

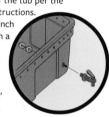

STEP 3 Cover the bottom of the tub with an inch or two of river-run gravel and top that with a layer of mesh. Fill it two-thirds full with damp shredded paper and cardboard mixed with dead leaves, two handfuls of wood chips, and two handfuls of sand or eggshells.

STEP 4 Spread the worms in the tub and cover with more damp bedding. Replace the lid and put the tub in a vibration-free spot where the temperature can be maintained between 50 and 75 degrees F.

STEP 5 Wait one week and then add a pound of mixed chopped vegetable scraps, fruit rinds, coffee grounds, used tea bags, and/or rotting leaves (no meat or animal products). Bury this mixture along with a handful of cornmeal beneath a few inches of the bedding whenever the previous supply disappears, about once a week. Add shredded paper and leaves as bedding is depleted, and sprinkle the surface with enough water to keep the bedding damp but not wet. If properly maintained, the farm should supply you with bait indefinitely.

MATERIALS Opaque 10-gallon plastic storage tub with a tight-fitting lid • Watercooler-style plastic spigot (available at hardware stores) or wine cork • Sheet of mesh screening to fit tub interior • Shredded paper and plain cardboard (nothing glossy) • Dead leaves • Wood chips • Gravel • Fine sand or ground eggshells • 1 pound bait-shop red wigglers (about 750 worms) or European nightcrawlers (about 300).

20 PICK YOUR NEXT FILLET KNIFE

Minnesota guide Tom Neustrom has filleted thousands of fresh- and saltwater fish in his 36-year career. He carefully considers handle design, blade length, and blade flex to select the perfect cutter for a given species. Follow his advice, and you'll never hack up a walleye or crappie again.

BEND TO THE BONE Nothing is more important than how a blade flexes, says Neustrom. Flex allows you to work along backbones and over ribs without unintentionally cutting either. Most of the work, he says, is done with the blade's wider half, so you typically want a knife with 15 to 20 percent flex (bend) close to the handle. The tip should flex well, too, for delicate skinning.

GRAB HOLD, SAFELY A composite or rubberized handle provides a surer grip with wet, slippery hands than does wood. What Neustrom cares about even more is the shape. A notch for your index finger or a guard on the hilt at the base of the blade helps ensure your hand doesn't slip up toward the blade. These features also improve knife control, so you'll make fewer mistakes.

Fish Length	Blade Length
5–10″	6″
10–15″	7½″
15–25″	9″
25–40″	10½″
40+″	12+″

21 PICK THE PROPER ICE-COLD CREEPER

When lakes and ponds freeze, out come tackle-shop signs advertising cute-sounding larva baits like butterworms and mousies. Many anglers assume they're all the same, grab a container of one or another, and head off to drill holes. But you'll catch more fish if you know which tiny creepy-crawler is best for your target species. Here's a breakdown of the four most common ice "worms" and how to fish them the right way.

● **SPIKE 'EM** Spikes, the pale larvae of the bluebottle fly, closely resemble maggots you might find hanging out in your garbage can. Due to their tiny size, spikes are best for catching smaller fish with smaller mouths, like perch and sunfish. Top off a Marmooska or Caty Jig with a spike or two, and you've got a lethal panfish combo.

● **GET A MOUSE** The larva of the drone fly is also known as a rat-tailed maggot—but mousie sounds better. Slightly larger than spikes, mousies secrete a white liquid when pierced that bigger perch and crappies can't resist. Thread three or four of them onto a No. 2 Swedish Pimple and jig it throughout the water column until you get a bead on the fish's holding depth.

● **BUTTER UP** The tebo worm, or butterworm, is the larva of the Chilean moth. Not native to the United States, it is sold here as both pet food and bait. While butterworms catch plenty of panfish, they are deadly for hard-water

trout. Pierce two or three on a ⅛-ounce Kastmaster spoon and jig it aggressively to lure them in, pausing occasionally to let them eat the bait.

● **WAX ON** Wax-moth caterpillars, like butterworms, are also sold as pet food. Waxworms have a soft body and are larger than spikes and mousies. They're considered an all-around favorite, as they catch everything from crappies to trout when dressed on a Swedish Pimple or a Kastmaster. But they also catch pickerel and walleyes when hooked on a Rapala Jigging Rap.

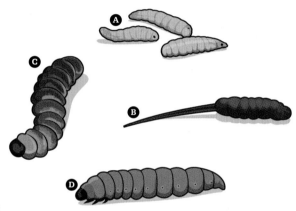

22 FEED THE KNEAD

Remember the deliciously salty taste of Play-Doh from when you were a kid? Fish love it, too. Here are three ways to put this nontoxic putty to use on a hook.

TROUT Neon Play-Doh balls make great salmon egg imitations, but you can also mold a pinch around a fresh mealworm to make it stand out in stained water.

CATFISH Cats will eat a hunk of Play-Doh mixed with garlic powder. Packing this mix around your sinker can also lure fish to traditional hook baits as the putty dissolves.

FLOUNDER Hook a minnow, then stick a ball of Play-Doh on the point, covering the barb. It keeps the livie from sliding off and amps visual appeal.

23 CATCH A BUG

Whether you call them crawdads, crawfish, or mudbugs, crayfish are one of the most lethal bass, catfish, and big-trout baits you can put on a hook. They also happen to taste great steamed with a little Cajun seasoning. Both are terrific reasons to get out and catch some craws. All you need is a set of fast hands, a piece of raw chicken, or an inexpensive trap. Here's what to do.

LIFT-AND-GRAB Though not very efficient, this method is probably the most fun. Just wade into any flowing, rocky creek, and start lifting stones to find craws underneath. Stand on the downstream side of the rock and lift toward yourself so the current flushes away the silt. Crayfish swim backward, so attack from the rear, whether using a dip net or your hands. If the latter, scoop with your palms or grab just behind the head.

TRAP Baited with shad or chicken backs, a crayfish trap funnels your quarry into a small opening to feed. Once in, they have a hard time getting out. Leave traps overnight in slow streams, in shallow still waters, or in eddies within fast streams. To keep captured craws from destroying the bait before more of their friends join the feast, slip the bait into a nylon stocking before loading the trap.

DIP Great for slow- or still-water cray fishing, dipping works exactly like the crabbing method common on the coast. Tie a raw chicken leg to a nylon cord, and dip the bait among the rocks, letting it soak for a few minutes. Crayfish will grab hold of the tough skin and stay attached if you lift the bait slowly up off the bottom. Quickly scoop them into a small dip net, but be quick; crayfish usually let go as soon as they break the surface.

24 GO DARK AND DEEP

When smallmouths scatter along rocks and weeds in their post-spawn funk, try turning to the seductive synergy of a jig-and-crawler combination. You can fish deep and cover a lot of territory, and the crawler seems to be the perfect touch for this transitional time, when the smallmouths have yet to lock on to a preferred forage. Dark jigs—black, brown, and purple—seem to match the nightcrawler's color. Try using a whole crawler and jig with a marabou feather skirt. When you get hit, drop the rod for 2 or 3 seconds before setting.

25

MAKE A DOUBLE-SIDED WORM CAN

Instead of digging down to the bottom of a coffee can to find worms, replace the metal end of the can with another plastic lid in which you've punched a dozen tiny airholes. When the worms burrow down to the bottom, simply turn the can over and open the other end.

26 SWEEP FOR 'EYES

Walleyes take a wide variety of worm rigs across their range. Whether you slowly troll or drift with the current or wind, one thing's for certain: The sinker had better be rapping the bottom. And distinguishing bottom from a bite can be tough. The trick is to ease the rod back to the strike (maybe a foot) and feel for life at the end of the tightening line. If it's there, set the hook with a sweep rather than a jerk. Once in a while you'll find yourself hooked to those slow, hearty tugs and that lovely weight of spring.

27 PICK THE BEST REEL FOR THE JOB

Anglers love to debate spinning vs. baitcasting reels. But really, it's less a matter of one being better than it is that spinning and baitcasting are two very different things. Spinning in freshwater usually means lighter line and lighter lures—usually 12-pound-test or less.

Baitcasting is typically done with heavier line and lures. The experienced angler uses both, depending on the circumstances. Going for a big brute of a muskie? Baitcasting is probably your best bet. Jigging for perch in a river? Try a spinning outfit.

BAITCASTING REEL

The spool on a baitcasting reel revolves on an axle as it pays out line. By applying thumb pressure to the revolving spool, an angler can slow and stop a cast with pinpoint precision. Baitcasting reels require skill and practice and are a favorite of bass anglers, many of whom insist the reels afford more sensitive contact with the line than spinning reels. Baitcasters get the nod from trolling fishermen, too, for the revolving spool makes it easy to pay out and take up line behind a boat and also reduces line twist.

LEVEL-WIND GUIDE Attached to a worm gear, this device moves the line back and forth across the face of the spool evenly to prevent line from getting trapped under itself.

SPOOL Holds the fishing line.

SPOOL TENSIONER A braking device to reduce spool overrun and resultant "bird's nests" line snarls.

STAR DRAG Adjusts tension on a stacked series of washers and brake linings that make up the reel's internal drag.

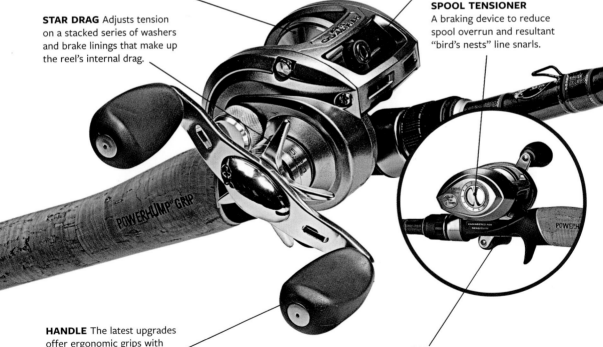

HANDLE The latest upgrades offer ergonomic grips with grooves for better control.

FREESPOOL BUTTON Allows the spool to turn freely for the cast.

REEL FOOT Slides into mounting slots of the rod's reel seat.

SPINNING REEL

Spinning reels have fixed spools that do not rotate—the line uncoils from the front of the spool, pulled by the weight of the lure. Since the cast lure doesn't need to have enough force to spin a rotating spool, spinning reels can utilize very light lures—ultralight spinning reels can handle lures as feathery as $\frac{1}{32}$ of an ounce—and backlash is rarely an issue. The downside to spinning reels: Stopping a cast isn't a straightforward task. And spinning reels are notorious for twisting line. It's best to pump the rod up and reel on the way down to minimize twist.

BAIL Serves as a line pickup device to return the line evenly on the spool after the cast.

DRAG ADJUSTMENT KNOB The drag is a system of friction washers and discs. Front-mounted drags are typically stronger than rear-mounted drags.

SPOOL Holds the fishing line. A skirted spool covers the main reel shaft like a skirt to prevent line entanglement.

GEAR HOUSING Protects the internal gears that connect the handle to the spool.

ANTI-REVERSE LEVER Prevents the reel handle from turning as line is playing out.

HANDLE Activates the gears to retrieve line. Spinning reels come in a wide range of gear ratios, which is the number of spool revolutions to the number of gear handle revolutions. High-speed retrieve reels have gear ratios in the 4:1 class or higher. Lower gear ratios support more cranking power.

28 RAID YOUR MOTEL ROOM

Everybody swipes those little bottles of shampoo and body wash, but there are other freebies and helpful hacks to be found in your basic hotel room that could improve your day on the river. The next time you check in, check out these tips.

206

SOAP STONE Don't hit the river with a dull knife. If there's a ceramic soap dish or coffee mug on the bathroom countertop, flip it over and sharpen your blade on the unglazed bottom edge. You'll leave behind some dark marks (that's the metal you're grinding off), but it's on the unseen bottom. But these aren't free souvenirs. Leave them behind for the next guy.

EAR CANAL TACKLE This idea came from an *F&S* reader: Use a foam earplug as a light-tackle bobber. Just thread the hook through the center and slide it on the line. Insert a length of coffee stirrer to make it a slip bobber. Don't see any earplugs in your room? Ask at the front desk. If you have the room by the ice machine, get an extra pair.

MUCK SACKS Most hotels will clip a few disposable drawstring laundry or dry-cleaning service bags to a hanger in the closet, and each bag fits one wet, muddy wading boot. Cinch them tight to avoid ruining everything else in your luggage in the event that you have to pack before your boots are clean or dry. Remember to unpack them as soon as you get home!

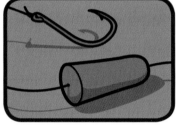

SPLASH ZONE The ice-bucket liner is a great extra layer of protection for your cellphone if you need to handle it with wet hands. Place the phone inside, flush with the corner of the bag, and fold the rest away from the screen so only a thin layer of plastic is between you and your texts.

SHOWER-PROOF Similarly, the free shower cap in your room can protect your DSLR camera from rain or splashing. Put the top part of the cap against the display screen and let the elastic edge close around the front, away from the lens. It's much more important to keep the electronics dry.

LAGER LATCH Toast your savvy repurposing by cracking a beer open on the door latch. Rest the top of the bottle cap against the base of the bar portion of the latch and close the hinged part so it catches the lip of the cap that's facing you. Press the bottle toward the door and pry off the cap.

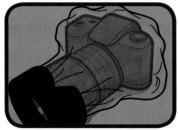

29 SLAP SOME SKIN

Long before the advent of soft plastics, striper men used the skin from dead eels to make their lures more lifelike. What many modern fishermen don't realize is that soft plastics are not a replacement for eel skins. Adding a skin to an already effective plug enhances the lure's profile and gives it a subtle, fluttering action. The process is tedious, but an eel-skin plug can be a true secret weapon. Here's how to make one.

PEEL AN EEL Make a shallow cut around the eel's body just below the pectoral fins. Loosen the skin from the meat with the tip of a knife and secure the head of the eel by holding it with a rag. Grab a flap of the skin with pliers and slowly pull it toward the tail (1), taking care to avoid tearing. Ideally, the skin will peel away without any meat attached.

But if there's some left, remove it by gently scraping with the knife. Some fishermen prefer the bluish-white color of an inverted skin; others, the natural olive of the outer skin. It's worth trying both.

SLIP SOME GRIP Remove the hooks from a needlefish, popper, or minnow plug and slide the eel skin over the lure's body (2). Wrap a piece of Dacron around the skin near the lure's head and secure with a few overhand knots. Trim as much excess eel skin above the Dacron as you can and fold the rest backward over the line. Next, make a small incision in the belly of the skin to expose the hook hanger, and reattach the hook. An eel skin should trail by only 3 or 4 inches (3); otherwise the hook will foul. After fishing, rinse the plug, toss it in a zip-seal bag, and freeze it for the next trip.

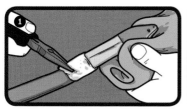  

30 TROT LIKE A PRO

Commercial trotlines will catch you a few catfish, but diehard longliners are largely do-it-yourselfers. They know how to modify their rigs to make them more efficient, easier to deploy, and less of a pain to store. These four pieces of gear are key to their success and can easily be worked into your trotlines.

CALL THE BRASS Tying the anchor directly to the trotline can make deployment and storage problematic, with a big weight always hanging and banging around. Instead, tie a large brass dog-lead clip to the tag end of your main line. Now you can run the line out weight-free, snap the anchor on when you're ready, and bombs away.

GANG UP Two hundred feet of line festooned with 30 permanent droppers invites tangles. So tie 3-inch stainless steel gang-rig clips to each dropper, which allows the hooks to be baited, attached, detached, and

stored separately. Tie off the main line, run it out, and drop your weight. Return to the start, and clip prebaited droppers at regular intervals.

REEL IT OFF Quickly spool your main line—without hooks, thanks to the gang clips—onto a plastic extension-cord reel for off-the-water storage. At the fishing hole, 250 feet of trotline unreels as fast as you can backpaddle or run the old 6-horse Johnson in reverse. It's the best $10 you'll ever spend on a piece of trotlining equipment.

START A SMEAR CAMPAIGN Considering how much catfish rely on scent to find food, keeping your hands free of unnatural odors is trotlining 101. But you can also use their sense of smell to your advantage. Rubbing Catcher Co.'s Smelly Jelly Sticky Liquid on your droppers and main line can make a big difference in the number of fish that end up in the cooler.

31 FISH TO LIVE

Survival fishing isn't as simple as the manuals suggest. That doesn't mean you shouldn't carry a survival fishing kit, but the emphasis should be on gear that fishes while you rest. First choice is a trotline, which consists of a series of hooks attached by short leaders to a main line, which is easier to handle than monofilament. Attach leaders to the main line with swivels, string them one at a time, and use overhand knots as stoppers to keep the leaders spaced. Tie one end of the main line to a branch and weight the submerged end with a rock. Hide the hooks in any natural baits you can find. Salmon eggs work really well if you can get them.

You'll also want a treble hook, which can be bent and then lashed to a stick with snare wire to make a gig or gaff. The wire also can be bent into small loops to make rod guides and wrapped at intervals along a willow switch or another limber stick. You'll find that it is much easier to fish with a cork and worm—or even to cast flies—if your rod is equipped with guides so that you can control the line with your hand.

32 PERFORM EMERGENCY GUIDE REPAIRS

A broken guide shouldn't be the end of a perfectly fine rod, or a great fishing trip. For strength, durability, and speed, nothing beats a strip of shrink-wrap to attach a new guide. In the fall, local marinas or boatyards have scraps from winterizing that you can pick up for free, and you can buy an assortment of guides at local tackle shops. Make a repair kit and keep it in your boat.

STEP 1 Cut a triangular piece of shrink-wrap long enough to wrap three times around your rod. The width of the base should extend beyond the foot of the guide.

STEP 2 Cut off the threads and foot of the broken guide with a razor.

STEP 3 Select an appropriate-size replacement.

STEP 4 Tape the new guide to the rod blank.

STEP 5 Wrap one foot with shrink-wrap.

STEP 6 Heat with a lighter, but be careful not to get the flame too close or you risk melting the shrink wrap.

STEP 7 Repeat steps 1 through 6 on the second guide foot.

33 LET THE ROD DO THE WORK

Spinfishermen and baitcasters can throw a line with greater distance and accuracy by leaving half a rod's length of line hanging from the rod tip when casting. This extra length causes the rod tip to flex deeper when the cast is made, generating more power from the rod with less effort from the wrist and arm. The reduced physical exertion permits better hand-eye coordination.

34 HAVE A CANE-DO ATTITUDE

You could use one of those fancy side-scan sonar depthfinders with the new underwater fish-eye orthographic readouts. Or you could go cut a switch of bamboo and do a little cane-pole fishing. If you choose the latter, a decent cane pole is as close as the nearest stand of bamboo. Ordinary backyard bamboo works just fine for panfish, bass, and small catfish. Make a cane pole our way, with the line anchored to the pole along its entire length, and you'll be able to land anything that doesn't pull you into the pond first.

STEP 1 Cut a straight piece of cane about 10 feet long. Trim the leaf stems as close as possible. Saw through the fat end at the bottom of a joint so the butt end will have a closed cap. Smooth the rough edges with sandpaper.

STEP 2 Tie a string to the slender tip and suspend the cane as it dries to a tan color. (This could take several weeks.) Straighten out a curved pole by weighting it with a brick.

STEP 3 Using an arbor knot, attach 20-pound line a few inches above the place where you'll want to hold the rod. Lay the line along the length of the pole and whip-finish the running line to the rod with old fly line at two spots—a few feet apart—in the middle of the rod and at the tip. (You're doing this so that, if the rod tip breaks, the line will remain attached to the pole.) Attach a 2-foot monofilament leader. Total length of the line from the tip of the rod should be about 14 to 16 feet. Finish with a slip bobber, split shot, and a long-shank hook for easy removal.

35 KNOW YOUR: BLUEGILL

Most anglers cut their teeth as kids chasing these easy-to-catch scrappers at the neighborhood pond or creek. Bluegills will eat anything from a fresh, lively cricket to a ball of stale white bread on a hook. Don't want to use bait? Any little fly, small spinner, soft-plastic grub jig, or tiny crankbait will do. But these aggressive fish aren't all child's play; serious grown-up anglers invest a lot of time hunting the biggest of the big in lakes and reservoirs across the country, as bluegills can break 2 pounds and are excellent on the table. The current world-record bluegill weighed in at an amazing 4 pounds, 12 ounces. If it's jumbo fish you're after, start a search around weedbeds, humps, and brush piles in 5 to 10 feet of water. If you just want to catch a whole mess and don't care about size, find the local public dock, cast a worm under a bobber, and start having fun.

36 PUT ON THE BRAKES

When it comes to setting the drag, lots of fishermen don't have a clue. The general rule for monofilament lines is that your drag setting should be about one-third of your line's breaking strength. Say you're fishing with 12-pound-test mono. That means you should tighten your reel's drag until it takes 4 pounds of force to take line from the reel. You can play with a drag knob and tug on the line while guessing at the setting, but it's far better to actually measure it. Try a simple 20-pound spring scale hooked to a line loop at the reel.

There are times when you need a tighter drag setting, but that applies only to comparatively heavy tackle. Some hardcore bass anglers lock down their drags when fishing thick cover—both to get a solid hookset and to haul big fish out of the weeds. In testing different freshwater baitcasting reels by tightening the star-drag knobs as hard as possible by hand, I found that they actually don't lock down at all. I could pull line from the reel in most cases with 8 to 10 pounds of force. With lighter lines, you'll need to back off the drag a bit or risk disaster. Also, be sure to set your drag based not on the line strength alone, but on the weakest link between the reel and your lure or bait, such as a knot.

37 STAY RUST-FREE

It doesn't take much moisture in your tackle boxes and bags to turn your tools, hooks, and terminal tackle into a pile of rust. Luckily, you never need to worry about it, thanks to modern technology at a reasonable price. Flambeau's Zerust tray dividers and capsules emit a harmless, odorless vapor that forms a protective barrier around your tackle. Change out your old dividers for Zerust dividers, or drop a few capsules in your bags, and you'll fish rust-free for years.

38 FEATHER A SPINNING REEL 50 FEET

An open-face spinning reel may not have a baitcaster's reputation for minute-of-angle accuracy, but you can still cast lures into tight spots from a decent distance with these popular rigs. The secret is to feather the outgoing line against the lip of the spool, much as you slow the revolution of a baitcasting spool with your thumb. It feels a little goofy at first, especially since you have to cast with both hands on the reel. But then you get used to the technique, and you start dropping lures into lily-pad openings the size of a cheeseburger bun, and you'll remember that disentangling your spinnerbaits from low bushes felt a lot goofier. Here's the drill for right-handed casters:

WIND UP Start with the reel handle pointing up (A).

BAIL OUT Place your left hand under the handle and cup the spool in your palm (B). Open the bail with your left thumb or the fingers of your right hand. With your left hand, reach around the bottom of the spool, and extend your left index finger.

HOLD THE LINE Trap the outgoing line against the spool rim with the tip of your left index finger (C).

Now comes the goofy part: Make a standard cast while keeping the outgoing line pressed against the spool rim. Your left hand will travel with the spinning reel. Hold the line with your left index finger.

CONTROL THE CAST Release the line to send the lure toward the target. Use slight finger pressure against the spool lip to slow the line (D) and then stop the lure at the precise moment when your lure is in the zone you want to hit.

39 OVERHAUL YOUR REEL IN 15 MINUTES

Think of your reel like your car's engine. Run it hard year after year without proper maintenance, and it won't be long before it seizes. This quick procedure is like an oil change for your baitcaster or spinning reel. Do it before the season, and you'll crank in fish all summer long.

STEP 1 Remove your old line (even if it's new) and recycle it.

STEP 2 Unscrew the drag cap and remove the spool. Then take off the handle cap and unscrew the winding handle in a clockwise direction. Lay the parts out on a clean work space in the same order in which you have dismantled them.

STEP 3 Rinse the entire reel with hot water to remove any sand or grit. Once it's completely dry, spray a nonflammable solvent (gun solvents work well) on metal parts to remove the dirty grease and oil. Let it dry and then wipe the reel with a clean cloth.

STEP 4 Put one drop of oil in all holes, the shaft, and exposed bearings. Then dab threaded surfaces and gears with grease. Only apply reel-approved products. Don't use WD-40, which leaves a hard-to-remove finish when heated. Less is best with oil and grease. Extra lubricant can slow the reel down. Reassemble, spool new line, and go fish.

CHARACTERISTIC	NYLON	VS	ADVANTAGE
LONGEVITY	Deteriorates in UV light (sunlight)	Not affected by UV	Fluorocarbon lasts longer
WATER ABSORPTION	Absorbs water and weakens slightly	Does not absorb water	Fluorocarbon is stronger when wet
DENSITY	Close to that of water	About 60% denser than nylon; sinks readily	Nylon can be made to float or sink in fishing
COLD WEATHER	Becomes stiffer	Unaffected by temperature extremes	Fluorocarbon is a good ice-fishing line
KNOT STRENGTH	Moderate to high	Moderate to high	A draw; depends on knot type
ABRASION RESISTANCE	Moderate to low	High	Fluorocarbon is best in heavy cover
PRICE	Low to moderate	High	Nylon is more affordable

41 LEAD THE WAY

In most circumstances, clear fluorocarbon line is less visible to fish than nylon monofilament of the same size. (It is not completely invisible underwater despite what you might have heard.) If you're after leader-shy fish such as winter steelhead in low, clear water or sharp-eyed false albacore in the salt, using fluorocarbon line makes perfect sense. Some kind of low-visibility fluorocarbon leader is also a good idea for trout, bass, and other fish made wary by fishing pressure. Abrasion resistance is also a huge plus. When these lines get nicked or scratched from being dragged across structure by a heavy fish, they are much less likely to break than comparable nylons. You have lots of knot options for making leaders. I usually use a four-turn surgeon's knot to attach a fluorocarbon flyfishing tippet, for example, and back-to-back Uni knots with heavier lines.

42 MATCH YOUR FLUOROCARBON TO YOUR FISH

If you're fishing for largemouths in thick cover or stripers around underwater rocks, a fluorocarbon leader will fend off abrasion. When I'm nymphing for trout, I often add 3 feet of 5X or 6X fluorocarbon tippet to a standard tapered-nylon leader. The nylon butt stays at or near the surface to make control of the drifting fly easier, while the fluorocarbon tippet sinks readily with the nymph and is less evident to fussy trout. I don't use fluoro tippet to fish dries because it will sink and pull the fly underwater. For bass and walleye fishing with spinning or baitcasting gear, I like superbraid lines because of the acute sensitivity their low stretch affords. All superbraids are opaque and require the addition of a clear leader, for which fluorocarbon is almost perfect. Attaching 3 feet of 12- to 20-pound clear fluorocarbon to 50-pound superbraid gives me a more abrasion-resistant leader that fish will have a tough time seeing. The only flaw in the equation comes when I am working surface lures, for which fast-sinking fluoro is a disaster.

43 TIE A PALOMAR KNOT

This is the most widely useful—and the easiest—of all terminal knots used in freshwater and inshore saltwater fishing. It works well with both nylon monofilaments and superbraids.

STEP 1 Extend about 6 inches of doubled line through the eye of the hook or lure.

STEP 2 Tie a loose overhand knot using the doubled line on either side of the eye. The hook itself will hang from the middle of the knot.

STEP 3 Pass the loop over the hook. Wet the knot with saliva and then pull on the doubled line (but not the loop) to tighten. Trim closely.

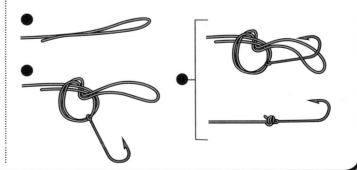

444 GET INTO HEAVY METAL

BULLET SINKER	EGG SINKER	DROP SINKER	WALKING SINKER	PINCH-ON SINKER
MODELS: Lead, brass, steel, or tungsten; painted, free-sliding, or self-pegging. **USES:** Casting or pitching Texas-rigged soft plastics. **RIGGING:** Run the line through the sinker's pointed end and tie it to a worm hook. **TIPS:** Use the lightest sinker needed to maintain bottom contact or to penetrate cover. Let the sinker slide free for open water; peg it to the head of the bait amid thick cover.	**MODELS:** Lead, steel, or bismuth. **USES:** Carolina-rigging soft-plastic bass lures; drifting and bottom-fishing live bait for everything from trout to stripers. **RIGGING:** Run line through the sinker and tie it to a two-way swivel. Attach a leader and hook to the other side. **TIPS:** This allows a fish to run with the bait without feeling the weight. Over a snag-filled bottom, pinch a split shot on the line in place of the swivel.	**MODELS:** Lead, steel, or tungsten; round, teardrop, or cylindrical. **USES:** Fishing small soft plastics in deep water. **RIGGING:** Tie a drop-shot hook to the line with a Palomar, leaving a long tag line to attach the sinker. **TIPS:** After the sinker touches down, gently pull the line taut without moving the sinker. Then drop the rod tip and let the lure free-fall slowly to the bottom.	**MODELS:** Lead or steel; Lindy-style or banana-shaped (bottom weighted). **USES:** Presenting live bait to walleyes. They're either dragged over the bottom behind a drifting boat or trolled. **RIGGING:** Thread the line through a walking sinker and tie it to a swivel. To the other side, tie a 3- to 6-foot 6-pound-test leader with a live-bait hook. **TIPS:** Banana-type models are more resistant to snags.	**MODELS:** Lead or tin; round, clam, bullet, or elongated. **USES:** Getting lures, flies, and bait deeper for trout, bass, catfish, and other species. They're most often used in stream and river fishing. **RIGGING:** Pinch the shot or sinker to the line above the hook or lure. **TIPS:** Pinch-on weights are best used for casting. Clam and bullet shapes are more snag resistant.

445 TAKE SOME PUNISHMENT

Looking to take heavy hitters like tarpon, muskies, tuna, or giant stripers on a popper? Opt for lures that are through-wired, as screw-in hook eyes are liable to be ripped out. Likewise, extra-heavy split rings are less likely to twist open from a brutal shot or extended fight. Finally, replace factory trebles with heavy-gauge trebles, as bent-out hooks account for a large majority of brute fish lost on topwaters.

446 GET YOUR GROOVE ON

Everything from smallmouths to pike will crush topwater walking baits—provided you can work them in a smooth cadence. If the line rides up toward the top of the line-tie eye, the nose will rise slightly during the twitch, which can make the lure jump. To fix this, use a small rounded file to create a shallow groove on the inside of the line-tie eye close to the bottom. It will prevent your line from sliding while keeping the bait's nose down on the retrieve to help you achieve a consistent walk.

47 ADJUST YOUR BOBBER TO THE FISH

BLUEGILLS When bluegills are on or near spawning beds in early spring, set your bobber to fish shallow with only 2 or 3 feet of line, holding your bait a few inches off the bottom. Later in summer, when bigger bluegills have moved to offshore bottom humps 10 to 12 feet deep, slide your bobber stop up the line to fish the same terminal gear at those depths.

TROUT For both resident stream trout and steelhead, adapt the tactic to moving water. To work a run of moderate current that's 4 feet deep, set your bobber so your worm, salmon egg, or small jig is just above the bottom as the bobber drifts with the current. Cast up and across the stream and then hold your rod high; keep as much slack line as possible out of the current to avoid drag on the bobber while following the drift with your rod. When the bobber pauses or darts underwater, set the hook.

WALLEYES Put a wriggly leech on a size 6 or 8 hook, add some small split shots, and set your slip bobber to fish at the same depth as the outside edge of a deep weedline. Ideally, a light breeze will drift both your boat and the floating bobber slowly along the edges of the vegetation, so you'll be covering lots of water with very little effort.

BASS Set your slip bobber shallow to fish a frisky 3-inch live shiner along shoreline structure. When you come to some deeper structure off a shoreline point, it takes only a few seconds to adjust your bobber stop and fish the same shiner 10 feet deeper and right on the money.

48 PLAY THE BAITING GAME

After you've made the effort to catch fresh live bait (or buying it from a gas-station vending machine), having it constantly fall off the hook can lead to a short, aggravating day of fishing. Be sure to rig your bait on the correct hook styl.

	Circle	Light Wire with Ring	Aberdeen	Bait-holder	Kahle
BASICS	Turned-in point impales fish in the corner of the mouth.	The ring on this hook lets baitfish swim freely.	Encourages bites and penetrates easily.	Two spikes on the shank of this worm dunker's fave hold long bait in place.	The large gap and turned-in point lock larger bait in place and hold fast.
BAITS	Live or dead baitfish and cutbait.	All live baitfish, from fathead minnows to shiners and herring.	Shiners hooked up through the lips or under the dorsal fin above the spine.	Red worms for panfish; crawlers for walleyes, trout, and catfish.	Crayfish, large shiners, and other live baitfish.
PRESENTATION	Bottom rigs work with dead bait and cutbait. Use a free line for live baitfish.	Any live-baitfish tactic, including bobbers, free lines, and bottom rigs.	Using a long pole, dip the Aberdeen hook and minnow combo in pools.	Any bait fishing tactic that involves frisky live bait.	Fish shiners under a bobber or on a free line.

GAIN SOME WEIGHT

The weight you choose to rig a soft-plastic bait can make that lure a killer—or a dud. Compared with yesterday's sinkers, today's models are more sophisticated and specialized than ever, so it pays to invest in a variety of them. Here are six types you need in your tackle box, so you can always sink to the bass's level.

1. BULLET WEIGHT Environmentally friendly tungsten bullet weights are smaller than equally heavy lead and louder when your Texas-rigged bait bumps cover.

2. INTERNAL TUBE WEIGHT Compared with a bullet weight, this sinker gives tubes a more natural appearance and a smaller profile. For skittish bass, both advantages can pay.

3. SPLIT SHOT Split-shot rigs are deadly for lure-shy bass. Bullet Weights Egg Shot slides over cover more easily than round split shot, reducing snags.

4. WEIGHTED HOOK A weighted hook lets you alter a bait's action.

5. CAROLINA SINKER Noisy Carolina rigs usually work better. On Lindy's Carolina Mag Weight, magnetized steel balls separate and collide with the slightest movement to draw more bass. The weight comes preassembled.

6. DROP-SHOT WEIGHT Drop-shotting excels for finessing clear-water bass. They're denser than lead and help you "feel" what's on the bottom. The narrow, line-gripping eye eliminates the need for a knot.

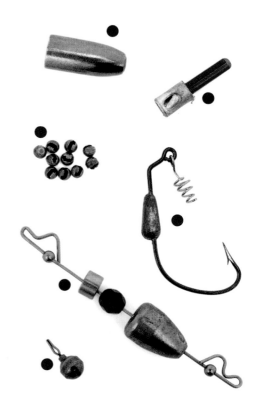

50   TIE A CLINCH KNOT

This versatile terminal knot is excellent for securing your line to a hook, lure, or swivel; it's perhaps most commonly used to fasten the leader to a fly.

Pass several inches of line through the hook or lure eye (1). Next, loosely wrap the tag end around the loop you've made (2). Wind the leader several times around the loop, then pass it through the opening just below the hook (3). Pass the leader through the far end of the loop (4), and then tighten down and trim as necessary (5). The hook itself will hang from the middle of the knot.

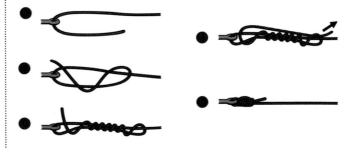

51 MAKE IT SNAPPY

Snaps that hold lures are as important as the lures themselves.

DUOLOCK SNAP Available in wide variety of sizes, duolock snaps open wide to easily slip through the eye of any lure. Just make sure you use one strong enough for the size fish you're targeting, because they can pull open if over-stressed.

COASTLOCK SNAP Typically made of heavier-gauge wire than duolock snaps, Coastlocks are staples in the saltwater world when tuna, marlin, and other big-game species are involved. Their design makes them very hard for a hard-fighting fish to pull open.

CROSS-LOK SNAP Slighlty stronger than duolocks because of their design, cross-loks—even smaller models—can handle a lot of pressure. These snaps are often found on pre-made wire leaders for bluefish or muskies.

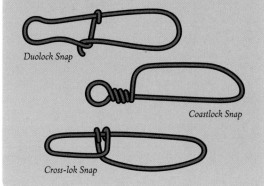

Duolock Snap

Coastlock Snap

Cross-lok Snap

52 PROPERLY SHARPEN A FISHHOOK

Have you sharpened any lure hooks lately? Has a fish pulled a split ring open on you in the last few years? If not, it's probably because razor-edged hooks and superstrong split rings have become standard on many new lures. You're going to do more harm than good by attempting to improve the new generation of chemically sharpened hooks, but less expensive versions normally need touch-ups. Here's how to do it right.

STEP 1 Hold the hook you want to sharpen by the shank between your thumb and forefinger so that the bend faces inward and the point is away from you. Grasp a metal file in your other hand.

STEP 2 Brush the left side of the point away from you and down the file in one long stroke. Give it another stroke if you desire, but file any further and you'll weaken the point.

STEP 3 Repeat the first two steps for the right side and the outside of the point.

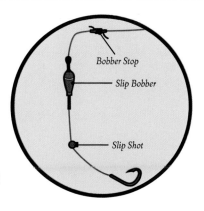

53 RIG A SLIP BOBBER

Rigging a slip bobber is a breeze. First, fasten a bobber stop on your line. Some commercial ones are on string that comes pre-knotted around a tube. Thread your line through the tube and then slide the knot off the tube and tighten. Or try what I like best: a bit of rubber tubing so small that it impedes casting very little when wound on your reel. If your slip bobber has a large hole at the top, add a small plastic bead on your line to keep the stop from sticking inside the bobber. Thread on the bobber after the bead and then tie a hook to the end of your line with two or three small split-shot sinkers spaced a few inches apart a foot or so above the hook.

Bobber Stop

Slip Bobber

Slip Shot

No one fly catches all the fish all the time. That's a fact of flyfishing, and it's why there are thousands of different patterns. Fish, ever whimsical, sometimes refuse to eat on Friday the fly they ate on Tuesday. Fishermen, ever inventive, constantly create new patterns to compensate. Despite this, some standard patterns have evolved. Tested by time, water, and fish, these are the old reliable flies you need.

BLACK GHOST This classic Maine-born streamer is killer for trout holding in fast water.

EGG FLY Not a fly so much as a ball of yarn, salmon egg patterns hook everything from stocked trout to native steelhead.

HARE'S EAR NYMPH Weighted or unweighted, these match-all bugs fool trout in any water style.

GRIFFITH'S GNAT When trout are eating super-tiny bugs, it's hard to beat this classic midge pattern.

DAVE'S HOPPER Most people are inclined to pick larger sizes to match big grasshoppers, but the smaller sizes may get you more strikes.

ZONKER A formed lead-foil underbody acts acts as a keel, which serves to keep this sexy streamer upright when stripped and twitched.

BLUEWING OLIVE These little mayflies are ubiquitous on rivers nationwide, and hatch almost year round.

BEADHEAD PRINCE NYMPH Fish this generic nymph under an indicator in fast riffles and eddies. And hang on!

BLACK WOOLLY-BUGGER
This universal streamer matches everything from leeches to baitfish and often produces when all else fails.

ELK HAIR CADDIS Simply the best caddis imitation you can find. I carry light and dark styles in sizes 12 to 20.

BREADCRUST This generic wet fly caddis imitation scores big trout solo or when swung in tandem with a small streamer.

ROYAL WULFF Split parachute wings let this classic dry ride high through fast water. Use it with a dropper nymph.

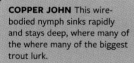

COPPER JOHN This wire-bodied nymph sinks rapidly and stays deep, where many of the where many of the biggest trout lurk.

PARACHUTE ADAMS Arguably the most versatile dry fly ever tied, the Parachute Adams's white post also makes it easy to follow on the drift.

MUDDLER MINNOW One of the best generic baitfish imitators, this streamer shines in slow or fast water.

55 TIE A FIVE-MINUTE FLY

The Woolly Bugger is the perfect pattern for a learning fly-tier. It's big, so you can see what you're doing, and it involves only a few inexpensive materials. Most important, it's a proven producer for trout, bass, and almost anything in between. The savvy angler always has at least a few Buggers in the fly box.

STEP 1 Wrap a piece of black 6/0 thread along the length of a size 10 elongated hook. Always wrap the thread away from yourself, over the top of the hook.

STEP 2 Secure one large black marabou feather at the front of the hook and wrap all the way back to the bend. You want to leave enough exposed to create a tail.

STEP 3 Connect a 2-inch piece of fine copper wire by the tail and also a strand of black chenille. Wrap the thread forward then the chenille, but leave the wire behind. Tie off the chenille with a half hitch.

STEP 4 Now tie on a saddle hackle feather (black or grizzly), palmer it back (i.e., wrap with spacing), and secure this with a couple of wraps of the wire. Trim the leftover hackle. Wrap the wire forward and tie it off with the thread. Trim the excess wire.

STEP 5 Finish the fly with a tapered thread head. Use a whip-finish knot, apply a dab of head cement, and you're done.

56 GET THE RIGHT SNIP GRIP

Mike Schmidt of Angler's Choice Flies ties roughly 15,000 bugs per year. Cranking out that many means being fast, and one of his tricks is that he saves loads of time by never putting his scissors down at the vise. Schmidt loops his scissors far back on his ring finger. This grip allows him to keep the scissor tight against his palm so he can close his hand around them, which stops them from interfering with other tools held by the thumb and forefinger. When he needs to cut, he simply slips his thumb in the other scissor arm loop, turns his hand to the side, and snips.

57 KNOW YOUR BUGS

Instead of grabbing a fly and hoping that you're close, get some inside information by seining a stream before you fish it. First wade out to where fish typically hold. Firmly grasp a small hand seine downstream of your feet on the creek bottom and turn over a dozen or so rocks. Bring up the net and look closely. Also check the surface flow in the current below if fish are actively feeding around you. You should pick up hatching insects, as well as any terrestrials that have the fish turned on. You don't need to be an entomologist to figure out what to do with what you seine.

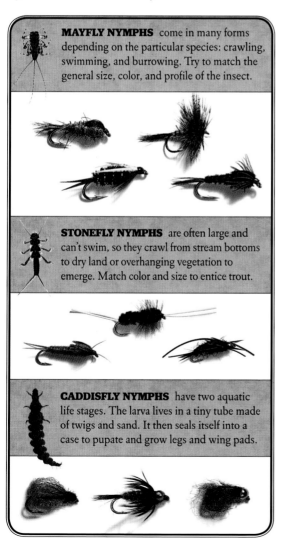

MAYFLY NYMPHS come in many forms depending on the particular species: crawling, swimming, and burrowing. Try to match the general size, color, and profile of the insect.

STONEFLY NYMPHS are often large and can't swim, so they crawl from stream bottoms to dry land or overhanging vegetation to emerge. Match color and size to entice trout.

CADDISFLY NYMPHS have two aquatic life stages. The larva lives in a tiny tube made of twigs and sand. It then seals itself into a case to pupate and grow legs and wing pads.

58 GIVE YOUR FLIES A STREAMSIDE TRIM

We've all been there: trout rising in every direction and not a fly in the box that'll draw a strike. The solution? Carry a small pair of scissors, and when trout get picky, use these three trimming tricks to make your bugs look buggier, and score more hookups.

DRY FLIES The problem with many dry flies fresh from the shop is that they have too much hackle; no mayfly or caddis I've seen has 80 legs. In hard-fished waters, a  low-floating fly tends to be a better producer, particularly in slow pools or during an evening spinner fall. In these situations, try clipping off all the hackle on the underside of the hook shank so the fly floats flush to the surface.

WET FLIES Wet flies imitate both an emerger and a drowned adult bug. The former drifts with its exoskeleton dangling; the latter often looks  bedraggled. That's why wet flies tend to catch more fish after they've been chewed up. Hurry that process by clipping the hackle unevenly, wrecking any fresh-from-the-vise symmetry. As a finishing touch, mash the fly into the mud once or twice.

NYMPHS A nymph's gills waft and pulse as the bug swims along with the current. To imitate this natural movement, use the point of your scissors to pick out some of the fur  along the side of the fly's abdomen and thorax. This gives your nymph the translucent look of the real thing, as the flared hairs add a touch of movement.

59 PRACTICE ANIMAL MAGNETISM

The long, flexible hair from a deer's tail is widely used in making bucktail jigs as well as streamer flies like the Clouser Deep Minnow. Deer body hair, meanwhile, is shorter, stiffer, and hollow. It can be spun around a hook shank with thread and trimmed to make floating bass bugs. In either case, you can have the satisfaction of catching fish with lures and flies made from your own trophy, if you happen to hunt. Here's a quick cut to get you there.

CUT AND CURE Start with a fresh deer tail cut at its base from the hide. Slice open the hide to expose the tailbone and remove the bone, starting at the base and working on the underside. Scrape away as much fat and tissue as possible. To get the right deer body hair, cut a few hide pieces about 4x4 inches in both white (belly) and brown (back or side) shades, and scrape. Coat the scraped hide with salt and allow to cure, which will take a few days.

COLORS TO DYE FOR After the hide dries, gently wash your bucktail or body-hair patches in lukewarm water, using a standard household detergent. Rinse thoroughly to get rid of grease and grit. Air-dry the natural-colored hair, unless you plan to dye it, in which case keep it wet while you ready a dye bath. Deer hair is easily colored with common fabric dyes such as Rit or Tintex. Believe it or not, one of the best dyes to use for some colors such as orange or purple is unsweetened Kool-Aid.

The most useful color for both flies and jigs is natural white; save at least one tail without dyeing it. For, say, smallmouth bass jigs, you'll probably want to dye some tails in green, brown, and orange shades so your jigs will imitate crayfish.

Trophy Bucktails:
(A) Bucktail jig; (B) Mickey fin; (C) Frankie Shiner; (D) Hot Lips saltwater jig; (E) Clouser Minnow

60 JIG YOUR BUCK

Making a bucktail jig is easy. Clamp a jighead by the hook bend in a fly-tying vise or locking pliers. Fasten some fly-tying or polyester sewing thread right behind the jighead. Separate and grab a ⅛-inch-diameter clump of white bucktail with your thumb and index finger. Cut this clump at the base of the fibers. Hold it next to the jig—hair tips to the rear—to gauge desired hair length, then trim the butts accordingly. Now hold the clump so the butts are just behind the jighead and secure the butt ends of the hair fibers to the hook shank with six to eight tight turns of thread to anchor the hairs onto the hook. Continue adding clumps of hair all the way around the jig. Finish with a few half-hitch knots or, ideally, a whip-finish knot. Finally, coat the thread wraps with hard-finish nail polish.

62 TIE A CLOUSER MINNOW

The Clouser Minnow catches trout, smallies and largemouths, and saltwater fish. And as you're about to see, it's a cinch to tie.

STEP 1 Lock a hook into the vise. Create a base with white 3/0 thread, starting near the hook eye; attach a dumbbell-weighted eye with figure-eight wraps. The eyes should be on top of the hook.

STEP 2 Dab head cement at the base of the dumbbell wraps. Place a few strands of Flashabou in front of the dumbbell and wrap back, with the Flashabou lined up on the bottom of the shank.

STEP 3 Rotate the vise and repeat with a strand of colored bucktail (chartreuse is great).

STEP 4 Secure the bucktail in front of the head and whip finish it.

61 CATCH A TROUT'S ATTENTION

Flies either imitate natural bugs or they attract the attention of fish. A new synthetic called Ice Dub, when wrapped into the body of a fly, does both. Classic nymph patterns like the Hare's Ear and Prince look just as realistic when they are tied with Ice Dub, yet they also flash and draw eyeballs—especially in low-light conditions—better than the same patterns tied with natural fur and feathers. In flyfishing, seeing is half of the believing equation for trout, and Ice Dub commands notice better than anything else.

63 MAKE IT REAL WITH RUBBER

Worm-imitating flies catch everything from panfish to trout. But instead of casting the San Juan worm pattern everyone else does, add realism to yours with a nonlubricated latex condom. Once you get past the awkward purchase, use sharp snips to cut long, thin strips out of the latex. Tie a strip to the bend of a long-shank worm hook, and dress the fly with dubbing or chenille in the color of your choice. Then tightly wrap the latex toward the head. This lets the body colors show through and mimics the sheen and squishy look of the real thing.

64 JOIN THE BASS BUG REVOLUTION

The essence of flyfishing for bass is a kind of laid-back antidote to trout fishing's match-the-hatch intensity. Bass bugs are fanciful rather than factual, full of wanton wiggles as they pop, slide, or slither among the lily pads of summer. Here's a close look at some of the best.

TOP PICKS Poppers and sliders are both essential patterns for topwater fishing, and new dense foam bodies float better and last longer than older cork versions. Soft silicone-rubber legs, meanwhile, add lifelike movement that drives bass nuts. Cup-faced poppers make lots of surface noise when twitched, stirring up lethargic fish. Sliders, on the other hand, make a slow and quiet surface wake when stripped with intermittent pauses. Not all modern bass bugs are high floating. The Polk's Dirty Rat swims with only its nose above water when retrieved—just like a mouse. There's also the Chubby Gummy Minnow, a fly caster's version of the soft-plastic jerkbaits used by conventional bass anglers. Its soft, shiny body is a great imitation of the threadfin shad that are common forage in many lakes.

FLY LURES Fly anglers are now imitating other bass lures, and the results can be terrific. They're heavy enough to sink but not so much that they rocket to the bottom. Because bass often hit while the fly is sinking, a slow drop can be a good thing. There are equivalents for soft-plastic worms, too, based on a long, flexible strip of wiggly rabbit fur. That soft fur has more bass-tempting wiggle in the water than even the softest of plastics. The fly also has a lightly weighted head to give a jiglike action when retrieved. Rabbit-fur flies do raise one critical point: Fur soaks up lots of water, and the weight becomes very difficult to cast with lighter gear. Although smaller, lighter bugs can easily be cast with trout tackle, bigger flies require a heavier line and rod. Eight- to 10-weight rods are not too big for larger bugs, and they're best coupled with a bass-taper fly line. This is not dainty stuff. When a 6-pound bass smashes your bug, those same heavier rods have enough power to keep the fish from diving back into cover. So not only will you have the fun of awesome surface strikes—you might even land the fish, too.

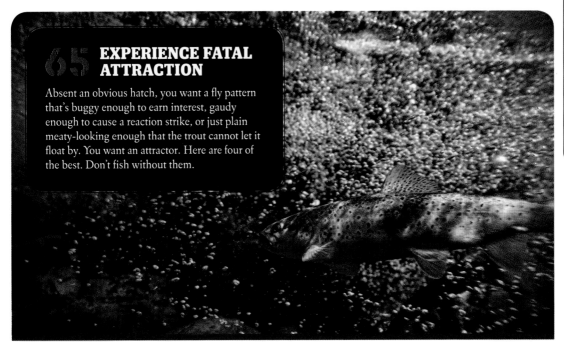

65 EXPERIENCE FATAL ATTRACTION

Absent an obvious hatch, you want a fly pattern that's buggy enough to earn interest, gaudy enough to cause a reaction strike, or just plain meaty-looking enough that the trout cannot let it float by. You want an attractor. Here are four of the best. Don't fish without them.

THE PATTERN	Rubber-Legged Stimulator	Autumn Splendor	Twenty Incher	Mercer's Lemming
WHY IT WORKS	Replicates a range of natural insects, from stoneflies to caddis to hoppers.	A brown body gives it crayfish appeal, and the rubber legs drive trout wild.	It's a Prince Nymph on steroids with soft hackle wing accents to oscillate in water.	No natural food packs more protein power than mice; a big meal for big fish.
WHEN TO FISH IT	Spring through fall, especially midsummer.	It's not a fall-only pattern. Fish it year-round.	Year-round, but it's most deadly in spring and summer.	Summer nights when big trout are on the prowl.
HOW TO WORK IT	Dead-drift the fly tight to banks. The seductive legs will do the rest.	Bang the banks, then retrieve the fly with fast, erratic strips.	Make it the lead fly on a double rig and dead-drift it through deep runs.	Make short, erratic strips toward the shore, above runs, and around cover.
TYING TWEAK	For dirty water, increase the flash with a sparkle-dubbing body.	Remove the conehead weight for softer presentations to lake fish.	Mix and match head-dubbing colors to find the real money mix.	Dab a spot of glow-in-the-dark paint on the head so you can see it at night.

GET THE INSIDE SCOOP ON FLY REELS

A spinning reel that costs $30 is going to function mechanically the same as one that costs $1,000. Fly reels, however, are different. If you're in the market for a new one, understanding the advantages and disadvantages of the two most common styles of internal gears can help you determine how much to spend and which reel is best for you. It ultimately boils down to what species of fish you intend to hook, and how hard that fish is going to fight.

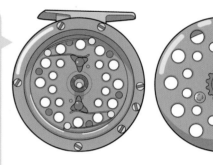

CLICK-PAWL DRAG In the early days of flyfishing, all reels featured a click-pawl drag. In a simple configuration, a gear fixed to the back side of the spool locks into triangle-shaped clickers held in place with tension on the inside of the reel frame. When the spool turns, the clickers keep up tension to stop the line from overrunning, as well as to stop the spool from moving in reverse. Some click-pawl reels feature adjustment knobs that allow the angler to change the amount of pressure on the clickers, thus making it easier to reduce tension when stripping line off to cast, and adding it when a fish is pulling against the reel. Click-pawl drags are still popular today, but they are mostly found on inexpensive reels. Click-pawls also are typically reserved for chasing smaller fish, such as stream trout and pond bass. It doesn't make much sense to spend a ton of money on a click-pawl for small-water applications, as the reel is little more than a line holder.

DISC DRAG Disc-drag fly reels are certainly more than line holders. These reels use a series of stacked washers sandwiched between plates covered in materials like cork or carbon fiber that be can compressed or decompressed via a drag adjustment knob to increase or decrease tension. Disc-drag systems factor in the amount of heat generated when a fish is spinning the drag quickly, as well as the torque applied during a hard run. It's disc-drag reels that can cost a pretty penny depending on the material used in construction. But if you're chasing salmon, steelhead, striped bass, or tuna that are going to take a lot of line off the reel, you'll want the reliability of a solid disc drag. Many disc drags are also sealed within the reel frame by a metal housing. This is particularly important to look for if the reel will be used in saltwater, as the housing keeps water out of the drag, thwarting corrosion and making sure moisture between the discs doesn't compromise the drag's performance.

67 UNDERSTAND YOUR FLY REEL

The fly reel has three basic purposes: to store line and backing, to provide a smooth drag against a running fish, and to balance your rod's weight and leverage. Even the most complex flyfishing reels are simpler than an average spinning reel, but it still behooves you to understand how to best utilize this vital piece of gear.

Flyfishing reels don't revolve during a cast, since fly anglers strip line from the reel and let it pay out during the back-and-forth motion called "false casting." In the past, fly reels have served largely as line-storage devices with simple mechanical drags. Advancing technology and an increase in interest in flyfishing for big, strong-fighting fish have led to strong drag systems that can stop fish as large as tarpon. Other recent developments include warp- and corrosion-resistant materials and finishes and larger arbors—the spindles around which the line is wrapped—that reduce line coils and help maintain consistent drag pressure.

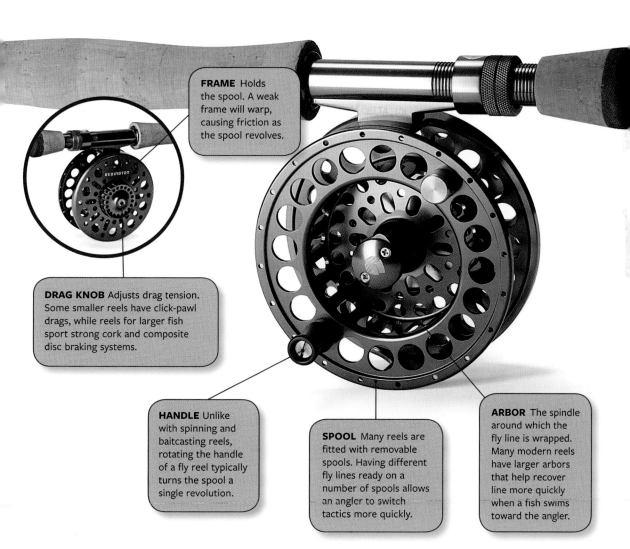

FRAME Holds the spool. A weak frame will warp, causing friction as the spool revolves.

DRAG KNOB Adjusts drag tension. Some smaller reels have click-pawl drags, while reels for larger fish sport strong cork and composite disc braking systems.

HANDLE Unlike with spinning and baitcasting reels, rotating the handle of a fly reel typically turns the spool a single revolution.

SPOOL Many reels are fitted with removable spools. Having different fly lines ready on a number of spools allows an angler to switch tactics more quickly.

ARBOR The spindle around which the fly line is wrapped. Many modern reels have larger arbors that help recover line more quickly when a fish swims toward the angler.

68 GET IN LINE

Unlike a spinning or conventional outfit where the reel and the bait's or lure's weight dictate how far you cast, when it comes to flyfishing, the reel won't gain you distance and what's tied to the end of the line doesn't matter. What you're actually casting is the line, and the fly you choose simply makes it more or less difficult to cast that line properly. The type of water, proper presentation of certain styles of fly, and the pursuit of different species sometimes call for specialty fly lines. These are the four most common; picking the right one will up your success with the long rod.

INTERMEDIATE LINE Often clear or lightly colored, intermediate line is heavier than floating line but lighter than a full-sink line. This line is designed to sink slowly, allowing you to present flies to fish holding in the middle of the water column. The coloring helps it blend into the surroundings underwater, and it is widely used by saltwater flyfishermen chasing wary species like striped bass and freshwater anglers who strip streamers in clear lakes and deeper rivers for everything from trout to smallmouth bass to muskies. Though you can use an intermediate line to present trout flies in streams, one disadvantage is that it's harder to see the line in the water, which can make detecting subtle strikes tricky.

SINK-TIP LINE Sink-tip lines offer the ease of casting of a full-floating line, but with the addition of a 5- to 12-foot tip section that sinks. These lines are popular for streamer flies that are stripped back to mimic baitfish in the water, but can also be used to fish nymphs and wet flies in deeper rivers and lakes. A sink-tip line is ideal for fishing water in the 5- to 10-foot depth range, but can work in shallower water when you need to get your fly into the zone quickly. If, say, you are floating in a drift boat and want to strip a streamer through a deep pocket, a sink-tip line will let the fly sink into the pocket fast, giving your fly maximum time in the strike zone when you have only a few seconds in which to make your presentation.

FLOATING LINE The vast majority of flyfishing situations call for a full-floating line. Whether you're presenting dry flies on a trout stream or bass bugs on a lake, floating lines cast the easiest and most accurately. Even if they need to fish a wet fly or nymph below the surface, most fly anglers aren't fishing areas deeper than 6 feet or so, or are targeting fish holding higher in the water column. The 7- to 12-foot leader you'd use with a floating line is typically long enough to allow your flies to reach the proper depth. Floating line also acts as its own strike indicator; when swinging a fly below the surface, keep an eye on the point where the fly line meets the water and watch for tics and stops. It's important to treat floating lines with dressing to keep them supple and slick for good castability. If they crack or lose their coating, they may not float as well. You can also find specialty floating lines that perform best in warm or cold water.

FULL-SINK LINE Though it's not very fun to cast, full-sink lines exist for special situations, and for the anglers who like to push the limits of flyfishing. In saltwater, a full-sink might be in order to get a fly down 20 feet or more in a hurry to a school of bluefin tuna. In freshwater, anglers use full-sink lines to get streamers to the deepest, darkest holes in lakes and rivers where monster trout and bass live. Sinking lines are generally configured by grain, which translates to weight, thus telling you how many feet or inches per second that line will sink. The drawback to a full-sink line is that it has no versatility, so while one hole in the river may call for it, you'll likely be hanging flies in the rocks all day in areas of shallower depths. But if you think there is a huge pike on the bottom in 25 feet of water at your favorite lake and you insist on catching it on the fly, a full-sink might be the only way to get a streamer in front of its face.

69 BUCK THE WIND

Don't overload your fly rod with a heavier line to make longer casts into strong wind. Instead, try going one level lighter than the rod's recommended line weight. This will underload the rod, causing it to flex less and allowing you to cast a tighter line loop. Rather than being dispersed over a wide arc, the energy of your cast will flow toward your target, extending distance.

70 MASTER SHORTER CASTS

Long casts, while impressive, are often overkill. What matters most in the real fishing world is accuracy under pressure. This exercise helps you master shorter casts—get it right and you will hook more fish, from trout rising in the river to bonefish cruising the flats. It's a great two-person game you can play in the back yard.

Set out five targets (trash-can lids, hula hoops, doormats, whatever) at 40 feet. When the caster is ready, the timekeeper calls a random target, one through five. Using a stopwatch, he or she counts four seconds. The caster must hit the target before time is called. Mix it up and then trade places.

HOW TO IMPROVE A BAD SCORE

LINE IT UP This drill makes judging distance second nature, so you focus on aiming the cast, not measuring line. Start by paying out 20 feet of line, draping 10 from the end of the rod and coiling 10 near your feet. Then hold the fly in your off hand. (Factor in a 9-foot leader between the line and the fly, and you're most of the way to 40 feet.)

BACK CAST CORRECTLY To get that slack line airborne, you'll first need to roll cast away from you, off target, and release the fly. Next, fully load the rod on the back cast. If you start by yanking backward and pulling the fly out of your hand, you'll only get yourself tangled. Strip out the remaining line as you make one false cast.

GO THUMBS UP Once the line is in the air, focus on the target. Use your thumb to direct the cast. The rod tip ultimately tells the line (and fly) where to go, and the thumb tells the rod tip what to do. When you shock the rod and make your final cast, if the target is lined up at the tip of your thumbnail, odds are your fly will land on the money.

71 STRIKE FOR LESS

Don't want to spend $75 on an indicator fly line for nymphing? You can make your own for about $5, with minimal time and effort. Buy a spool of 30-pound Sunset Amnesia shooting line (sunsetlineandtwine.com) in red. Attach a 6- to 12-inch piece of the Amnesia to the end of your fly line via a nail knot. Next, tie a perfection loop in the tag end of the Amnesia for easy leader connection. The line is super bright and has zero memory, so it won't kink or coil. When the Amnesia stutters during a drift, set the hook.

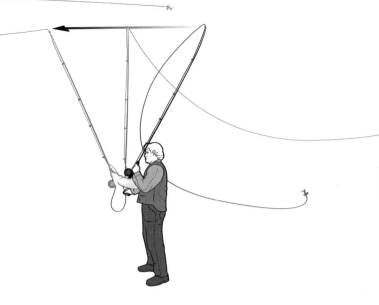

72 LOSE THE TAILING LOOP

A tailing loop occurs when the fly and leader dip below your line on the forward cast, usually causing a tangle. It is to a fly caster what a slice is to a golfer: an all-too-common problem caused by a simple mechanical flaw.

The vast majority of tailing loops are caused by overpowering or "punching" the rod on the forward stroke. It's human nature. Trout are rising; you're making your false casts and have a nice loop going. All you need is that extra 10 feet, just a little more oomph, and dang! Bunched up again. When you overpower the rod, you flex it too much and actually shorten its length in midstroke. This changes the path of the tip and the line, causing the tailing loop.

How to fix this? Try imagining that you have a tomato stuck on the end of a stick, and you want to fling that tomato into a bucket, say, 20 feet away. If you whip the stick, you'll end up splattered with red mush. But if you gradually fling the tomato off the stick, you might get it there. Same deal and same feel with the fly cast. The motion must be a gradual, controlled acceleration to an abrupt stop.

If you still have trouble developing this feel, practice in your backyard. First, tilt the rod sideways and cast from waist or chest level on a flat plane in front of you so you can watch the line. Start with short flicks of line. You should see and feel good U-shaped loops as well as bad tailing loops. Eventually the good loops will become uniform, and you'll be able to lift that cast overhead, still feeling how the line shapes. Once you get the feel for this, you'll stop tailing, your loops will get tighter, and your casts will go farther.

73 CONTROL YOUR WRIST

The No. 1 mistake novice fly casters make is going back too far on the back cast. The only tip-offs are the noises of line slapping the water or the rod tip scraping the ground behind them. This happens, more often than not, because the caster is allowing his wrist to cock too far back.

Remember this: The arm is the engine; the wrist is the steering wheel. Yes, sometimes it's "all in the wrist," but that pertains to matters of aiming the cast, not powering it. When you let your wrist power your cast, you will crash.

To correct this, get a large, thick rubber band, wrap it around your casting wrist, then insert the rod butt inside the band when casting. If the band is flexing too much, the odds are that you are breaking your wrist too far.

If you are wearing a long-sleeved shirt, tuck the rod butt inside your cuff. It will have the same effect.

74 POINT YOUR SHOTS

It's axiomatic that the fly line, and thus the fly, follows the rod tip. Taking that one step further, the rod tip follows the thumb, which is the strongest digit and the one most anglers place on top of the grip for power and direction. Lee Wulff used to cast with his index finger on top, because he felt it gave him better control. He was an exception to the rule. No matter. As long as you keep your thumb—or index finger—pointed at the target, your cast will go where you want it to.

75 KEEP FLIES IN MINT CONDITION

Aside from sparing your fishing buddies from your coffee breath, there's another reason to eat Altoids: The empty tin makes for an ideal fly box. And if one of those pals who's suffered your coffee breath before is new to flyfishing, apologize with one of these. It's the perfect beginner's fly box.

◀ **STEP 1** Clean the mint dust from the tin. Next, cut the following from a shoebox: one 3½ x ¾-inch strip to fit lengthwise inside the tin, and two 2⅛ x ¾-inch strips to fit widthwise.

▶ **STEP 2** Cut two notches halfway through the longer strip. Do the same down the center in each shorter strip. Insert the shorter strips into the longer piece at the notches.

▲ **STEP 3** Wrap the cardboard with duct tape. The tape strengthens the cardboard, protects it from water damage, and gives the grid a snugger fit inside the tin.

76 FISH THE CYCLE

In 1496, Dame Juliana Berners described fly imitations for about a dozen mayflies in her *A Treatyse of Fysshynge wyth an Angle*. And so it began. There are more than 500 species of mayflies known to North America, and no telling how many mayfly patterns. Here's how to match the fly to the mayfly life stage.

	Nymph	Emerger	Dun	Spinner
ABOUT THE PHASE	As nymphs feed and molt, they move about the stream and become dislodged in the current. Trout whack them.	Mayflies beginning to hatch rise to the surface, crawl to water's edge, or shed skin underwater. Trout go wild for them.	Young adults drift on the surface until their wings dry. Still weak, they fly to a protected area to molt a final time.	This is the final adult breeding stage. When the dying insects fall to the water, wings outstretched, trout go nuts.
FLY TO MATCH	1. Pheasant Tail Nymph 2. Copper John	3. Klinkhammer 4. Emerging Para Dun	5. Sparkle Dun 6. Comparadun	7. Angel Wing Spinner 8. Krystal Spinner
FISHING TIP	This is when mending means the most, to drift cleanly through riffles and runs.	If you see a trout head bulging out of the water, it's likely feeding on emergers.	If duns don't work on top, let them sink into the film	Use a dropper rig with a larger fly as an indicator and a small submerged spinner trailer.

77 BE A HEAD CASE

Not sure which topwater fly to fish? Here are some notes on how to pick the right foam fly for any popping situation.

CUPPED Cupped heads excel in quiet still waters. The deeper the cupped mouth, the louder the bloop it makes.

REVERSE This style is great when you want a subtler still-water presentation or need less resistance in fast water.

CREASE Crease flies sit low, combining delicate splashes with subsurface jerkbait action that fools finicky fish.

FLAT This head throws a lot of water with little resistance, making it ideal in ripping currents.

BUILD A SMALLIE WADING KIT

Wet-wading a smallie stream? Here are all the lures you'll need for a great day on the water.

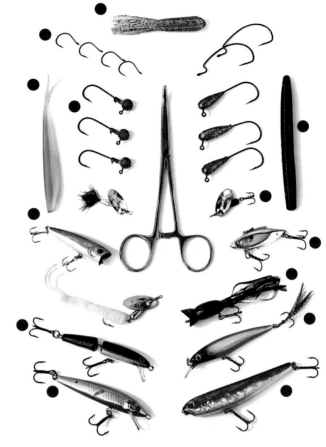

1. STRIKE KING BITSY TUBE These 2³/₄-inch baits have an unusual amount of range, imitating everything from darters to crayfish to hellgrammites. Let them tumble over the bottom, or jig them hard.

2. HOOKS Wide-gap worm hooks in size 2/0 come in handy for rigging baits weedless. I also carry some size 4 finesse hooks for wacky-rigging soft plastics—or just in case I happen to find a live crayfish scurrying around the rocks.

3. ZOOM FLUKE A Fluke shines when a subtle presentation is in order. I rig the 4-inch bait—pearl white is my preference—on a weedless hook, cast upstream of the zone, and let it flutter down with the current like a dying baitfish.

4. JIGHEADS Whether for stuffing a tube or jigging a Fluke in a deep hole, a small assortment of plain round and tube jigheads is a must-have. I generally carry ¹/₁₆- through ¹/₄-ounce weights.

5. YAMAMOTO SENKO Wacky-rig a 4-inch Senko and drift it, weightless, through seams and eddies with your rod held high and a finger on the line.

6. PANTHER MARTIN SPINNER Panther Martins get down astonishingly fast in strong current, and a single-hook model tipped with a grub kills on the swing.

7. MATZUO NANO POPPER This 2-inch bait is my go-to popper on smallmouth streams. It splashes down softly and can be worked subtly on light gear.

8. RAT-L-TRAP When you come across a deep hole and just can't turn a fish in the middle of the column, a 'Trap ripped tight to the bottom often scores.

9. ARBOGAST HULA POPPER When smallmouths get more dialed in to sipping bugs than chasing baitfish, I break out a 1³/₄-inch black Hula Popper.

10. RAPALA JOINTED ORIGINAL FLOATER Sometimes a joint can make all the difference in drawing strikes, especially in broken water, where I want the current to impart the action.

11. RAPALA X-RAP This stickbait on steroids is hands down my favorite small-stream hard bait. It shines in faster water, where a few forceful jerks make it slash violently.

12. RAPALA ORIGINAL FLOATER In slow stretches where you want to work a stickbait with a little more finesse than usual, there are few alternatives that can do better than an Original Floater.

13. CABELA'S FISHERMAN SERIES WALKING DAWG The scooped mouth on this 3¹/₂-inch walker throws a little more water than a classic Spook.

79 MAKE AN ESSENTIAL REPAIR KIT

Meet your newest fishing buddy. It's got everything you need to mend a broken rod tip, patch your leaky waders, and fix broken lures. About that backlash in your baitcaster? You're on your own.

WHAT'S INSIDE (1) lure markers; (2) reel oil; (3) superglue; (4) wader-repair kit; (5) lighter; (6) electrical tape; (7) split rings; (8) split-ring pliers; (9) hook sharpener; (10) rod wrap thread; (11) dental floss; (12) Fuji guide sets (spinning/baitcasting); (13) epoxy; (14) razor blades; (15) paper clip; (16) spare rod-tip guide; (17) shrink tubing.

80 MAKE THE ULTIMATE ICE-FISHING BUCKET

GET A BUCKET Start with a standard plastic 5-gallon bucket with a lid to haul gear and provide a seat.

ADD BUNGEE CORDS Wrapped near the rim, they secure jigging rods and tip-ups to the side of the bucket.

ORGANIZE Stash all nonmetallic items with a small tool belt fastened around the bucket. Now you've got a great place to stash things like hand warmers, tissues, plastic boxes, bobbers, and snacks.

VELCRO IT Attach a cushion or a piece of 3-inch foam to the lid. Using Velcro rather than glue allows you to remove the foam easily if it needs to be cleaned or replaced. And it will.

GET A GRIP The handle can also be a storage spot. Get a golf towel (one that comes with an attached clip) and snap it on. Tie on other items that you will use regularly, such as line clippers and a bottle opener.

GET ATTACHED To create handy holders for metal items, buy an assortment of inexpensive magnets. Attach them to the bucket's sides with an all-purpose glue, such as Gorilla Glue. Set the magnets wherever needed to keep pliers, hooks, and lures in easy-to-reach spots.

81 PICK THE MOST IMPORTANT TOOL

The tool that can save your life won't cost nearly as much as all your essential tackle. For $5 to $10, buy a pair of ice picks. These sharp spikes are mounted to handles and tethered together on a lanyard that hangs around your neck, letting the picks dangle in easy reach on either side of your chest. Should the ice break and you fall in, get to the edge of the hole, grab the picks, reach out, and jam them hard into the stable ice. Now you have a way to pull yourself out of the hole. Even if you ice fish with friends, you should always have picks around your neck. It's a cheap way to ensure you'll be ice fishing another day.

82 BEAT THE WINTER WIND

More than any other tough winter condition, New Hampshire ice fishing guide Tim Moore hates high wind. "It's my personal belief that fish respond to the noise and change in pressure created by the wind," he says. "Sound travels faster in water than in the air, so the sound made by the wind blowing across the ice goes right to the fish." Moore also believes the wind compresses the ice and puts more pressure in the water, similar to how high barometric pressure affects fish. He says during windy conditions, the fish are not going to move very far. Moore focuses his attention on basins that run 20 to 40 feet deep when hunting white perch, and on windy days, he plans on drilling a lot of holes until he finds the fish, because he knows they won't be cruising around. The real key to success, however, is a portable ice shelter. While a shelter can be cumbersome to keep moving as you look for fish, Moore says it's a necessity. He points out that with added pressure and noise in the water, bites are going to be subtle and difficult to detect. If your line is vibrating in the wind on the open lake, you're going to miss fish, and on tough, windy days, you need to make every bite count.

83 KNOW YOUR: NORTHERN PIKE

Northern pike are the perfect example of a gamefish anglers either love or hate. Fishermen after bass or trout often see pike as a nuisance that steal lures and baits, decreasing the chances for the target species to get hooked. However, that voracious attitude and willingness to attack almost anything that moves have created legions of dedicated pike nuts. These fish can grow past the 40-inch mark like their cousin the muskie, and the current world-record pike weighed 55 pounds. Pike are also not nearly as temperamental and hard to fool as muskies. Whether stocked or naturally occurring, they can be found in most reservoirs, lakes, and rivers in the northern half of the United States, with their range extending into Canada and up to Alaska. Find a weedbed or rocky ledge close to deep water and any live baitfish or stickbait will get crushed.

84 MIND YOUR MONITOR

On a party boat, the captain will let anglers know at exactly what depth fish are holding so that they can count down accordingly—and he'll keep an eye on when that holding depth changes within a drift. Small-boat anglers, however, don't always check their finders. "Guys will mark fish at 17 feet, drop lines, and stay at 17 feet for an entire drift," says walleye expert Ron Boucher. "It's critical to keep checking the monitor. Sometimes I'll find fish at 6 feet on one side of a reef and 20 on the other side, a short drift away."

85

GET BETTER SONAR RECEPTION

Don't fasten the transducer and receiver of your electronic fishfinder directly to your small jon boat. Instead, mount them on short wooden boards extending below the level of turbulence caused by the hull. Use carpenter's clamps to fasten the boards where you want them, and move this setup around to find the best reception points.

Whether you're after steelhead, trout, or stripers, coldwater wading can be miserable if you don't suit up properly. These four tricks help me focus on casting instead of on which appendages may be frostbitten.

BOOT UP Forget stocking-foot waders and opt for boot-foot waders one size larger than you'd normally wear. The thick boot shell makes a better barrier between your foot and the water, and the extra space within the boot traps warm air while you walk. A pair of good wool socks is all you need inside.

STAY TUCKED Buy your base-layer tops in tall sizes. There's nothing worse than coming untucked or having your thermal shirt ride up, creating cold spots, especially if bare skin bumps directly against the inside of your waders. If you de-wader to re-tuck, you're just going to lose all the body heat you've built up.

MIND YOUR CORE Keeping your core toasty leads to better warmth all over. I like a fleece-lined pullover above my base-layer top and a windproof jacket over the fleece. Fleece-lined pants are the best under waders; don't wear jeans. If your body is warm, a pair of fingerless gloves should keep your hands comfy.

TOAST YOURSELF If you plan to gear up streamside, you're making a big mistake. When it's cold, I put everything—including my waders—on before I leave the house. When I'm 10 minutes away, I'll crank the heat in the truck and roast myself. It gets your core warm quickly, and it's much better than freezing while dressing.

87 MAKE A GREAT MICRO-LIGHT SPINNING OUTFIT

To score bigger 'bows and browns, you'll need the right gear to reel them in. Here's some advice on what to look for next time you're in the shop.

LOSE YOUR SEAT A light trout rod with a Tennessee-style cork handle—which has no fixed reel seat—will improve sensitivity and take a bit of bulk out of your stick. When you attach the reel, anchor the foot first with 3/4-inch masking tape. Next, cover that tape with electrical tape. The masking-tape base will prevent cork damage.

REEL SMALL To keep overall weight low, you want a compact reel that will balance with the rod. Such a setup will increase accuracy and control when casting tiny lures. Look for reels classed for 1- to 4-pound-test. A small reel that can handle years of big-trout punishments shouldn't cost you more than a dinner for two on a Friday night.

USE FINE LINE Trout are notoriously line-shy. A big mistake anglers make is using line that's too heavy. This is an especially bad idea in clear streams. Use no more than 4-pound-test on a microlight outfit; you'd be wise to opt for fluorocarbon-coated monofilament.

MAKE IT NATURAL To up your catch rates, eliminate any elements from your presentation that might make your offering look less than natural. Take the time to tie directly to your lure whenever you make a change. A shiny swivel's added visibility can turn off a picky trout, and even the smallest snaps can affect the action of a tiny lure, especially in fast current. If you're using worms, dough baits, or shiners and need additional weight, opt for split shot instead of a barrel swivel and an egg sinker. Also, use the smallest shot possible that gets the bait down to the fish. The lighter lead reduces the sound of the weight knocking off rocks, keeps you from getting hung up on the bottom, and helps you detect strikes much faster.

88 KNOW YOUR: BLUE CATFISH

Head to the South and it won't be hard to find a diver who swears he's encountered a blue big enough to swallow a man in the local lake, or an angler who swears she hooked a blue so big there was no hope of winning the fight. Though man-eaters are unlikely, these fish do frequently top 100 pounds, with the world record standing at a brutish 143 pounds. Blue cats are natives of the Mississippi River drainage but have also been introduced to Eastern rivers and Southern lakes. To drop a jaw with a blue cat, you've got to catch one heavier than 40 pounds, and to do that, most anglers lean on fresh-cut shad baits or live shad. Despite popular belief that catfish love stinky, rotting baits, most blue cat aces will tell you the fresher the bait, the bigger the cat. Many catfish pros lean on heavy gear usually reserved for saltwater pursuits.

~~~

89 GRUB A SPINNER

Light in-line spinners perfectly mimic the baitfish found in smaller rivers. Here's how you can catch more with a single-hook model. Thread a small white or chartreuse curly-tailed grub onto the hook and position yourself at the head of a long run. Make a long cast downstream and let the spinner hang in the current, advancing it forward a foot or so every half minute. Even reluctant fish will often get annoyed and smack it.

90 TREAT THEM RIGHT WITH RUBBER

Studies show that nets with rubber bags are ideal for all species of gamefish. Nylon nets (especially those with knots) and mesh cloth nets have been proven to damage fins and remove a fish's protective slime coating, leaving it prone to disease and infection until the coating reforms. Rubber nets are far gentler, which is especially important with the more delicate species such as trout.

Over the last few years, rubber "ghost nets" have become very popular. They cause minimal damage to the catch and fishermen widely believe the translucent color further reduces stress, as it blends better with the water than a traditional black or green bag. As a bonus, lures, flies, and bait hooks won't tangle in a rubber net nearly as easily as they will in a cloth net.

91 WADE AFTER YOUR BASS

The biggest advantage a wading angler has is the ability to stay put and pick a stretch of water apart for the most and biggest smallmouths, as opposed to getting a few fleeting casts from a drifting boat. Just don't risk injury or worse at the mercy of swift current; if you're not comfortable reaching a spot, skip it.

Here's the most practical and efficient way to be sure you comprehensively cover stream eddies, where smallmouths like to station themselves and feed. Position yourself three-quarters of the way up the eddy closer to the head. From here, you'll be able to make four presentations with a spinner, crankbait, or jig in a single cast. Start by casting upstream of the eddy head (A) and working the lure downcurrent. After a few cranks, as your line is pulled along the eddy, work the lure straight across.

Turn the reel handle a few more times and stop, allowing the lure to swing down toward the eddy's tail (B), then retrieve straight upcurrent for the recast (C). In this manner, your lure is presented down, across, on the swing, then directly upcurrent in one sweep, and you can quickly determine which presentation the bass like best.

92 DRIFT A HELLGRAMMITE

Hellgrammites arguably catch more big smallmouths than any other bait. The trick is presenting one naturally with the current. If you drift one cross-current with a split shot, the weight often hangs. Instead, drift it unweighted.

Position yourself 30 or 40 feet upstream of your target. Face downcurrent, keep your rod low, and begin peeling line off the spool (D). An unweighted hellgrammite will be close to the bottom by the time it nears the fish. Keep feeding line so the bait won't spin or stop. If the line coming off the reel increases in speed, your hellgrammite just got picked off. Hook the hellgrammite through the collar, the rigid body section behind the head; the bait will often slide up the line after a hit, so you can reuse it several times.

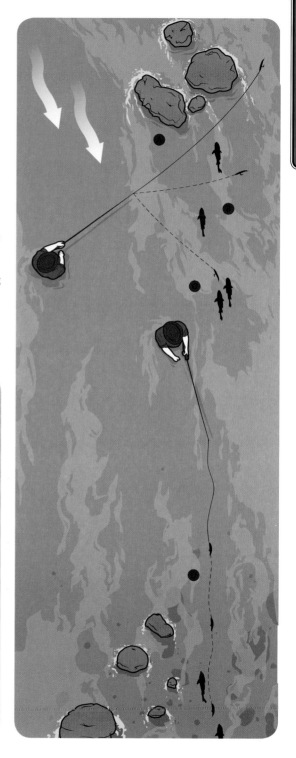

93 RELEASE YOUR ANCHOR QUICKLY

It can be difficult to land large fish from a boat anchored in strong current if you can't slip anchor quickly. To make a quick-release system, tie a loop in the anchor line and attach a buoy or plastic jug to the loop, which you will place around the bow anchor cleat. When you hook up, slip it off the cleat and toss it overboard. After you've landed the fish, retrieve the anchor and buoy.

94 KNOW YOUR: RAINBOW TROUT

Originally native to the West Coast from California to Alaska, rainbow trout are now one of the most widely stocked species in the country, available in everything from neighborhood lakes to the mountain streams of the Rockies and Appalachians. Wild rainbows are particularly prized for their brute fights and aerial acrobatics on the line. Unlike brown trout, which will sometimes lie low and be choosy about meals, rainbow trout, by and large, are more aggressive. These fish will strike streamer flies and jerkbaits with crushing blows. At the same time, stocked rainbows can be fooled with a simple garden worm or be keyed into a very specific bug hatch, gently sipping flies off the surface. Of all the places these fish live, Alaska is still considered by many to be rainbow Mecca. The trout here get fat on salmon eggs, and frequently hit the 20-pound mark in rivers like the Kenai.

95 CAST FROM A KAYAK

For easy casting from a kayak, install a movable anchor system. Mount pulleys near both ends of the craft and run a ³⁄₁₆-inch braided nylon line through them and tie the ends to a strong metal or plastic ring. Insert your anchor line and tie it off to a deck cleat. Use the pulley line to move the ring forward or back, adjusting the anchor pull-point until the kayak lies in a comfortable casting position for your target area.

96 TIE A TRUCKER'S HITCH KNOT

This versatile knot is great for tying down heavy or unwieldy loads for transporting. Use it to tie your canoe or kayak to roof racks.

STEP 1 Loosely loop your rope as shown, leaving the tail end free.

STEP 2 Feed the tail end through your anchor point and then through the loop you made in Step 1.

STEP 3 Loop the free end into a half-hitch knot.

STEP 4 Tighten all knot points down well for safety.

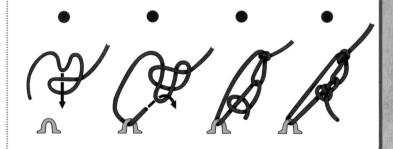

97 AVOID RIVER OBSTACLES

When two people are canoeing downstream, the best way to steer around danger is for the bow paddler to use draw strokes to the right and left. The stern paddler should make both draw and bracing strokes to pull the body of the canoe in line with the bow and hold it as the craft drifts past treacherous areas. Use forward power strokes only to avoid emergencies.

98 PACK AND PADDLE FOR POWER

To paddle a canoe into a headwind, arrange the load so that the canoe is slightly bow-heavy. The bow will sink deeper into the water, making it less likely to be blown off course. The lighter stern end will follow as the wind pushes it straight behind the bow. To run downwind in open water, reverse the load. You won't have to correct your direction as often as the wind bears on the stern.

99 TIE A CANOE TO YOUR RACKS

STEP 1 Place the boat on the rack upside down and centered fore and aft. Tightly cinch it to the racks, using one cam-buckle strap per rack. Do not crisscross tie-downs; be sure to snug your tie-down straps or ropes directly against the gunwales where they cross under the racks.

STEP 2 Tie two ropes to the bow, and the end of each rope to a bumper. Repeat for stern anchors. Do not use the same rope or strap to create one long V-shaped anchor. Pad lines where they run across a bumper edge.

STEP 3 Test by grabbing the bow and shifting hard left, right, up, and down. You should be able to rock the entire car without shifting the canoe. Do the same for the stern. Stop, test, and tighten as necessary after 10 minutes of driving.

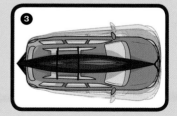

100 GET UP THE CREEK

Creek channels provide some of the best action on the nation's many reservoirs. Learning to hug these structures with your boat goes a long way toward better fishing.

Start by driving at a slow to medium idle speed in a lazy "S" pattern (A) while watching your console-mounted graph for and sharp dropoffs. As you go, toss out marker buoys to delineate the edge of the dropout you plan to fish. Once you've marked a stretch with several buoys, kill the outboard and use your trolling motor to reach the middle of the channel. Cast a diving crankbait, jig, or plastic worm perpendicular to the structure, into the adjacent shallower flat. Then work the lure back toward you, down the channel ledge, into deeper water.

If this doesn't work, reposition your boat so it's directly above the dropoff and cast parallel to it, methodically working the bait back along the channel ledge.

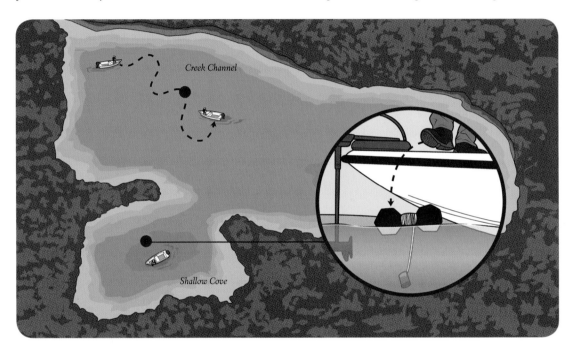

Creek Channel

Shallow Cove

101 BE SNEAKY

Most bass are caught in less than 8 feet of water. But you won't catch them there unless you can slip a big, flashy boat within casting range—without spooking them. Here's how.

RUN SILENT When you approach skinny water, turn your outboard motor off and raise it using the power trim so the skeg doesn't drag bottom. Keep part of the skeg in the water, however, so it acts as a rudder.

GET LOW Lower the trolling motor quietly. Don't drop it like an armload of bricks! Adjust the motor's shaft height so it doesn't bang into stumps and rocks.

STAY STEADY Avoid constantly hitting the on-off switch as you navigate. Instead, keep the trolling motor on a slow to medium speed. Bass will adjust to a constant noise, but an intermittent noise can spook them.

MARK YOUR SPOT As you work shallow structure, such as a stump flat, keep a marker buoy near your foot. When you hook up, immediately kick the buoy into the water (B). This way, if you drift off this spot while fighting the fish, you can get right back on it—and catch more bass.

102 GO, SPEED RACER (SAFELY)

Today's bass boat is a marvel of efficiency—incredibly fast, stable, and smooth on the water. The fastest bass boats are capable of speeds in excess of 75 mph, but it takes skill and seat time to drive them well. Here's how to pilot your rig safely from a dead stop to top speed.

First, have your boat dealer's service center adjust the steering to remove any "slop" (excessive play) in the wheel and make sure the engine height is right for your specific boat-outboard-propeller combination. Next, adjust the gear in your boat so the load is evenly distributed. Skip any of this, and you're apt to have handling problems.

Now get on a big, calm body of water away from boat traffic. Fasten your outboard's kill switch to your life jacket. Crank the engine, trim it all the way under, and when the coast is clear, accelerate. The bow will rise, then fall, as the boat gets "out of the hole" and on plane. Continue accelerating while applying power trim judiciously to lift the bow. Be very careful not to overtrim!

As you practice getting a bass boat to speed, instead of running in a straight line, try piloting the boat in a gradual, sweeping arc to the left. This counters the propeller's torque and makes balancing the boat on its pad easier.

103 PUT ON A COAT OF ARMOR

Though there are plenty of breathable jackets and bibs on the market, sometimes it's hard to beat old-school PVC when it comes to fighting the elements. Problem is, PVC rain gear can dry out and crack over time if you use it often and don't take care of it properly. To make sure my PVC jacket and bibs stay reliable when I'm taking cold fall spray over the bow, I give them a rubdown with Armor All. The same formula that keeps your dashboard shiny will keep PVC rain gear supple and hydrated. A thin coating with a soft rag is all you need to help extend the life of your rubbers—and reapply before you tuck them away for winter.

104 DIAGNOSE AND CURE A SICK MOTOR

Among the many early signs of spring is the fisherman standing at a boat dock, having just launched his boat for the first time after winter storage. All too often, he's scratching his head and wondering why in hell his outboard motor won't start. Here are some troubleshooting tips and tricks for anyone with a basic set of tools and some rudimentary tinkering skills.

SLOW TO START First, make sure your starting battery isn't dead. Next, check that the kill switch is in the "run" position. The kill switch itself might have corroded slightly over the winter. In general, corroded electrical connections are a common problem. When you find a wire terminal that's green and crusty, it's time to clean or replace it. Next, check the battery-cable connections to the engine block and starter solenoid and the fuse panel. You may have a blown fuse. Then give the rest of the boat's electrical wiring a onceover. Finally, don't make one of the most common mistakes—forgetting to open the vent on your fuel tank.

ROUGH AT IDLE While the motor is idling, turn the low-speed jet screw in and out for a bit on each carburetor to loosen any debris. See your service manual for jet-screw locations and factory settings. If this doesn't do it, there might be an ignition problem. Clean or replace spark plugs as needed. When I first start my motor, I always check to make sure there's a telltale stream of cooling water being discharged from the rear. If that stream isn't happening, the motor has to be shut down immediately before it overheats.

DEATH AT SPEED Sometimes a motor that seems to idle just fine at the dock will surge or just plain die when you're under way at midrange rpm. While running the motor in the problem rpm range, have a buddy rapidly squeeze the fuel-primer bulb a few times. If this extra shot of fuel smooths the motor out, then you've got a fuel delivery problem. It might be as simple as a partly clogged fuel filter, which can be an easy fix.

105 AVOID FOULED OUTBOARDS

Avoid contaminating your outboard's fuel system by purging the gas line before you start a motor that hasn't been run recently. Disconnect the fuel line from the engine and hold the connector over an empty container. Use a screwdriver to depress the plunger in the connector and squeeze the primer bulb repeatedly to pump out contaminated fuel that has been lying in the line.

106 SAVE GAS

Wasted fuel means less time on the water per tank and, of course, wasted money . . . gas prices don't seem to be going down any time soon.

GET CLOSE Launch close to the area you intend to fish.

SLOW DOWN Minimize running flat out. Once your boat is on plane, throttle back to 4,500 rpm or so and use power trim to reduce drag and fuel consumption.

LOSE WEIGHT Not even the pros need to bring 400 pounds of jigs and worm sinkers. So pare down your tackle. Also keep your live well plugged until you've caught a fish to avoid dragging extra water weight. Remember, a gallon of gas weighs 6 pounds, and many bass boats have fuel capacities exceeding 50 gallons. Unless you really need to, don't fill your tank beyond one-half full. Finally, weigh in your fishing buddy before each trip; if he gains any pounds, hit him with a fuel surcharge.

107 BACK YOUR TRAILER EASILY

Backing a boat trailer down a ramp isn't all that hard, but it does take practice. The key fact to keep in mind is that the trailer will always go in the opposite direction to the tow vehicle. This causes a great deal of confusion for newbies and is one of the main reasons you see guys wrestling a trailer that seems to have a mind of its own. Here's an easy way to master this maneuver:

GO SOLO Before you go anywhere near the water, practice your moves in a big, empty parking lot—the kind of place you'd go to teach your kid how to drive. Shift into reverse and then place your left hand on the bottom of the steering wheel. When you move your hand to the right (which turns the steering wheel and the front tires to the left), the trailer will move to the right (A). When you move your hand to the left . . . you guessed it. The wheel and front tires go right, the trailer moves left (B).

TAKE IT SLOW Most beginners back up too fast at first. Go slowly and, if the trailer starts to move in the wrong direction, stop. Pull up, straighten the trailer, and start again. Trying to correct a wayward trailer in motion will only make matters worse. Once you master the parking lot, you're ready for the ramp.

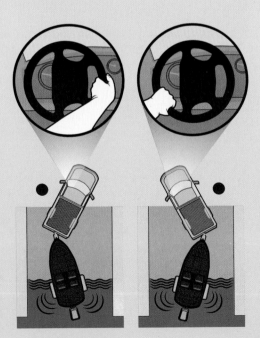

108 FREE AN EMBEDDED HOOK

Getting hooked is a rite of passage for anglers. It's going to happen eventually, and I'm not talking about a jab. I mean in past the barb. Now, anytime you get stuck with a heavy-gauge hook, or the hook is planted in your head or face, go lines in and find some professional medical attention right away. But if you've got a Woolly Bugger in your thumb, a crankbait hook in the leg, or a spinnerbait in your arm, there's no need to quit fishing. Here's how to remove the hook sans screaming and get back in the action.

STEP 1 Snip the lure or hook free of the main fishing line to get rid of any tension. If possible, detach a treble hook from its lure and clip away any of the hook points that are not stuck in your person. Next, cut a 15-inch strand of line off your reel and tie the ends together to create a loop. This is what you'll use to remove the hook.

STEP 2 Double the loop of fishing line, then pass it under the bend in the hook close to your skin. The line should be resting against the hook bend. Push down on the eye of the hook. This raises the point—better aligning it with the hole it made when entering. Now take a deep breath, because next comes the moment of truth.

STEP 3 In one quick, sharp tug, yank the line straight back. (This step is often better executed by a fishing partner.) As with a Band-Aid, the faster you pull the less it hurts, often popping right out without causing pain. If the wound is bleeding, apply pressure until it stops. Use antiseptic ointment and bandage before you get back to fishing.

109 KNOW YOUR: STEELHEAD

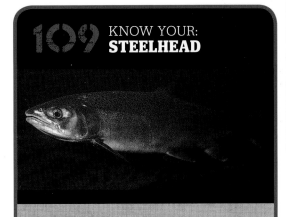

Steelhead are actually rainbow trout; what makes them different is that they live in saltwater and run back into freshwater rivers to spawn. Because they have to tough it out in the ocean and dine on more nutrient-rich saltwater forage, they grow very large and fight a whole lot harder than the average freshwater rainbow. Their name comes from their steel or chrome colorations, not found on other rainbows. True salt-running steelhead are native to the Pacific Northwest, but in the 1960s, they were also introduced to the Great Lakes. Though these fish don't make it to the ocean, every spring and fall they run up rivers and creeks that drain into lakes from New York to Michigan. Hooking a steelhead isn't all that difficult; they fall most often to natural salmon egg sacks, salmon egg flies, streamer flies swung in the current, or crankbaits. The real challenge is landing one, as they're known to rip miles of line off a reel, run into root snarls and rock piles, and do whatever they can to shake the hook. Most steelhead hooked in rivers require the angler to chase them downstream for a chance at netting.

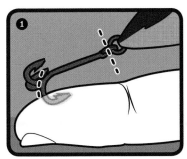

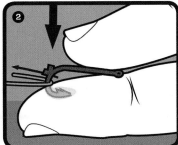

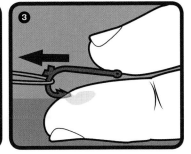

Pike can rarely resist a flashy spinnerbait pulsing overhead. But a few simple modifications can make these tried-and-true classics even more appealing to trophy-size predators, and better equipped to handle their ferocious attacks. So, if you're ready to catch bigger pike and buy fewer new lures, try these hacks.

LEAD OFF Most pre-tied commercial wire leaders aren't made for the open eye of a spinnerbait. The snap tends to slide down the lure's shaft when you cast, causing it to roll on its side during the retrieve. To thwart pike teeth and keep the bait running true, I pre-tie 18-inch lengths of 40-pound fluorocarbon directly to my spinners and then add a small barrel swivel to the tag ends. It makes lure swaps superfast.

GIVE IT A PINCH With a forest of teeth, a layer of slime, and a habit of thrashing, pike are difficult, not to mention downright dangerous, to unhook. And twisting your spinnerbait free can bend it out of tune. So make the job easier by pinching down the barb with needle-nose pliers before your first cast—which will help you drive that hook home in the first place. Jaw spreaders make unhooking even less of a hassle.

BLAZE A TRAIL Adding a soft-plastic trailer to your spinnerbait helps fill out the bait's profile and increases the amount of vibration the lure puts out. And the stronger the vibe, the more your bait mimics a struggling forage species. Also, giving pike a chunk of soft plastic to clamp down on prevents the skirt from shredding so quickly. My go-to spinnerbait trailers are twister tails, lizards, and paddle tails.

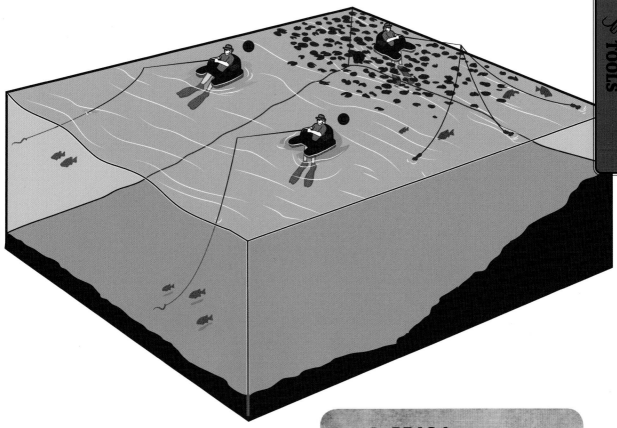

111 BELLY UP TO A BASS

Belly boats are not only cheap; they also offer an element of stealth not easily achieved in a motorized boat. You can quietly kick into hard-to-reach pad clusters and stick-strewn coves where big bass live. In addition, a belly boat lets you present lures in new ways.

Anglers on bass boats typically set up on the outside of lily-pad clusters, tossing lures into the pads and working them back to open water. With a belly boat, you can reverse that approach to hook more fish. Kick your way gently into the pads (A) just far enough to get your lure into open water with a long cast. Once you're in place, keep still and wait 10 to 15 minutes for the area to settle, as you might have spooked some fish.

Cast frog lures or buzzbaits into open water and retrieve into the pads. With frogs or poppers, be sure to stop the retrieve right on the edge of the vegetation for a moment or two to simulate forage trying to move into the cover. This tactic is particularly deadly early in the morning, when forage species begin moving, so get out before dawn breaks.

112 DRAG A WORM

The slow speed at which a belly boat moves while you kick is just right for dragging a long soft-plastic worm with a curly tail. Trolling would be too tiring to do all day, but pulling a lure as you move from spot to spot can both catch you more fish and help you find areas where bass are holding in deeper water.

Keep a 6- to 10-inch curly-tailed worm rigged with a wide-gap hook within reach. When you're ready to move, tie it on with no weight, make a long cast, then let out another 15 feet of line. As you kick, hold the rod low to the water. At maximum speed, the worm will gently flutter behind you in the middle of the water column (B). If you slow down, it will fall. If you want to probe deep structure, just stop kicking and let the lure touch down (C). When you start moving again, the worm rising up off the bottom can provoke a strike.

113 RECORD IT RIGHT

The first time I saw a GoPro for sale in a tackle shop, I knew it wouldn't be long before these tiny video cameras became nearly standard tools in the modern angler's arsenal. Spend a few minutes on YouTube, and you'll see I was right. But the average fisherman just straps one to his head and calls it a day. These three easy tricks will bring your videos up a level.

● **NET A GOOD SHOT** Everyone wants to nail that deal-closing shot. The problem is, most people put a GoPro on the landing net's handle. Most of the time, it never makes it underwater where the action is happening, because the majority of fish are netted off the surface or just below. To make sure I get the right view, I mount my camera on the hoop itself, halfway between the handle and the front rim. In this position, thanks to a GoPro's wide-angle lens, you'll see the fish both during the last leg of the fight as it comes to the net and during that final gotcha scoop from underwater.

● **CENTER YOURSELF** There's nothing inherently wrong with putting a GoPro on your head, but you move your noggin a lot more than you'd think while casting or fighting a fish. If you can keep your head locked in one spot, great. If not, your movie might conjure nausea. The center of your body moves a lot less, so mounting a GoPro to your chest produces more stable footage. Don't want to buy the expensive GoPro chest harness? Strap your head mount around your fly fishing chest pack. It works just as well and makes the camera easier to put on and take off.

● **PUT IT ON A POLE** I've stuck a GoPro on everything from rod handles to oar handles to extend my reach and capture that perfect underwater shot, and I've found that it's best to have a dedicated pole. Nothing works better in my experience than a 6-foot heavy-duty garden stake from Home Depot. It'll cost you $3, it's light, it can easily be trimmed, and the little nubs that help the stake stay firmly in the dirt also provide a surer grip for your camera mount.

114 TAKE SOME FISHING TRIP ADVICE

Twenty minutes after we launched on the Delaware River, the worst fishing guide I ever hired told me he hated his job and that I was stupid for expecting to catch muskies there in April. He failed to mention either of these fun facts when I first called him—and before he cashed my deposit check. That was seven years ago, and if I had taken the time to vet the guy first instead of trusting a business card, I might not have endured such an awkward, hopeless day. I swore I'd never make that mistake again.

The best reference for a guide or lodge is a thumbs-up from a buddy. If you don't have that, you can get a good idea of the kind of guide you'd be dealing with by spending a few hours online. Pick your species, pick your location, then digitally pick apart the area's outfitters. Here's how I run a background check.

GET SOCIAL Nowadays, a guide's social media pages are more critical marketing tools than his website, as they often give better insight into his business. Facebook allows a guide to post up-to-the-minute or daily reports. My friend and trout guide Joe Demalderis posts at least one photo to Instagram every day from the water—whether it's a shot of a client's fish, hatching bugs, or just scenery. This kind of consistency gives you an idea of how often a guide is on the water. The more he's booked, the more likely it is he's popular and reputable. Scroll back through a guide's feed and make some mental notes. If there were big gaps between posts during prime time, take warning.

CLEAR THE WEBS While many guides rely solely on social media to book trips, smart lodges and outfitters still maintain websites. If I click on one and it looks like it was built in 1995—with star-field background and GIFs of jumping fish—I'm skeptical. In my opinion, outfitters that don't care about updating don't really care too much about attracting new clients. I look for clean, modern web designs that are easy to navigate, with information that doesn't appear to have been written by a third grader. Bios of the operation's guides are important to me, too, as are quality photos of the accommodations. Video tours are even better.

FIRE AT WILL The best thing you can do with an unfamiliar outfitter or guide is ask tons of questions. Email is a good way to communicate, but the phone is better. You're potentially putting up a lot of money, which gives you the right to talk through every step of the program. No matter how small or detailed a query, it should be answered thoroughly and courteously. If it seems like you're bothering the guy when you ask how old his boat is, or about meals the lodge serves, or about what tackle you should bring, then maybe he doesn't want—or deserve—your business.

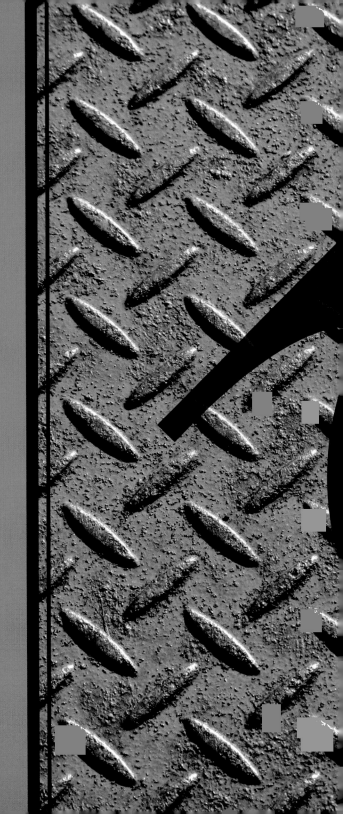

TECHNIQUES

IN MY OPINION, THE MOST GLORIOUS MOMENT IN FISHING IS

not when your catch makes it to the net, but rather when it eats. That split second when a fish commits to crushing your lure, sipping your fly, or slurping up a well-placed bait is the true victory. You've fooled the fish. You've won. This victory becomes even sweeter on the toughest days when nothing seems to be biting. You change lures. You change retrieve speeds. You tweak your colors and then all of a sudden, BAM! That's the moment that anglers live for.

If you're reading this book, I assume you know how to cast, bait your hook, and choose a lure for the fish you're chasing. The question is, do you know how to cast as effectively when the wind is gusting to 40 miles per hour? Do you know how to bait that hook for clear versus dirty water? Do you know where to stick that hook into a bait to ensure your target species gets the point when it eats? Do you know how to change the action of a lure by presenting it differently than you normally would, or how to make it effective during a time of year when you'd normally never use it?

The answers all speak to your repertoire of techniques, the expansion of which will not only make you more productive in the places you fish most often, but will also make you better prepared to break down new water you encounter. The techniques presented in this chapter are from some of the best anglers, guides, authors, and tournament fishermen in the business. They may have never wet a line at your favorite spot, but their insights will make you more effective there than ever before.

115 CRANK UP YOUR SPRING

It's springtime. You've got a tackle box full of crankbaits and a whole lake in front of you. Question is, how do you make this popular lure work best during this transitional time of year? This guide will help.

SEASON AND LOCATION KEY

○ **EARLY SPRING**
Water Temperature:
40°–55°
Time of Year: February–March in the South; March–April in the North

● **SPRING**
Water Temperature:
55°–70°
Time of Year:
March–April in the South; April–May in the North

POINTS Fan your casts to the points of creek mouths and within the first quarter of creek arms; use a balsa wood–body crank. You may need spinning tackle to cast it, but it's worth it. Plastic lures may cast farther, but nothing beats the sexy wobble of a balsa wood crankbait, especially early in the season.

GRAVEL AND ROCK Run a ¹/₂-ounce lipless rattle bait over gravel and rock bottoms near the mouths of creeks. Make regular bottom contact. Sunny banks are generally more productive, as rocks trap heat.

BANKS AND RIPRAP Sweep 45-degree-angle banks and riprap with a suspending crankbait, which will hover in place when you pause the retrieve. This gives sluggish bass ample time to respond. Any time you come across shallow brush, stumps, or wood, switch to a ³/₈-ounce diving crank and bounce it off the structure.

SUBMERGED GRASS Work over the deep edges of submerged grassbeds, which are just now beginning to grow, with a shallow-diving crankbait or lipless crank. In many lakes, grass is present down to 10 to 12 feet, though in

especially clear lakes it could be 18 feet or deeper. Tick the top of the vegetation with your lure to mimic baitfish fleeing the cover; this can trigger reluctant bass to attack.

⑤ **WOOD COVER** Crank a tight-wiggling ¹/₄-ounce bait in orange and a wide-wobbling ¹/₃-ounce in pearl red eye over wood cover. This includes stumps lining creek channels that cut through flats, brush, and windfalls along the bank and next to boat docks.

⑥ **GRAVEL AND CLAY BANKS** Pull bass from chunk-rock, gravel, riprap, and red-clay banks with a

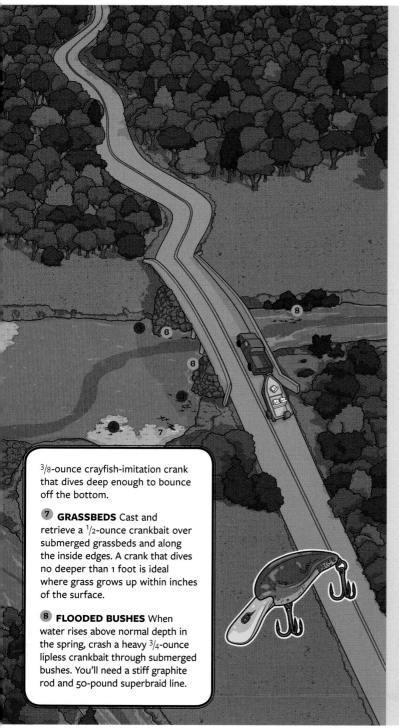

116

BUILD A BETTER TUBE RIG

One of the best bass baits you can fish in grass and other cover is a Texas-rigged tube with a bullet weight. One major drawback: The weight, or the cover, can push the fat-headed tube down the hook's shank, where it causes frequent snagging and missed strikes. This simple rigging trick combines a tube hook and a swivel to keep the tube in place.

STEP 1 Thread a $\frac{1}{4}$-ounce tungsten bullet sinker and a No. 12 swivel to the main line, and then tie off to a 3/0 extra-wide-gap offset hook. Now run the hook through the nose and out the side of the tube.

STEP 2 Push the hook point through the open end of the swivel. Slide the swivel up the hook's shaft to the bend near the eye. The sinker will sit on top of the swivel.

STEP 3 Finish Texas-rigging as normal. The swivel will keep the sinker from pushing down on the tube and keep the tube from sliding down the hook—even when a bass nabs it.

$\frac{3}{8}$-ounce crayfish-imitation crank that dives deep enough to bounce off the bottom.

7 **GRASSBEDS** Cast and retrieve a $\frac{1}{2}$-ounce crankbait over submerged grassbeds and along the inside edges. A crank that dives no deeper than 1 foot is ideal where grass grows up within inches of the surface.

8 **FLOODED BUSHES** When water rises above normal depth in the spring, crash a heavy $\frac{3}{4}$-ounce lipless crankbait through submerged bushes. You'll need a stiff graphite rod and 50-pound superbraid line.

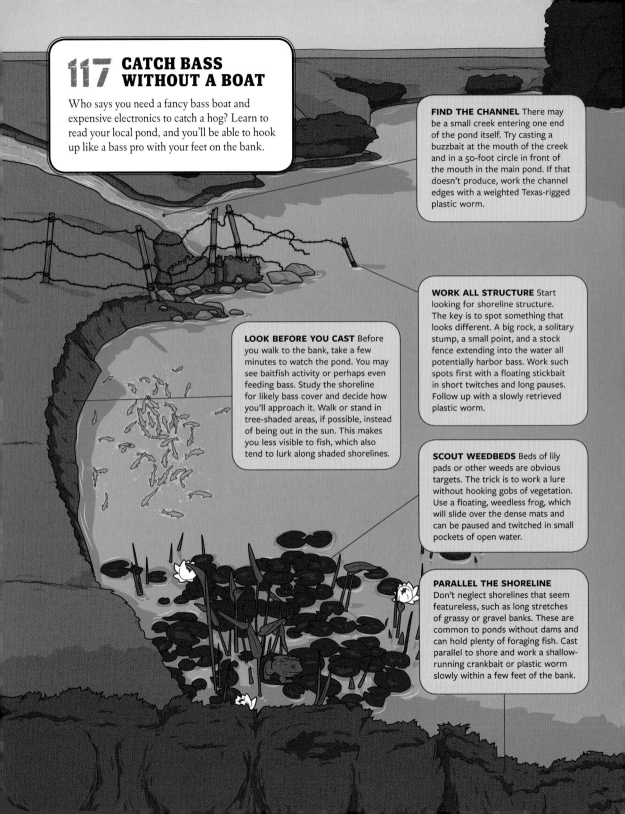

117 CATCH BASS WITHOUT A BOAT

Who says you need a fancy bass boat and expensive electronics to catch a hog? Learn to read your local pond, and you'll be able to hook up like a bass pro with your feet on the bank.

FIND THE CHANNEL There may be a small creek entering one end of the pond itself. Try casting a buzzbait at the mouth of the creek and in a 50-foot circle in front of the mouth in the main pond. If that doesn't produce, work the channel edges with a weighted Texas-rigged plastic worm.

LOOK BEFORE YOU CAST Before you walk to the bank, take a few minutes to watch the pond. You may see baitfish activity or perhaps even feeding bass. Study the shoreline for likely bass cover and decide how you'll approach it. Walk or stand in tree-shaded areas, if possible, instead of being out in the sun. This makes you less visible to fish, which also tend to lurk along shaded shorelines.

WORK ALL STRUCTURE Start looking for shoreline structure. The key is to spot something that looks different. A big rock, a solitary stump, a small point, and a stock fence extending into the water all potentially harbor bass. Work such spots first with a floating stickbait in short twitches and long pauses. Follow up with a slowly retrieved plastic worm.

SCOUT WEEDBEDS Beds of lily pads or other weeds are obvious targets. The trick is to work a lure without hooking gobs of vegetation. Use a floating, weedless frog, which will slide over the dense mats and can be paused and twitched in small pockets of open water.

PARALLEL THE SHORELINE Don't neglect shorelines that seem featureless, such as long stretches of grassy or gravel banks. These are common to ponds without dams and can hold plenty of foraging fish. Cast parallel to shore and work a shallow-running crankbait or plastic worm slowly within a few feet of the bank.

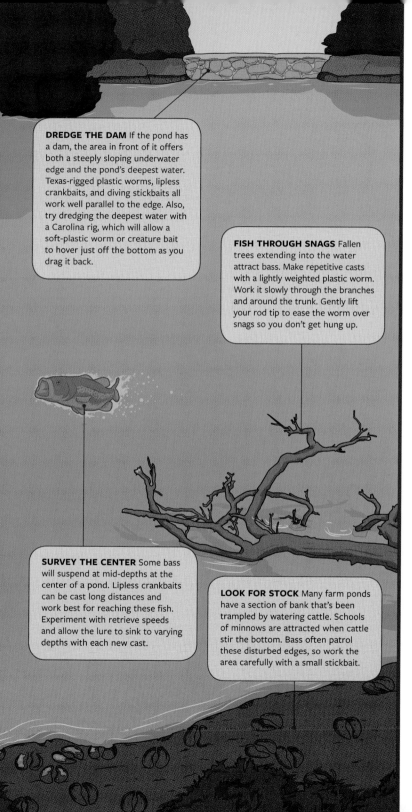

DREDGE THE DAM If the pond has a dam, the area in front of it offers both a steeply sloping underwater edge and the pond's deepest water. Texas-rigged plastic worms, lipless crankbaits, and diving stickbaits all work well parallel to the edge. Also, try dredging the deepest water with a Carolina rig, which will allow a soft-plastic worm or creature bait to hover just off the bottom as you drag it back.

FISH THROUGH SNAGS Fallen trees extending into the water attract bass. Make repetitive casts with a lightly weighted plastic worm. Work it slowly through the branches and around the trunk. Gently lift your rod tip to ease the worm over snags so you don't get hung up.

SURVEY THE CENTER Some bass will suspend at mid-depths at the center of a pond. Lipless crankbaits can be cast long distances and work best for reaching these fish. Experiment with retrieve speeds and allow the lure to sink to varying depths with each new cast.

LOOK FOR STOCK Many farm ponds have a section of bank that's been trampled by watering cattle. Schools of minnows are attracted when cattle stir the bottom. Bass often patrol these disturbed edges, so work the area carefully with a small stickbait.

STOCK UP ON ESSENTIALS

A basic pond-fishing kit will fit easily in your pocket and is designed to work with a medium-weight spinning outfit spooled with 8- to 12-pound-test monofilament. Thousands of other choices exist, but these few lures will guarantee at least some success on ponds anywhere in the country.

1 A weedless, floating frog in a natural color.

2 A lipless crankbait in chrome with a blue back.

3 A $3/8$- to $1/2$-ounce topwater buzzbait in white or chartreuse.

4 A pack of 6- or 7-inch straight-tailed plastic worms in green or pumpkin and a few size 3/0 offset-shank worm hooks; an assortment of bullet-shaped worm weights in $1/16$- to $1/4$-ounce and some round wooden toothpicks for weight pegging.

5 A floating twitchbait or stickbait in black and silver.

119 SHARPEN YOUR BLADES

Having trouble patterning bass, walleyes, and crappies in fall? According to Stephen Carey of Fish Sense Lures, blade baits are the answer. "When the water temperatures start to drop, baitfish that are sensitive to the quick change begin to die," he says. "There is no better match for a dying baitfish than a blade bait." Success comes from a combo of setting up in the right area of the lake and having the magic touch.

PLAY THE ANGLES A good blade-bait bite starts when water temps fall into the low 50s and lasts until the first ice of the season. During this cooling period, fish prefer to feed by moving vertically because it expends less energy than roaming large areas. According to Carey, that makes banks or channel edges with 45-degree drop-offs prime targets for a fall mixed bag. Fish will hold on the drop, moving up or down to feed depending on the position of the baitfish in the water column. Any structure near the bank or channel edge, such as chunk rock or wood pilings, holds more heat as fall presses on. These are likely places to find both baitfish and gamefish.

HOP TO IT Blade baits can crush fish on a straight retrieve, but Carey hops his across the bottom, working down the slopes from shallow to deep water. He says it's critical to experiment with the height of your hops, the length of the pause in between, and hop speed until you figure out what makes the fish respond best. A typical height is about 12 inches, and Carey notes that fish often eat the bait right off the bottom while it's sitting still.

GET THE FEEL Whether you throw a blade bait on spinning or casting gear, Carey says a medium-heavy rod with a flexible tip is the best option. "Having a tip with a little give is important because it lets you feel the fish inhale the bait," he says. Carey spools with 12- to 17-pound-test monofilament, because braid lacks abrasion resistance and fluorocarbon tends to get stiff in cold water, reducing your ability to feel takes.

120 BANG LOUDLY FOR LARGEMOUTHS

In the spring, prespawn largemouths are often found in creek channels or transition zones in close proximity to the shallow flats they'll use to spawn. This time of year, the water is often cold, and although these staging fish are hungry, sometimes it takes a little extra coaxing to get them to chew. If you're targeting them around hard structure—particularly stumps or submerged wood— all it takes is a little extra noise to trigger that smash.

Start by tying on a crankbait, as these hard lures are much less likely to hang up in the wood than similar lures like a jerkbait. As you retrieve, purposely reel the lure into the structure, allowing it to bang off the stumps, sticks, or brush. When bass are lethargic in the early season, they may not want to chase your crankbait. However, that hard bang, followed by the puff of silt or

algae that often comes off submerged wood, frequently draws an instant reaction from the fish.

If you don't get hit right after the connection with the wood, stop the retrieve entirely for a few seconds. The thump will get the fish's attention, but an attack comes as the crankbait slowly begins to float back up.

121 GET A FROG IN YOUR THROAT

All topwater strikes are special, but few eruptions compare with that of a Goliath largemouth inhaling a hollow-body frog in the lily pads. Frogging over pads give you a great shot at a topwater trophy, and this vegetation also tends to hold large numbers of fish. Fishing heavy cover effectively, though, requires proper gear and an understanding of how to bring a frog to life. Here's what to do to raise a giant.

GET SOME BACKBONE Leave the medium-action spinning outfit with the 8-pound line in the rod locker. Getting a toad from the pads needs more winching power. Try a heavy-action baitcasting rod measuring 7 or 8 feet that can handle 1/2- to 1 1/2-ounce lures and heavy line. Match your stick to a quality reel with lots of line capacity. A Shimano Compre 7-foot 2-inch heavy-fast rod with an Abu Garcia Revo SX-HS low-profile is my go-to outfit for frogging. Spool with 50- or 65-pound braid to wrangle fish from the thick vegetation. There are countless frog options on the market, but those with rubber-tassel legs are my favorites, as they maintain action at any speed.

CRASH THE PAD Not all lily pads are created equal. This is especially true if you're hunting for giant bass. Huge expanses of lively green pads look tempting but often aren't worth your time. In sprawling pad beds, bass can be almost anywhere, and the heavy growth makes

them difficult to extract. Smaller beds tend to concentrate fish and are easier to work from different angles. Look for ones with other elements, such as stumps, logs, or a deep ditch, which can be identified by a void in the surface vegetation. If you can pinpoint a bed with any of these characteristics that also happens to be growing in deeper water, you may have just hit the jackpot.

CROSS THOSE EYES Drawing strikes and planting hooks with hollow-body frogs takes practice. Long casts give the best opportunity to contact a fish and give it enough time to track your bait and strike. A long cast also makes a hard landing, which can be key to getting a fish's attention right away. After the frog smacks down, hop it across the pads, letting it sit still for a few seconds anytime it reaches an open hole. Shaking the rod slightly to get the legs moving while it's resting can seal the deal with a tracking bass. The hardest part is waiting to set the hook when you see the explosion. If you swing instantly, you'll just pull the frog away. Instead, pause for just a moment to allow the bass to turn its head and compress the bait, then take up the slack line and set as hard as you can. To make it easier for the hooks to grab, bend them up slightly and sharpen them frequently. Also, be sure to periodically squeeze the water out of your frog to stop it from sinking.

122 WAKE 'EM UP

We know guides who have caught 60-pound stripers, and a surprising number of lunker bass as well, by "waking" a large plug across the surface. Bass will get right in with a pack of stripers to bird-dog a baitfish school and drive it to the surface. Try using a 7½-foot baitcaster and 20-pound mono, and cast a jointed Red Fin across a tributary point, gravel bar, or hump. With the rod tip at 10 o'clock, reel just fast enough to make the tail slosh back and forth, throwing a wake across the surface. Keep your drag loose; your next strike could be anything from a 7-pound largemouth to a 40-pound striper.

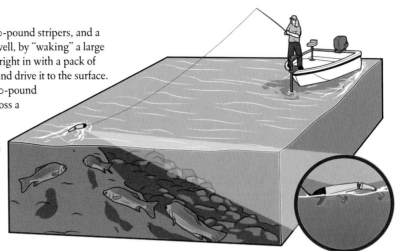

123

MAKE IT POP, NOT HOP

Traditional hollow-body frog lures are designed with a V-shaped head, allowing them to walk and glide through lily pads and vegetation. They are certainly proven big-bass catchers, but there are advantages to different, more new-school designs. In particular, hollow frogs with popping mouths do a great job of scoring bass that are reluctant to eat a traditional-style frog. When paused, a popping frog will make a lot more noise with just a short twitch of the rod, allowing you to keep the lure in the zone while ramping up the surface commotion. In cleaner or more open water, popping frogs can also be worked more aggressively than standard frogs, allowing you to throw more water and attract fish from farther away but still maintain a weedless presentation.

124 DO THE DOUBLE DOG

When bass begin attacking schools of baitfish in summer, target the aggressive feeders with a one-two punch combining a noisy topwater lure with a dying baitfish imitation created with a tube bait. Using two lures on a three-way swivel, this twist on the old walk-the-dog technique has both attention-grabbing commotion and "match-the-hatch" realism.

Look for signs of bass feeding on baitfish: swirls, shad jumping at the surface, or big schools of suspended fish on your depthfinder. Make a long cast to your target,

using a walk-the-dog retrieve to zigzag the lures across the surface. It should look like the big walking bait is chasing the little shad-imitating tube.

Bass may be reluctant to hit the noisy topwater lure, but it gets their attention. Frequently, fish that don't pound the walking bait will follow it or make a halfhearted strike. When that happens, stop your retrieve. The tube flutters down like a dying baitfish, and bass jump at it.

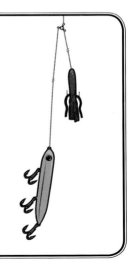

125 STRIKE IN THE NIGHT

Big bass lose their wariness once the lights go out, and if your lake is under pressure during the day, topwater action can be stellar after dark. The two most productive nighttime bass lures are black buzzbaits and jitterbugs, but since you won't see the strike, you can't just swing away when you hear the hit. Here's how it's done.

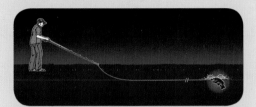

RESIST THE SET It's dark, so when you hear the strike, you won't know if the fish just knocked the lure or pulled it under. Despite what your instincts tell you, don't set. Do absolutely nothing for a moment.

BE SURE Reel just enough to pick up any slack. Then wait for the rod to load. If the fish drops the lure and you rear back, you'll have hooks flying at your face. Make sure you feel the fish first.

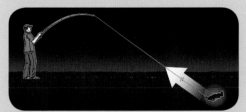

TAKE IT SLOW Sweep the rod up slowly. The bass has had time to "walk away" with the lure and apply pressure against the line, so there's no need to swing with all your might.

126 MAKE THE PERFECT PITCH

Pitching is an underhand baitcasting skill that's perfect for delivering bass jigs or weighted creature baits in heavy cover. It's effective from about 10 to 50 feet. You can make a pitch while standing on a boat deck, and you can practice indoors with a hookless casting weight because extremes of force and distance aren't required.

THE SETUP Heavy-cover fishing requires strong line—20- to 25-pound-test mono (1). Start with a ¾- to 1-ounce lure in your non-casting hand, about even with the reel. While keeping slight tension on the line with your off-hand, put the reel in free-spool and press your casting thumb against the spool to prevent any movement.

THE SWING Hold the rod at waist level, extended straight out in front of you (2). Your casting-arm elbow should be bent and relaxed. Let go of the lure to start a pendulum-like swing. As the lure swings, raise the rod upward and outward by about a foot. Release thumb pressure on the spool so the lure flies with a low trajectory. If it lands right in front of you, you released the spool too soon. A high-flying lure means you let go too late.

THE LANDING As the lure reaches the target, thumb the spool to slow its flight and lower the rod slightly so the bait hits the water with a gentle blip (3). Remember that you're swinging the lure to make this cast, not throwing it.

127 FIND BASS IN THE GRASS

Bass love submerged aquatic grass—so much so that they cling to it even late into fall. As the water chills, the surface mats formed by this vegetation over the summer break up and die, and the bass go deeper and feed in whatever grass remains.

Ⓐ WALK A STICKBAIT In late fall, most of your bites will come 7 to 12 feet deep. Should a warming trend cause baitfish to rise to the surface, however, you could enjoy some topwater action as pods of baitfish ripple the water. Walk a large stickbait over the grass with a sluggish sashay. Try Lucky Craft's Sammy 115 in a shad pattern.

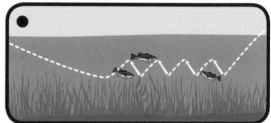

Ⓑ TWITCH A SOFT STICKBAIT If the bass won't smack a topwater plug (they'll typically feed at the surface until the water temperature drops back below 50 degrees), pick them off with a soft stickbait. A pearl 5-inch Strike King KVD Perfect Plastic Caffeine Shad is a good one. Rig it Texas-style with a 5/0 offset hook and give it a pokey twitch-pause action.

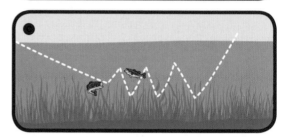

Ⓒ RIP A RATTLER When the autumn bass are feeding a bit deeper in the grass, repeatedly rip a rattler—a ½- to ¾-ounce XCalibur One Knocker works well—through the top of the grass and let it fall back a foot or so. Most strikes happen on the drop. A stiff baitcasting rod and 50-pound braided line will snap the lure free of the grass.

Ⓓ SLIDE A JIG Get down to bottom-hugging grass bass with a pointy jig that slides through the greenery, such as Terminator's Pro Series. Dress the hook with a plastic chunk, make 20-foot pitches, and let the jig sink straight to the bottom on a semi-slack line. Fish the lightest jig—usually ¼ to ¾ ounce—needed to penetrate the grass.

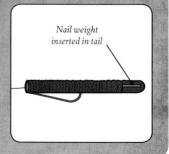

128 WORK A WORM IN REVERSE

Instead of a standard Texas-rigged worm presentation, take a 4½-inch french fry (stick worm) and insert a 1/32-ounce nail weight, the kind normally used with soft jerkbaits, in its tail. Then rig the worm on an offset hook, cast around likely cover, let it settle to the bottom, and retrieve with light twitches of the rod tip. When you pop the worm off the bottom and drop it, the nail in the tail actually makes the bait move away from you as it glides back down, much the way a live crayfish backs up when it's frightened.

Nail weight inserted in tail

129 CATCH BASS IN THE COLD

Bass suspending in hyper-chilled water are extremely lethargic and often won't strike a moving lure. But dangling a small hair jig resembling a tiny minnow in front of their noses for a long time often gets them to open up. Position the jig 8 to 12 feet under a bobber and present it on a whippy 8-foot spinning outfit spooled with 4-pound line. Cast to a steep rock bank and allow the jig to sink. In choppy water, hold the rod still; waves will give the jig action. If it's calm, jiggle the rod tip slightly, pause, and repeat.

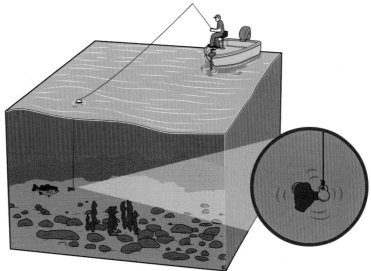

130 DO SOME HEAVY LIFTING

Many anglers use tiny finesse baits in deep, clear bass lakes. Instead, try large, heavy baits to trigger violent strikes. Here are two favorites of the bass pros. Fish them on a medium-heavy baitcaster.

DOUBLE-HOOK SPOON Tie on a ½-ounce slab spoon in white, gold, or silver, and drop it all the way to the bottom. Fish the spoon vertically with 1- to 2-foot jumps that let it pound the bottom when it touches down. It may seem overly aggressive, but the hits will be violent.

FOOTBALL JIG Try a ¾-ounce peanut-butter-and-jelly football jig dressed with a 4-inch trailer in cinnamon–purple jelly. Cast the jig out and let it drop to bass suspended 30 to 40 feet deep before swimming it through the area. You can also try bouncing the jig over deep lake points.

131 KNOW YOUR: LARGEMOUTH BASS

The largemouth bass is, without question, the No. 1 most sought-after gamefish species in the United States. That's because these fish adapt to and thrive in almost any climate. Whether you live in the northern reaches of Maine or the southernmost point in Texas, guaranteed there is a tiny pond, river, creek, or giant lake nearby that holds largemouths. What also makes these fish so appealing is that an angler fishing from the bank with a live minnow and a bobber has as much chance of catching a trophy as the fisherman with a new bass boat and an arsenal of the hottest new lures. Ten pounds is considered a lifetime achievement for most bass anglers, but this species grows much larger, with a 22-pound, 4-ounce monster caught in Japan in 2009 standing as the current world record.

132 SHRINK YOUR JIG

In clear water, a standard jig-and-pig is as subtle as a fat guy in a Hawaiian shirt. Smart pro anglers are instead downsizing their jigs for spooky bass. Rigged with a small pork or plastic chunk, smaller jigs are a ringer for a live crayfish. These diminutive lures are especially deadly during spring in clear, rocky lakes, when bass are feeding on crayfish emerging from their winter hibernation. Flip them around boat docks and let them sink slowly.

133 BUZZ A GRUB

Everybody fishes plastic grubs, but only a handful of pros have recognized how effective these short plastic worms can be when they're fished in the style of topwater buzzbaits. Choose a grub with a strong swimming tail so that a fast retrieve really stirs up the water when pulled across the surface. Rig it weedless on a jighead as light as $1/8$ ounce. You can fish it anywhere, especially through shallow weedbeds. Also, when you stop reeling, the lure will sink, and you can keep working it like a mid-depth crankbait or even on the bottom like a jig or plastic worm, all on the same cast.

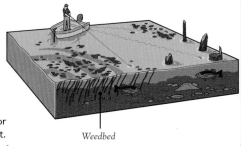

Weedbed

134 TUNE UP YOUR POPPING GAME

It's not easy finding a smallmouth angler that doesn't love watching one of these fish destroy a popper on the surface. While time of year and water temperature have a lot to do with how much or little popper success you find, water clarity often matters more. Here's how to fine-tune your popping game based on the color of the waters.

CLEAR WATER Clear water can often be the most difficult, as the fish will have plenty of time to study a popper before striking. In these conditions, downsize your lure and also lean on a long fluorocarbon leader. Make a few subtle pops and stop; the hit often comes during the pause.

STAINED WATER A little stain is a good thing for topwater action, as the fish tend to react very quickly without clear-water wariness. Pop with moderate force, maintaining a steady cadence. Change speeds until you get the fish to react.

DIRT WATER When visibility is limited, upsize your popper to make more noise. Start by making a few aggressive pops, but work slowly between movement to give fish time to find the lure.

135 PUT A DIFFERENT SPIN ON IT

Spinnerbaits may be the most versatile bass lures of spring and early summer. Here are three techniques and modifications that the pros rely on to get the most out of a spinnerbait.

Willowleaf   Indiana   Colorado

VARY THE RETRIEVE Never cast and retrieve a spinnerbait without changing your speed and direction. Raise the rod tip slightly as you're reeling—to make the lure climb—then lower it and stop reeling, which lets the spinnerbait fall slightly. Strikes come as the blades make that change, most often just as the lure starts falling. Even a rise and fall over a few inches can make a difference.

CREATE A NEW LOOK The three basic blade types are willowleaf, Indiana, and Colorado. In general, the slim profile of the willowleaf is designed to perform best at high speeds, which allow it to deliver a lot of flash. The rounder Colorado spins slowly and doesn't put out as much flash. The blade in the middle—the Indiana—is a compromise design that works best when retrieved at moderate speeds. If bass are hitting well but consistently missing the lures, change blade color (say, from silver to gold) before changing the type. To provide a completely different look, remove the spinnerbait skirt and replace it with a soft-plastic worm, a grub, or even a tube lure. Retrieve the lure just as you would one with a regular skirt.

RIP FOR BIG BASS Let the spinnerbait fall to the bottom in slightly deeper water and rip it up with a few fast cranks. Then stop reeling and let it fall back to the bottom. Repeat this for the entire retrieve. Ripping a spinnerbait often brings reflex strikes from heavier fish that may have been watching the lure on the bottom.

136 THAW OUT A TROUT

In early spring, when ice is melting, ponds and small lakes are great places to fish. And, with oxygen confined to the surface layer, most prey is in depths of less than 10 feet. Trout are rarely far away. The most effective tactic may be to fish from the bank when so many trout are within easy casting range. Start early, because the period during and just after ice-out can be absolutely hot. It's essential that you cast in the right places. This illustration shows you where.

1. CREEKS Rainbows, cutthroats, and baitfish stage off creek mouths prior to spring spawning. Hit these spots with streamers, spinners, salmon eggs, or egg flies. Fish may also move into creek outlets if they find spawning habitat, so try the first quarter mile of the creek, too.

2. CREEK CHANNELS In stream-fed, man-made still waters, look for creek channels cutting through shallow flats. The deeper water offers trout a natural ambush point. Hang bait in the middle or ply the edges with streamers, Woolly Buggers, or spinners.

3. WEEDBEDS Aquatic vegetation dies back in winter, depriving insects of cover and exposing them to trout. Work dragonfly nymph patterns just above the dead weeds, or bottom-fish with waxworms and hellgrammites. You can find the beefy grubs for bait underneath woody debris.

4. DEADFALLS AND TIMBER Downed wood is a magnet for insects, trout, and bait (such as minnows and nightcrawlers). Fish it with shallow-running stickbaits or a Woolly Bugger on the fly rod.

5. SHALLOW BAYS The first areas to warm up in the early spring, skinny-water bays can be prospected with leech streamers or weighted nymphs. Stay on the lookout for cruising trout and intercept them by casting well ahead of their line of travel.

6. MUDFLATS Bloodworms and bright-red midge larvae inhabit the soft, silty bottoms on the flats. Rig a small San Juan Worm under an indicator or a live redworm under a bobber, riding it just off the bottom. Cast and let it drift with the wind.

7. NEW GROWTH From shore, cast out into open water past the new growth of reeds or rushes. Use a strip-and-pause retrieve with a damsel nymph, gold-ribbed hare's ear, Prince nymph, or leech streamer on the fly rod.

8. BARS AND MIDWATER SHOALS Work these areas by casting to the shallow water and retrieving into the deep water. Try a fly pattern like a midge larva or pupa, allowing it to sink to the bottom on a 12- to 14-foot leader and working it back glacially slow.

9. ICE SHEETS As the thaw begins, look for open water between ice sheets and the shoreline, particularly in shallows adjacent to deep water. Some anglers cast baitfish imitations onto the ice shelf, then drag them into the water and begin their retrieve.

137 BULK UP FOR TROPHY BROWNS

Having one of those days where you hook double-digit numbers of trout is doubtless a lot of fun. But for some anglers, the real thrill is not quantity, but quality. Those on a mission for true trophy brown trout understand that the same little lures, baits, and flies that catch big numbers of small fish aren't necessarily the go-tos for the elusive giants. No matter which style of fishing you prefer, these are the offerings more likely to stick that hog brown.

STICKBAITS Forget little inline spinners. Even in smaller trout streams, the bigger browns are more apt to expend the energy chasing down a large meal. Five- to 7-inch stickbaits should be a big part of any big-brown hunter's arsenal. For shallower streams and rivers, opt for those that dive to 3 feet or less. Jerk these baits aggressively through seams and eddies and hang on. If a fish swipes and misses, then just keep the lure moving.

ARTICULATED STREAMERS Small woolly buggers catch tons of trout. Four- to 6-inch articulated streamers catch the "right" trout. While a 12-inch rainbow is likely to pass on a giant, meaty streamer, such as a Double Deceiver, a fat brown will blast it. To fish these patterns, beef up to a 7-weight fly rod, and don't be afraid to use a short sink tip, even in water only a few feet deep; the faster the fly gets down, the more time it has in the strike zone.

CRAYFISH AND HELLGRAMMITES A big brown will suck up a mealworm or nightcrawler, but there's a definite advantage to drifting large, natural baits that already live in the river. Hellgrammites are the aquatic larval forms of the dobsonfly, and while you may have to seine your own in the early summer, their scent is irresistible to big trout. Crayfish are another good bait for trophies when fished whole and live, especially in the fall, when browns fatten up for winter.

138 SPOT AND STALK TROUT

The secret to catching big wild trout often comes down to identifying a single target and then dissecting the fish's feeding rhythm. This kind of fishing requires patience and stealth. Here's how.

STALK INTO POSITION On broken pocket water, the rippled surface allows a closer approach (A). Cast from straight downstream to keep your line out of mixed currents, but beware of small "lookout" trout (B) that will spook into the head of the pool. If you're fishing slick pools or spring creeks, don't push too close. Anglers casting wet flies should post across and slightly upstream (C) of the fish for drifts that keep the leader, tippet, and any split shot outside the trout's view.

MATCH THE RHYTHM Does your trout rise to every morsel of food, or every few seconds, or every few drifting insects? Does the fish prefer prey off to one side or directly in front of its snout? Does it slurp up a mouthful of spinners or sip in singles? Pay attention to these patterns and factor them into your presentation.

CALCULATE THE ANGLES Count down the cast, and put the fly 2 feet in front of the fish. A tighter cast will spook it. A longer cast could require too much mending to stay drag free. If you mess up, resist the temptation to fire out a quick cast to cover up your mistake. Give the fish time to settle.

139 PICK THE PERFECT TWO-FLY TROUT RIG

Two-fly rigs let anglers present double the meal options to discerning trout. The best pairings, however, are no given. Trout streams and feeding behavior can be dynamic. What works in the morning can easily strike out by afternoon. Try these combinations when the time is right.

MORNING Tie a No. 6 weighted stonefly nymph to a 3X leader. Add 2 feet of 4X tippet to the bend in the nymph hook, and finish with a trailing No. 12 caddis pupa. Drift below a strike indicator behind rocks and in eddies where natural nymphs are. A large and small offering gives trout options prior to any hatch activity. Use a black or brown stonefly; dark colors show better contrast in low light.

MIDDAY As the sun gets higher, trout go surface feeding, eating live bugs and dead mayflies that have fallen back to the water after mating. Present both options: a No. 10 Irresistible with a No. 18 Adams a foot in tow. Clip the hackle off the Adams so it sits flat in the film like a dead mayfly spinner. The bulky Irresistible not only draws strikes but also helps you keep track of the location of the tiny Adams during the drift.

EVENING Low light brings big trout out of hiding. They may be interested in bugs, or they may attack smaller trout still sipping on the surface. To fool these toads, strip a No. 6 yellow Marabou Muddler; a No. 12 Leadwing Coachman brings up the rear by 14 inches (above). The streamer moves plenty of water to get a meat eater's attention, and the large wet fly imitates drowned aquatic insects that require less work to eat than snapping live bugs off the top.

1-10 PERFECT THE PARACHUTE CAST

The biggest trout hold in deep water, a situation that calls for heavily weighted flies. But simply adding more lead can be self-defeating. Heavy nymphs and streamers act unnaturally underwater, which can deter strikes. You need to get deep with as little weight as possible. To do this, use the parachute cast, which produces enough slack to let the fly sink unhindered by drag—only a small amount of lead will be needed to reach even the deepest fish.

STEP 1 Make a standard overhead cast, aiming for a point about 10 feet above the water.

STEP 2 Stop your forward stroke around the 12 o'clock position.

STEP 3 As the line passes overhead, snap the rod forward to the 10 o'clock position.

STEP 4 Instead of straightening out, the fly line will hinge toward the water, dropping or "parachuting" the fly and leader vertically onto the surface.

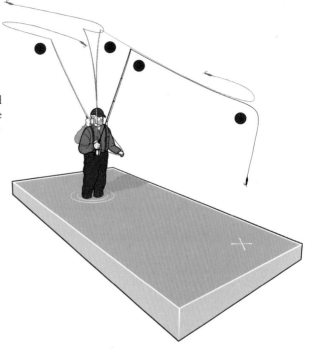

1-11 MASTER THE MEND

The key to the perfect drift is mending your line: basically, keeping your fly line upstream of your dry fly (or strike indicator when you are nymph fishing). Once the fly line gets downstream of the fly or indicator, it will grab the current and cause the fly to drag. Usually that's game over, and you lose.

An ideal "mend" involves lifting the fly line from downstream and placing it upstream, without moving the fly or strike indicator. The most common mistake, even among people who understand the importance of mending, is getting herky-jerky and trying to whip the line with the rod from chest level. Wiggling your flies around for the sake of mending defeats the entire purpose.

Fly rods are long for a reason. When you start the mend, lift the rod tip just high enough to pick the fly line off the water, but not so high that you disturb the leader (1). Next, with your rod tip straight up, swing it across your face from downstream to upstream (2). Then gently lay down your line to the upstream side of your fly or indicator (3). Sometimes, in faster water, you might want to "kick" that rod over with more force.

CURRENT

142 SHOOT THE BREEZE

Any flyfisherman can cast well on a calm day. It's how you deal with wind that separates the men from the boys. Here are three tips that can help you shoot the breeze with ease.

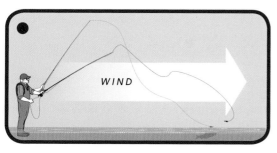

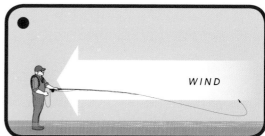

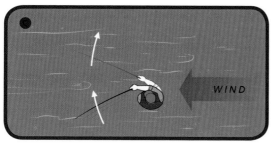

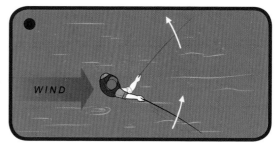

TRY SKITTERING Insects hovering just above the surface are trout magnets, and wind coming from behind can be used to skitter a fly. Make a downwind cast. Hold the rod nearly straight up (A) and allow the wind to move the fly around just above the water's surface. By raising and lowering the rod, you can make the fly dance on and off the surface, just like a real insect.

VARY LOOP SIZE If the wind is coming straight at you, throw a tighter loop (B). This reduces the amount of line affected by the wind and increases the speed at which the line unrolls—both of which help the line punch through the breeze.

ADJUST THE CASTING PLANE In a crosswind, cast sidearm in order to unroll the line under the wind. If the wind is from the rod-hand side (C), you'll need to cast across your body to keep the fly away from you. If the wind is from the off-hand side (D), all you need to do is perform a normal sidearm cast.

143 MOVE THEM WITH A MAMMAL

Ever have one of those days on the river where the fish are all keyed in to a specific hatch and either you just can't seem to match it or the trout are simply refusing your fly? Next time that happens, don't get frustrated. Instead of trying to play dainty and delicate all day, switch gears and tie on a large surface fly, like a mouse or frog pattern. While the change can seem counterintuitive, every once in a while, you'll be surprised by a big trout that suddenly loses interest in those micro bugs when a big steak suddenly passes overhead, even in broad daylight in clear water.

144 FLY IN THE COLD

Trout feeding patterns change when temperatures drop and insect life cycles slow down, so you'll have to alter your tactics a bit. One of these three approaches should coax a few fish from their icy lies.

SMALL AND SLIM (A) On most winter trout streams, tiny mosquito-like midges are the most active and available food form. Standard midge pupa patterns—such as Brassies and Serendipities—can be effective. So can slim-bodied nymphs, such as the Flashback Pheasant Tail. But size is often more important than the specific fly. Think small, and go for patterns in sizes 18 to 22 on 5X to 7X tippets.

HIGH AND DRY (B) Low, clear winter water can make those occasional rising fish ultra-cautious. A size 18 or 20 Parachute Adams or Parachute Black Gnat, or a Griffith's Gnat in sizes 18 to 22, will cover a hatch of midges or, on some rivers, blue-wing olive mayflies. Keep a low profile and use long, fine leaders.

BIG AND GAUDY (C) If the microflies aren't bringing them in, you might want to try the other extreme and go large—leeches and streamers up to size 4 or so. I hooked my largest winter trout on an ordinary No. 8 black Woolly Bugger. Fish near the bottom and dead-drift with occasional short twitches.

Flashback Pheasant Tail   Serendipity   Parachute Black Gnat   Bunny Leech

Brassie   Parachute Adams   Woolly Bugger

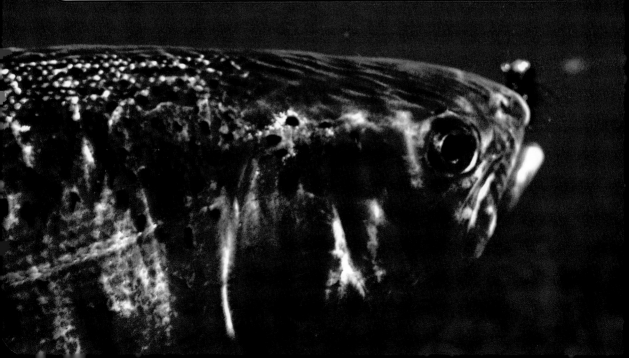

CURRENT

145 DREDGE A FALL STEELIE

Fall steelhead anglers typically cover water with cross-stream casts until a fish hits. Instead, try putting the fly right in front of the fish from directly downstream.

GETTING DOWN Pattern choice matters, but presentation is the real key. You need to put the nymph 4 to 8 inches above bottom, which means adding weight to your line. An unweighted fly moves more naturally than a weighted one, so try a slinky weight attached to the leader butt. The setup lets you easily change the weight as river conditions dictate.

DEAD-DRIFTING When water temperatures dip below 50 degrees, dead-drift a nymph on a 9½-foot (or longer) 7- or 8-weight rod with a small-diameter shooting line (A) rather than a traditional weight-forward floating fly line.

The small line allows for quieter entry of the flies on the cast (no line slap to spook fish) and offers less resistance in the water, which makes it easier to get a drag-free drift. Don't false cast. Simply pick up the line and shoot it directly upstream (B). Casting with the added weight is smooth and effortless. This is a great way to work a tree-choked stream that routinely snags back casts.

As a go-to rig, pros recommend an 8- to 10-foot butt section that ends with a bead and barrel swivel (C). A slinky weight slides freely on the butt section via a snap. To the swivel, tie on a 3- to 6-foot leader; onto this, knot a chartreuse caddis nymph. Run 17 to 24 inches of line from the eye of this fly, then attach a stone-fly nymph. The long, light tippet offers little water resistance and sinks quickly.

146 SUCCEED FLAT OUT

When the ice disappears and water temperature begins climbing, many gamefish migrate to shallow water. Bass and walleyes head to spawning areas, pickerel hunt for emerging weeds, and trout, panfish, and pike utilize the transition zone between deep and shallow water to look for food. One easy way to cover water and hook a mixed bag is flatline trolling. The best part: you can leave the weights and downriggers at home. Just take your favorite medium-action spinning or baitcasting outfit spooled with 8- to 10-pound-test mono, some stickbaits, and a few spoons.

KEEP IT CLOSE Start by working depth-transition areas in 5 to 10 feet of water (A). To avoid bowing and slack, send lures no farther than 75 feet behind the boat. The water is still cold; keep speed between 2 and 3 mph so sluggish fish don't chase a fast lure.

KEEP IT BENT When a fish hits, The boat's forward movement should do most of the work planting the hook. Lift the rod straight up (B) and give it a gentle tug just to make sure the fish is glued, and then start reeling.

KEEP IT MOVING Whoever is on the throttle should keep the boat in gear but moving slowly enough to avoid breaking the fish off or forcing the angler to reel against the drag (C). Stopping the boat fully will often give the fish enough slack to spit the hook.

147

FOLLOW THE CRAPPIE HIGHWAYS

As crappies follow creek channels to spawning water, they stop at staging or rest areas. Isolated wood cover, underwater stumps along bends, and points are all good spots to find fish. The warmer the water temperature, the closer they'll be to spawning areas.

Reservoir crappies typically winter on deep main-lake structures like river-channel dropoffs, submerged roadbeds, and offshore humps. They're often 25 to 50 feet deep. As the lake gradually warms in early spring, crappies gravitate toward shallower water, following predictable migration routes that lead to their eventual spawning areas.

This crappie migration takes place in waves rather than all at once. The initial activity occurs when a lake's waters reach 55 to 58 degrees. "The first wave often contains the biggest fish, so it pays to monitor the water temperature closely during this period and be on those crappie highways when the slabs roll in," says Kentucky Lake guide Gary Mason. "You'll find most of them in the 12-foot zone, holding tight to submerged brushpiles and stumps."

By the time the lake hits 65 degrees, expect to experience some truly awesome crappie fishing if you target this pattern. They'll move progressively shallower as the water warms, eventually ending up in the backs of tributary arms and coves, where they spawn in stake beds and sunken brushpiles once the water reaches the low to mid 70s. But you'll have already caught the biggest, baddest fish by then. You can leave the little ones to the batter-and-fry crowd.

148 CATCH MORE POND CRAPPIES

Small lakes and ponds accessible only on foot can offer crappie fishing just as good as large lakes and reservoirs. In fact, in some instances, they can often produce better fishing, as the crappies don't have much room to roam, making their location that much more predictable during any given trip. Follow these three tricks, and they can help you turn the action up with farm pond crappies.

MAKE MORE HABITAT It's no secret that crappies gravitate to brush piles, and if you build them, they will come. Don't be afraid to construct some new crappie hideouts by tossing dead brush, limbs, or even small downed trees in strategic locations. Focus your home building on deep banks, coves with some depth, and even shallow flats where crappies will move to spawn in spring.

GO SMALL As it's easier for crappies in a small, closed system to get wise to fishing pressure, scale your tackle down to be stealthier. I like to attack small ponds with a 5-foot trout rod and reel spooled with some 4-pound fluorocarbon. This setup allows me to cast light jigs far and accurately, as well as to slingshot jigs into tight spaces where heavier line or a longer rod might not reach.

CHANGE OFTEN Fish for a school of pond crappies long enough, and they will eventually start to turn their noses up at the jigs and lures they see most often. With that in mind, it's critical to change lures and colors frequently, even resting hot baits for a few days before using them again. I've seen multiday hot bites turn into a few nudges in small ponds after continually fishing the same style and colors of lures.

149 GET INTO THE GRASS

When crappies are spawning, guides recommend you concentrate on narrow bands of grass near the shoreline. The fish hold along the inside and outside edges of the greenery, with bigger fish favoring the deeper outside edge of the grass.

Your best strategy here begins with lure selection. The key is to cast a $^1/_{16}$-ounce jig dressed with a curly-tailed grub over the grass to the bank. Slowly reel the grub to the inside edge and let it sink to the bottom. If that doesn't get a strike, try pulling the jig over the vegetation and letting it sink on the outside edge.

To dupe postspawners, by contrast, you'll want to use a $^1/_{16}$- or $^1/_{32}$-ounce tube. You can fish these baits on 6-pound line and an 11-foot crappie rod with a spinning reel. Easing within a rod's length of trees standing in water 4 to 12 feet deep, or holes in milfoil beds, slowly lower the jig straight down into the water, about 6 to 10 inches. A crappie will often rise up and hit it. If that doesn't coax a bite, you may have luck by dropping the jig down 1 foot and holding it there for another 30 seconds. Repeat this process until the jig touches bottom. Then crank the jig up and fish another tree or hole in a grassbed.

150 CATCH CRAPPIES UNDER A BRIDGE

Postspawn crappies often stack up on riprap points on either side of bridges that cross creek arms. You'll tend to find them suspending around these points 6 to 10 feet deep in 7 to 15 feet of water.

To pick off these postspawners, expert guides suggest you try dropping a jig straight down on 8-pound-test copolymer line that runs through the guides of a 10-foot rod matched with a spinning reel. After the jig is down 6 to 10 feet, move the boat around the riprap points slowly enough for the line to remain vertical. You may well find that you start getting bites only after you stop working the jig up and down.

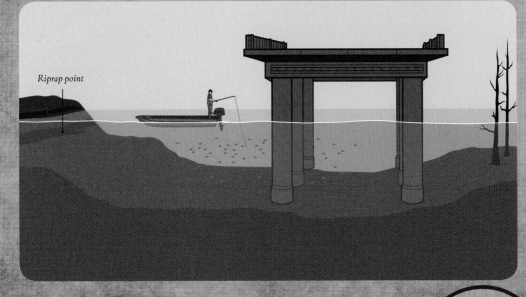

Riprap point

151 DANGLE A BUNCH OF LIVIES

When prospecting for crappies in a shallow lake, here's an easy way to target multiple depths at the same time with live bait. Tie a 10-foot length of thin 6-pound superline to the tips of 5 to 8 crappie poles—fancy fiberglass cane poles with no reels. At the end of each length of superline, tie a snap-swivel. From each snap-swivel, tie a 6- to 8-foot length of monofilament leader, and then add a ¼- or ½-ounce bell sinker to each snap. Spread the rods out in holders positioned around the boat (A), keeping some low to the water and raising some higher, to vary the depths (B). Add a lively fathead minnow to a small hook on the end of each leader and drop each line straight overboard. You want the lines to stay as vertical as possible as you drift with the breeze or nudge it along with the trolling motor.

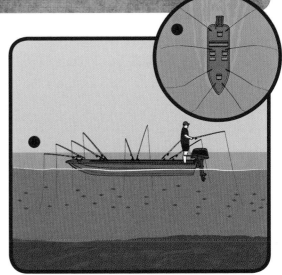

152 CATCH YOUR BIGGEST BLUEGILL OF THE YEAR

Anyone can catch bluegills when they're on the bed. But you can land some of the biggest fish of your life long before the nesting season—and before the lake gets slammed with competing anglers—when the water is still chilly. Find the fish, dangle a tasty morsel inches from their noses, and wait for a bite. It's like ice fishing on open water.

To catch these fish, you need a long cane pole or a jigging pole, some jigs, and waxworms. That, and some free time. A $^1/_{16}$- to $^1/_{32}$-ounce jig tipped with a waxworm is the proven standard. A plain, painted ballhead jig will do, but dressed jigs with marabou, tinsel, or duck-feather skirts slow the fall rate and provide added visual attraction.

For fishing cover visible from the surface, a collapsible 12-foot jigging pole works very well. A seasoned cane pole

also does the job. No reel is required, especially when you're fishing shallower than 10 feet. When you find the right depth, just tie that amount of line to your pole, and you're all set. You'll snag a lot of jigs in the thick stuff, so 6-pound braided line is handy for straightening hooks and saving jigs.

To probe submerged cover right under the boat in open water, make a near 180 in your tackle choice. Rather than a long crappie pole, a short, supersensitive spinning rod with an ultralight reel is best; my favorite rod length is 5 or 6 feet. I've even used ice-fishing tackle to fish rock piles. Small-diameter braid is still O.K., but finicky fish, clear water, and small spinning reels prone to tangling line may require a switch to monofilament.

153 ENJOY THE SUMMERTIME BLUES

Don't give up on slab bluegills once summer heat drives them from the shallows. Here are three killer tactics to catch big bulls in deep water.

MATCH A MAYFLY HATCH With the exception of the spawn, mayfly hatches mean the best opportunities to catch big bluegills. Cruise the lake and check any place where wind corrals the bugs into confined areas near deep water (A). "Target the banks that are closest to the channel, where the wind blows the larvae into the bank," says Ron Lappin, a retired Kentucky guide and panfish pro. "The higher the bank, the better the hatch is. Look for places where the wind can blow across a large area." Cast to the bank and use a slow retrieve, occasionally pausing to let a spinner or jig glide on a semi-slack line just above bottom.

PITCH AROUND PILINGS Bridge pilings across deep areas and large tributaries offer vertical current breaks where bluegills can rise from cooler water to feed near the surface (B). In these spots, Lappin fishes a drop-shot rig: He suspends a Brim Reaper bug on a No. 6 long-shank cricket hook 12 to 18 inches above a $^1/_{16}$- to $^1/_8$-ounce cylinder weight. Lappin fishes it on a 9-foot float-and-fly rod and suggests keeping the line length no longer than the rod. "A lot of pilings have steel cross members between them," he says. "That's where you'll get the biggest concentrations of bluegills."

CAST IN CURRENTS Most reservoirs have manmade current sources, such as a dam, its turbines, culverts, and locks (C). These attract bluegills and are best if they are in deeper spots or have a large concrete structure like a dock piling nearby. "You'll see bluegills almost swarming in these areas after the spawn," says Lappin. He floats a live cricket, rigged on a No. 6 cricket hook, under an acorn-size bobber (Pinch two split shot onto the line between the cricket and bobber), starting on the sunny side of the structure, then shifts to the shaded side, casting directly against the dam.

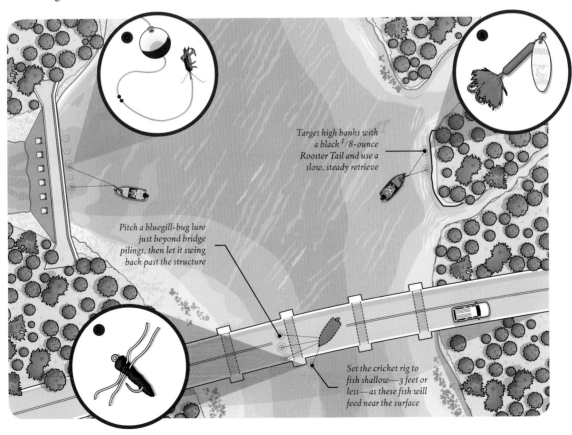

Target high banks with a black $^1/_8$-ounce Rooster Tail and use a slow, steady retrieve

Pitch a bluegill-bug lure just beyond bridge pilings, then let it swing back past the structure

Set the cricket rig to fish shallow—3 feet or less—as these fish will feed near the surface

154 TAG-TEAM WINTER PERCH

Jumbo winter perch tend to travel in pods numbering anywhere from a couple of fish to a dozen or so and tend to enter and exit the scene in a burst. These dine-and-dash fish call for certain tools and tactics. Try this "firefighting" technique with a partner—as one of you unhooks, the other instantly fires back down the hole to pick off another fish. Instead of nabbing one or two jumbos, you can catch several in a few minutes of fast action.

GO DEEP Deeper than 15 feet, you really need a lure that will get down fast (A). Opt for a heavier metal jig that's slim and hydrodynamic. If you want to tip it with bait, waxworms are a good choice since they don't resist water like a minnow.

WORK THE SHALLOWS In water less than 15 feet deep, use an aggressive flash spoon and something that gets up and down in a hurry but also sparkles enough to hold fish and draw other transient pods (B). Spoons that bear holographic decals work especially well.

MOVE QUICKLY Tag-teaming perch works best on big fish that advance with zeal but are sure to vanish, and it's effective both shallow and deep. The key is to get the second bait down as soon as the first fisherman reels up (C). Look for eat-and-run perch behavior particularly during peak feeding hours, like dusk and midmorning.

155 TAKE A SHOT IN THE DOCK

This slingshot technique sends a light jig into tight spaces—under a dock, overhanging limbs, or blowdowns. Use a 5-foot spinning rod and a closed-face spinning reel, preferably with a front trigger.

STEP 1 Let out enough line so the jig hangs parallel with the bottom rod guide. Hold the jighead in your left hand between your thumb and index and middle fingers, with the hook pointing out to avoid getting snagged on the release. In your rod hand, keep your right index finger on the trigger, which unlocks the spool.

STEP 2 Lower the jig to your left side and extend your right arm out, keeping the rod angled toward the water. As

your arm extends, it will create a bend in the rod. Do not create tension by pulling on the jig. Continue to bend the rod by extending your arm until the face of the tip-top guide is parallel to the water's surface.

STEP 3 Once the rod is fully drawn, your arms should not change position. When you're ready to aim, point the rod tip at your target spot by turning your entire upper body.

STEP 4 Release the jig and the reel trigger at the same time to shoot. If the jig goes high, you probably broke your left wrist when you let the jig go. If the jig whizzes back at your head, you fired the trigger too late. The jig should fly straight and low to the water.

156 BLACK OUT

Whenever you're dealing with wary fish in clear water, line spooking is often a concern, especially if you're using braided line or a super line that's colored instead of clear. Dark colors blend more smoothly with the surroundings underwater, so an easy way to make your clear-water presentation stealthier is to color the first 10 feet of your braid black. Use a razor blade to cut a slit in the tip of a permanent marker and keep it in your tackle bag. When you need to go dark, just run the line through the slit, give it a few seconds to dry, and fish on.

157 GO LONG, WIDE, AND DEEP FOR WALLEYES

In late spring to early summer, the big postspawn female walleyes are suspended in open water. To find these fish, cover as large a swath of water as you can—up to 200 feet wide, and from top to bottom. Set the shallowest baits far to the sides of your boat to avoid spooking fish feeding near the surface. This big trolling spread is as simple to rig as it is deadly on walleyes.

STEP 1 This setup requires four side-planer boards. Install three adjustable rod holders along each gunwale. The two flat-line rods lie parallel to the water at 90 degrees. The next two holders angle rods at 65 degrees. Those nearest the bow keep the rods up at 45 degrees.

STEP 2 Fish 10-pound monofilament on all six of the trolling rods except for one of two flat-line rods. Spool this one with 10-pound braided line, which has less resistance in the water and will get the crankbait on this rod running deeper than any of the others.

STEP 3 Fish the same lure on every rod. Long, slender crankbaits with large diving bills work well. In stained

water, try hot pink or orange. On sunny days, use metallics, and in clear water, try white or pearl.

STEP 4 Trolling at 1.5 to 1.7 mph, set the rods closest to the bow first and work down to the stern. Reels with line counters will help you achieve your desired distance when sending the lures back. The longer the line, the deeper the baits will run. If one depth seems to be producing results consistently, reset the other lines to match that depth.

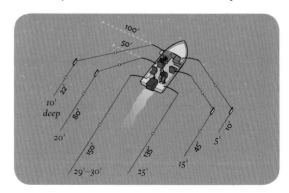

158 FISH A WEED-CUTTER RIG

Walleyes cannot resist the thump and glint of a blade whirling in tandem with a minnow, leech, or nightcrawler. Anglers commonly troll a spinner rig to present the meat-and-metal package to fish in open water. But some nonconformist pros have a different approach, actually casting the rig. Casting spinner rigs allows you to fish areas that you can't target when trolling, such as weedbeds. On a straight retrieve, the spinner's oscillating blade clears a path for the hook and bait. Walleyes rise from the dark and forested bottom to strike. Here's how to tie one up.

THE TACKLE Start with a 6- to 7-foot medium to medium-heavy spinning rod (A) with fairly stiff 10-pound mono or weed-shredding superline.

THE RIG Use a snell knot to tie a No. 2 to No. 4 wide-gap hook to a 12- to 24-inch leader of 10- to 14-pound-test fluorocarbon (B). The shorter leash (trolling spinner rigs

are typically 30 to 40 inches) casts smoothly, is easy to control in shallow and rough water, and permits quick hooksets. String six beads above the hook and add a No. 5 Colorado blade. Tie the free end to a barrel swivel. Slip a 1/8- to 1/4-ounce pegged bullet sinker onto the main line before attaching it to the barrel swivel's open end.

THE BAIT If you're using a minnow, run the hook down its throat and out the back of its head. Penetrate a leech just past the sucker or go with half a nightcrawler, hooked deeply through its thicker-skinned head (C).

THE TARGET Cover a weedbed by casting into any thin spots, particularly those along and just into the outer edge, and into clearings. Bring it back straight and methodically, to about halfway through the water column. A spinner blaring through the weeds will tend to elicit a quick reaction. Fish usually hit on instinct.

159 GET AN EDGE FOR RIVER STRIPERS

Many rivers experience spring runs of striped bass. In some cases, these fish might be coming straight out of the ocean, while in others, the bass might migrate out of a lake or reservoir to follow spawning shad. In either case, where they post up to feed will be similar.

While stripers have no problem feeding in a heavy current, they're not likely to hold directly in fast water. In most cases, the fish will sit behind trees or boulders or in depressions that break the current and offer them a holding location that allows them to exert minimal energy. When a shad or herring is washed overhead, the stripers can quickly dart out, feed, and return to their quiet spots. Of course, knowing where these fish hold is only part of the battle. These two tricks will get them to take a shot on artificial lures more often.

TAKE A SWING Over the years, I've noticed that one of the most important aspects of drawing a strike from a river striper is how your lure swings. These fish are less likely to chase a lure moving straight upstream or downstream as they are one swinging past in an arc with the current. With that in mind, choose diving plugs and soft plastics that dig and maintain a tight wobble with only the current acting on them. A lure that needs to be reeled quickly may not look appealing on a tight line swing and therefore might slip right over a striper's head without the fish moving even an inch to chase.

GO GRAY Stripers are pretty light-sensitive fish, and if your river is crystal clear during their spring run, getting bit on a bright, sunny day can be a challenge. That's why in the spring, I pray for overcast skies and rainy conditions when the water is clear. While you might get a quick bite at first and last light on a sunny day, overcast skies seem to get the fish to lose their wariness, often moving away from their haunts to hunt in riffles and across flats.

160 WEED OUT TROPHY WALLEYES

Many anglers consider June to be an unparalleled time for walleye fishing. The shallows teem with forage, and water temperatures range from the 60s to mid 70s, which is optimum to livable for a walleye. Weeds come up, lending protective cover and shade, and the walleyes take notice—and residence.

Certain weeds are better than others. True broadleaf cabbage establishes in 6 to 12 feet of water over sand, gravel, and marl. Walleyes prefer thicker, forest-like stands, but if those are not an option, a fistful of plants in a pasture of single weeds can draw them in like a magnet. Coontail is another gem, with its lattice of Christmas-green whorls. In its most dynamic form, coontail grows in dense mats in 5 to 9 feet of water.

Nothing outshines the jig-and-minnow rig here. It perfectly mimics what the fish are after, and you can fish it many different ways by varying your stroke and speed. My preference is a long-shank jig with a shiner. Thread the minnow on the hook to foil short nips. Use the electric trolling motor to crawl along and pitch the jig to weed edges or into a field of short vegetation. Swim and hop it back, bumping weed stalks and the bottom. Keep your line taut and the bait in constant motion. Weed-dwelling walleyes are aggressive fish; they'll catch up.

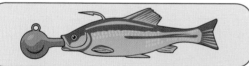

161 KNOW YOUR: WALLEYE

The largest members of the perch family, walleyes can be found throughout much of the United States in everything from small ponds and rivers to neighborhood lakes. Big fish, however, are found in more abundance in large, deep bodies of water such as reservoirs, lakes with serious acreage, or major river systems. Walleyes have exceptional night vision and frequently hunt after dark, making nighttime trolling with crankbaits highly effective. If trolling isn't your game, you can cast twitchbaits or bounce the bottom with leeches. Walleyes are also a primary target of ice fishermen because they readily strike even when the water is at its coldest. These fish have keen hearing as well as eyesight, which can make them extra-sensitive to engine noise. Pro tip: You're mostly likely to catch the biggest fish in a given area first, as the jumbos are the first to spook.

162 FOLLOW THE FOLIAGE

Believe it or not, there are other methods of figuring out when the fishing's hot besides looking up Internet reports. All you have to do is take a lesson from Mother Nature. If it's fall, for instance, and you want giant walleyes, all you have to do is figure out if your lawn needs a raking yet. According to walleye pro and guide Ross Robertson, no matter where you live in the country, the hot fall bite usually coincides with leaves falling from the trees. Around the same time leaves start fluttering down onto the yard, the air temperature is likely cold enough to lower local water temperatures to a range that kicks on walleyes' instinct to pack on the pounds before falling leaves give way to falling snow.

163 PLAY QUANTUM LEAP FROG

Want your frog lure to do more than just cruise through the pads? These three simple modifications will make that frog work harder (and catch more fish) than ever before.

SUCK IT UP I add a clear suction cup to the head of my hollow-body frogs to create a surface disturbance that mimics the sound of a frog plopping off a lily (A). Poke a hole through the middle of the cup, thread it over the hook eye, and secure it in place with superglue. When I work the frog, the cup creates enough popping action to attract more attention without spooking fish. If fish are wary, push the suction cup backward, like a broken umbrella, to reduce the pop and make the bait slide from side to side.

SINK AND SWIM *Big City Fishing* host Jamie Pistilli drowns his soft-plastic frogs by Texas-rigging them on a 5/0 hook with a split shot a foot up the line (B). This way, the buoyant frog hovers below the surface. Weave the bait through lily stalks and be ready for reaction strikes. "A straight retrieve at medium speed produces the most strikes," Pistilli says. "But make sure you always look for movement behind the bait before you yank it out of the water. Bass will follow right to the boat."

PLAY DOCTOR Pro Jonathon VanDam cuts half an inch off each leg on sinking soft-plastic frogs, to reduce the noise the bait makes in the water but maintains just enough kick for the frog to stand out (C). He pitches the frog to a hole in the grass and lets it fall. The flutter on the drop looks like a real frog swimming below the grass line. The short legs make the frog look "smart," VanDam says. A real frog doesn't want to draw attention by fully extending its legs when it swims.

164 TAKE A STAB IN THE DARK

Turn off the lights and grab a spear! In dark-house spearing, the sunlight penetrates the ice but not your shack, creating a window to the world below. South Dakota guide Paul Steffen, who skewers walleyes and pike on Lake Oahe, compares it to bowhunting: "When the fish comes to you, it's like a buck coming in. Your fists shake and your heart starts pounding." (Note: Check local regs for spearing, as well as laws on species and line limits.)

FIND ICY SITES Start by searching for bottom around 10 feet deep that gradually drops off to 40 or 50 feet of water. The mouth of a small bay with soft breaklines is a good start.

DRILL, BABY, DRILL Steffen augers four holes in the ice, then cuts out a 3x6-foot block with a saw. A plywood ice shack without windows (or a pop-up shanty) goes up and the hunt is on.

PLAY A BAITING GAME Steffen rigs two jigging sticks—one with a white 1-ounce Rat-L-Trap Magnum Force, the other with a white Kalin's soft plastic. "We use longer 4- or 5-inch grubs and lizards," he says, "anything with a lot of tentacles that shows motion in the water." He rigs a third rod to a fish decoy, which is dropped between the lures. "Use the smallest deke possible for walleyes, and the largest one for pike."

TAKE A STAB When a fish appears, ease the spear points close as you can—just over the back of the fish's head—then strike. A big splash will spook the fish. "The fish don't give many options. Sometimes they stop, often they don't. Be prepared."

Set your lures on the far sides of the hole, with the decoy in between—all three two-thirds of the way to the bottom

165 LEARN HARD LESSONS

Most anglers think of soft-plastic grubs when it comes to plastics for walleyes. I'm more into hard plastic in spring, because it's easier to tailor crankbaits and stickbaits to the various stages of the spawn. Here are my go-to lures, as well as the tactics that get them producing trophy walleyes.

PRESPAWN Perch and larger baitfish are favored meals of the biggest walleyes prior to the spawn. Nothing matches these food sources like a crankbait. Trolling over deep flats near spawning grounds is often highly productive. Spread lures through the water column, with particular attention to baits running halfway down, which often get hit more than others. You can also run a crank high in the water column to target any walleyes basking in the warm surface water. Reef Runner's suspending Skinny Stick is my No. 1 choice here; it truly hangs and maintains action trolled at slow speeds.

SPAWN Those in the know may be putting their boats in when most anglers are taking them out to head home.

During the spawn, large females often stop feeding by day and get very spooky, making night the right time for shots at these giants. Sneak into shallow areas with a rocky or hard bottom, using just your electric trolling motor, to set up for epic action in the dark. Once in position, fan-cast shallow-diving stickbaits, such as the Rapala Husky Jerk HJ12. If you're not getting bit working slowly, try a slightly faster steady retrieve with occasional twitches of the rod.

POSTSPAWN Postspawn female walleyes tend to hold deep in the water column, which makes crankbaits the best option right after the spawn, especially since spring runoff often dirties the water. You need lures that dive to depths in excess of 20 feet without assistance but don't need to be trolled quickly to work effectively. The Reef Runner 800 is my top pick. Many anglers troll these lures with heavy snap weights, but I've found that using the lightest weight you can get away with while still reaching your desired depth catches more fish, as it won't change action so drastically.

166 DO A FALL MINNOW DOUBLE-TAKE

In the fall, walleyes come out of their summer funk and feed ravenously before ice-up. Here's how to make the most of the occurrence, whether you're fishing lakes or rivers.

◀ **LAKE FISHING** Look for walleyes in lakes and reservoirs during mid-fall in water 25 to 45 feet deep where dropoffs of 60 feet or more are close by. Until ice-up, you'll get good results with a basic Lindy rig—a walking sinker and a leader with a hook—with a live 4- to 7-inch chub. The Lindy rig lets you drag a bait along bottom and the sliding sinker helps you feel delicate takes. You'll most likely need a 1-ounce weight to maintain bottom contact at these depths if there's any wind at all. Using a bow-mounted electric motor, slowly drag the walking sinker in a zigzag course along the lip of dropoffs where you've marked walleyes. Once you feel a bite, let it run for as long as 20 seconds, reel up the slack, and make a sweeping hookset.

▶ **RIVER FISHING** Walleyes gang up in the tailwaters of dams and in deep river bends when the water chills in autumn. Pros rely on $^1/_8$- to $^3/_8$-ounce standup jigs to catch these fish. The jig design puts the hook in an upright position to reduce snags. The teeter-totter action of the jig imparts more movement to the bait. Use the lightest jig that maintains bottom contact and tip the hook with a 5- to 6-inch sucker minnow. Then work the jig with a slow lift-drop action. Fish the jig vertically 10 to 30 feet deep on spinning tackle and 10-pound monofilament. Drift backward with the current, and use a bow-mounted electric motor to slow the boat and keep the line vertical. When you feel a hit, lift the rod straight into the air to set.

167 GO SLOW AND STEADY TO WIN A WALLEYE

One of the best methods for targeting walleyes is trolling with crankbaits and worm rigs. When walleyes are holding deep, getting the bait or lure in front of them might mean using extra weights on the line or diving planer boards. In either case, it's often necessary to feed out more than 100 feet of line to get your offering into the zone. With that much line plus the weight of your terminal tackle, how you handle a strike is of the utmost importance. Many trollers rear back to try to set the hook when a fish hits, but walleyes have delicate mouths; the force it takes to transmit a set all the way down the line may also pull the hook out. Walleyes typically set themselves when they bite because the lure or bait has forward momentum from the pull of the boat. Just grab the rod and wind slowly and steadily after the strike. If you pause or drop the rod tip, you risk putting slack in the line and loosening the hook. You never want to pump the rod, either. It takes some getting used to, but the slow, even crank will put more trophy walleyes in the boat.

168 LAND A PIKE OR MUSKIE FROM YOUR KAYAK

The stakes are higher when you're fishing from a kayak—after all, you can't get much closer to your fish! Here's how to land a toothy monster without falling overboard.

GETTING IN POSITION The key is letting the fish get tired enough to handle—but not so worn out as to prevent a healthy release. Straddling the kayak will give you leverage and better balance. Make sure that all landing tools are within reach but out of the way. Because you're so low to the water, a net is rarely necessary. With the fish beside the boat, turn on the reel's clicker. Keep at least a rod's length of line out; too much line tension loads up the rod and could result in getting yourself impaled by a hook.

LANDING YOUR FISH It's usually when you go to lift a pike or muskie that they thrash about. Keep your eye on the lure at all times. Holding the rod in one hand, grab the back of the fish's head, just behind the gill plates. You can pin especially big fish against the kayak. Once the fish is stabilized, pop the reel out of gear and set the rod in a rod holder. Use a fish gripper to lip the fish. Slide a hand below the belly to support the fish as you lift it out of the water.

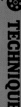

169 PACK THE PLIERS

Pike will bite through just about anything they're offered, so watch your fingers when handling them. If the pike is under 10 pounds, you can grip it across the back of the head, behind the eye, or over the back of the gill plate. Bigger pike should be netted and subdued with a firm grip while in the net. Needle-nose pliers are a must; jaw spreads can also come in handy. Pinch down the barbs of your lures to expedite extractions.

170 SCORE A WINTER PIKE ON THE FLY

If your local lake or river doesn't freeze completely in winter, pike are a viable option for fly fishermen even in the coldest months. The secret? Tailoring your presentation to sluggish fish and choosing your casting locations wisely.

THE FLIES Try flies that hover in the water column instead of sinking rapidly. Don't use patterns with heavily weighted heads, but those with bulky bodies of bucktail or synthetic materials and no added weight. Present a fly with "breathing" action that won't need moving far or abruptly to maintain some wiggle. In cold water, the slower you work, the better.

THE HOT SPOTS Keep in mind that pike don't really like current during the warmest times of year, so in rivers, finding pockets of slack water becomes critical, especially in winter. Slack holes or calm areas behind deadfall or rocks are where you're going to find the fish. In lakes, pike will continue to cruise the drop-offs around any remaining weedbeds, as well as any deep spots near the mouths of feeder creeks.

THE TAKE When the water is cold, don't expect a big pike to slam a fly the way it would in spring or summer. Hits in winter can be rather subtle, which means it's up to you to detect them. Do your best to keep as tight a connection to your fly as possible during the entire retrieve. One way to achieve this is by burying the first few inches of your rod in the water as you strip. If you feel any tick or resistance, however slight, set the hook.

171 GET MUSKIES AT THE WIRE

Muskie anglers love to debate the merits of a figure eight versus an L-turn at the end of the retrieve. They bicker over how often you need to execute one or the other: every time, or only when you see a fish following? Both methods quickly change a lure's direction, which is often the trigger that causes a following muskie to strike. The truth is that they both have a time and a place. Keep these rules in mind, and you'll have a better shot at hooking the next muskie that's hot on your lure's tail.

TURN FOR THE BETTER An L-turn is a quick sweep of the rod to the right or left when the lure is about 15 inches from the tip. This motion is far less physically taxing than a figure eight, so many guides suggest making an L-turn at the end of every retrieve. It never hurts because a fish swimming below the lure may not be visible until the last second. I've also seen muskies shoot out from under the boat to eat a lure that's just about to be pulled from the water. On clear days, even if you may not feel like you need one because of the visibility, an L turn can score surprise muskies.

FIGURE ON FACTS When to make a full figure eight at the end of the retrieve? In low light, or if the water's stained, you may not be aware you're being followed, so keeping the lure in the water for a few extra seconds is never a bad idea. If water clarity is poor, a figure eight also gives a trailing muskie more time to find the lure. In clear conditions, most guides make a figure eight only if they see a fish following, or if an L turn won't get a muskie to commit. Sometimes it takes several figure eights, or a change in speed, to draw the strike.

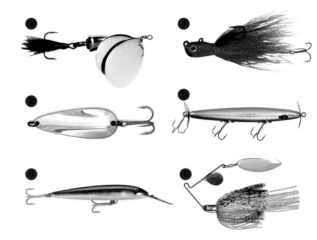

172 LURE A BIG, BAD PIKE

White, yellow, and chartreuse are great pike lure colors, probably because they resemble the belly of a struggling food fish. Try these on for size:

1. IN-LINE SPINNER In early spring, before weed growth becomes a factor, focus on covering water. Bigger spinners are a top choice here because the weight lets you cast them farther and the blades throw more flash. Retrieve the spinner steadily, just fast enough to keep it off the bottom.

2. SPOON Start by steadily and slowly reeling, just fast enough to keep the spoon wobbling. If that doesn't produce, try a "flutter retrieve," accomplished by imparting a jigging motion as you reel.

3. LARGE PLUG Begin with a steady retrieve. If that doesn't work, try stop-and-start reeling. Early in the season, use a shallow runner. As waters warm up, go to a crankbait or a soft-plastic swimbait that runs in the 10-foot range.

4. JIG As the temperature in the shallows reaches 60 degrees, pike begin to set up shop along 6- to 10-foot dropoffs. These are best fished with a jig in full, 2- to 3-foot hops. Pike often take the jig as it drops.

5. SURFACE PLUG In late spring, fish topwater lures over weedbeds in the calm water of morning or late afternoon. Over the years, the combination of a slim minnow shape and propeller fuss has been most productive for me.

6. SPINNERBAIT Draw a spinnerbait past sprouting weeds and stop the retrieve for a three-count just as the bait approaches a possible hideout. Add a twist-tail or rubber-worm trailer for action and color contrast.

173 READ A PIKE BAY

Mouths of swampy creeks (A) make good starting points, but you'll probably catch more pike in the flats just offshore. Find one where the depth is 3 to 10 feet. Pike might have traveled up the creek to spawn and will now be drifting out into the bay. These flats serve as staging spots for spawning panfish or baitfish or gathering spots for any trout (or juvenile salmon or steelhead) that may swim down following an upstream stocking.

Ice-out pike gravitate to secondary coves, areas that warm before the main bay. In fact, pike might have spawned in the marshy shallows or flooded timber (B) at the edges of such spots. Fish the flats at the mouths of these coves with in-line spinners.

Prominent shoreline structures (C)—beaver dams, flooded timbers, downed trees—always deserve at least a few casts. Work your way in, combing the flats in front with an in-line spinner.

As the spring sun warms the bay, weeds grow and pike orient to cover near dropoffs. Weedy points (D) make particularly good fishing spots, as do midbay weed shoals. Search adjacent waters with an in-line spinner, flutter-retrieve a spoon, or stop and start a spinnerbait along the edges of the weeds. If the water is calm, try your topwater lures.

Deeper weedlines (E) near access to deep water are the last spots on the spring tour. Find the 6- to 10-foot break. In general, pike over 10 pounds are the first to vacate the shallows for cooler water. This edge is the spot to try a jig-and-worm or, perhaps, to flutter-retrieve a spoon.

174 KNOW YOUR: CHAIN PICKEREL

The smallest member of the *Esox* family, pickerel may not reach the sizes of their cousins the northern pike and muskie, but in terms of light-tackle sport, they are ferocious predators that fight hard. Found in ponds, lakes, bogs, creeks, and rivers from Maine to Florida, and inland to Wisconsin, they are less finicky than other *Esox*, making them great targets for anglers of all ages. Find a shallow, reed-filled cove, a cluster of lily pads, or a submerged tree and there's a good chance a pickerel is near. They like to ambush their prey, often hovering or hiding in one spot, waiting for the perfect moment to strike. Catching one can be as simple as casting a live minnow under a bobber to likely holding areas, or as challenging as delicately presenting a streamer and watching them wake behind the fly before attacking. Pickerel are bony and not prized as table fare, but pickled they are a popular dish in certain regions, as the pickling process dissolves most of the bones.

175 GO SHALLOW FOR POSTSPAWN MUSKIES

In early summer, postspawn muskies are ill-tempered and ravenous, prowling the shallows, looking for something to clobber. Make it your topwater lure. Here's how:

FIND THEM First, you're going to want to hit the shallow muck bays where the fish typically spawn. Next, target nearby points, downed trees, weed-and-rock transitions, cabbage, and sand-and-gravel shelves. Pay special attention to where the wind is blowing into cover or structure. Shut your boat motor down about 75 yards away from the structure, and use your trolling motor to sneak to within about 100 feet of your target.

FOOL THEM Make a long cast. Bring a gurgling prop bait back with a steady retrieve, holding the rod tip low. Do the same with the dog-walker, but add repeated twitches that make the lure sashay from side to side. If you see a muskie following, don't stop the retrieve—speed it up. When the lure is about 10 feet from the boat, release the reel's spool and make a figure L or 8. (If you're just searching, do an L. If you've had a follower, do a full figure 8 or two.

LAND THEM The biggest mistake people make with topwater muskies is setting the hook too soon. Don't react to what you see, but wait until you feel the weight of the fish. Then come up and to one side with the rod tip—hard. Your drag should be screwed down so tight that you can hardly pull line out. Once you know you have a solid hookset, back the drag off to let the fish run. Then take your time and use a good muskie net to land your trophy.

176 STRIKE QUICK TO GET THAT MUSKIE

Most muskie hunters who send out live suckers are familiar with the quick-strike rig. This bait harness features two treble hooks connected by bite-proof steel wire. One hook is rigged in the bait's head, and the other is near the tail to thwart short strikes. The only problem with the traditional quick-strike is that it doesn't do much to promote catch-and-release. That's easily fixed with a tiny rubber band and a flip of the bait. Rather than rig a sucker headfirst, plant one point of the lead hook in the tail. Then, using a rigging needle, thread a small rubber band through the bait's nostrils to create an anchor point for the second hook. Muskies often attack headfirst, and with the treble seated in the rubber band, it can quickly break free upon the hookset, increasing the odds that the fish won't swallow the sucker and all that hardware. Not only will this help keep the muskie hooked just inside the mouth, but it will reduce the odds of the second hook's snagging its face or gills, which can hinder a quick release.

177 GET LUCKY WITH A DUCKY

Lures that imitate baby ducks have been around for a while, and though many anglers rope them into the gimmick category, it's a fact that big muskies feast on tiny ducklings. And even though serious muskie hunters seem to shy away from such lures, most will admit they'd love to catch a bruiser on one of these bobbing babies. Duckling lures will never replace gliders, bucktails, or jerkbaits in the muskie arsenal, but they still deserve space in your tackle box because these mini-fowl can be surprisingly effective. Here's how to use them to your best advantage:

PICK A STICK You'll want a shorter conventional rod that will force you to make shorter strokes and is stiff enough to deliver a clunky duckling but still soft enough to let you finesse it across the surface. Use it with a reel spooled with 50-pound braid.

QUACK ATTACK The secret to your attack is to work a floating duckling lure with subtle sweeps of the rod tip to make it track side to side. Ducklings don't swim in a straight line.

SET SOME DECOYS Can't find real ducklings in the area? Pick up some classic rubber-ducky toys, wrap them in mono with weights tied off to the ends, and toss them out as dekes. Cast your lure on the outside of the flock to make it look like the straggler. Will this actually work? I have no idea. But it sure sounds like fun to try.

178 GET FIT FOR FALL MUSKIES

Casting and working heavy jerkbaits that score trophy fall muskies can tax your muscles. Phys-ed teacher and Pennsylvania muskie guide Red Childress designed a preseason workout to keep him fit for throwing the big stuff. "I use Thera-Bands to strengthen my rotator cuffs," Childress says. "It's one of the easiest things to injure throwing for muskies." Tuck a rolled towel under your elbow and pull the band across your body. Turn and pull away from your body for a complete workout.

179

TRICK A PRESPAWN MUSKIE

Consistently catching prespawn muskies is a big challenge. Many anglers know muskies move into the shallows to spawn when water temps reach the 50s. The problem—these fish are all but impossible to catch because they're focused on breeding. Keep in mind that targeting muskies is illegal in some states until June or July, but where there is no closed season, here's how to get on the fish.

GO INSIDE OUT Forget plying the shallows, where muskies will be spawning. Target the water outside these areas where prespawn muskies will still be on the feed. Position your boat between the shallow flats and open water. Don't cast toward the shallow edge, like you would in summer. Instead, fish "inside out," keeping the boat in 8 to 10 feet of water and casting over the edge into the deeper water.

GLIDE ALONG Glide baits excel in cooler water for sluggish fish, as these lures can be worked at a variety of speeds and will hover on the pause. Phantom Softails or Hughes River Hugheys are phenomenal early-spring glide bait choices. Swimbaits are also proven prespawn options, and the Joe Bucher Swim'n' Raider is an old classic that's still around for a reason.

180

BANK ON A BUCKTAIL

There are literally hundreds of muskie lure styles available, and if you're new to the muskie game, selecting your arsenal can be daunting. Don't fret. The truth is it's hard to go wrong with a large in-line spinner—commonly just referred to as "bucktails" by muskie anglers—any time of year in any type of water.

Bucktails are available in many styles, but they all share common traits. A large blade or set of double blades provides serious thump and vibration as they're pulled through the water. Muskies rely heavily on their ability to pick up vibration from prey to feed, which is why bucktails are so effective. More importantly, using one requires no special skill. Simply cast, keep your rod tip low, and reel.

During warmer times of year, a fast retrieve often works best,

prompting lethargic summer or late-spring muskies to simply react out of aggression. When the water is colder, slow down your retrieve rate enough to just get the blades turning and you'll get bit.

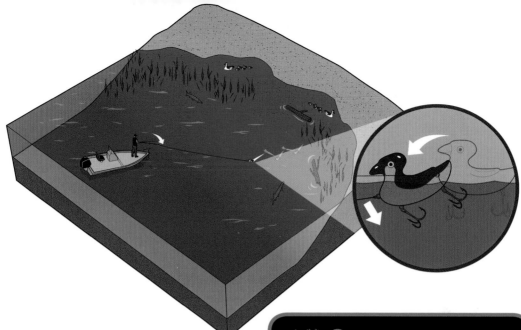

181 FLIP A MUSKIE THE BIRD

Start by scouting local waters and observing where ducks and their babies hang out most. Look in shallow bays and coves with an average depth of 10 feet or less. Areas with timber or reeds that protrude above the surface are ideal, as the structure provides shelter for the birds.

The real trick to making a duckling lure look natural in the water is to make it behave like a baby bird that got separated from the family—which often happens on very windy days—and is frantically trying to find its mother. Achieving that action all comes down to some crafty, calculated rod work. Real baby ducks don't move in a straight line, and muskies know this.

To take advantage of this fact, make a long cast, but thumb the spool before the bait lands. A live duckling weighs very little, so you want the lure to touch down with minimal splash, as would be the case with a duckling falling off a log or the bank.

Gently twitch the rod from side to side to make the lure move left and right. Don't overwork the rod, as ducklings don't move quickly or abruptly. After you've covered about 8 feet, give the lure a long pause.

Before you move the lure again, dip the rod tip in the water to pull the front of the lure downward. This makes the lure's bob more pronounced and helps mimic how a real duckling bobs, especially in a light chop.

182 KNOW YOUR: MUSKELLUNGE

Better known as muskies, this big, bad predator fish is the largest member of the *Esox* family, which also includes the northern pike and the chain pickerel. Part of the appeal for dedicated muskie hunters is the skill and patience it takes to get hooked up to what's commonly referred to as the "fish of 10,000 casts." Muskie anglers are like a cult, and many of them have little interest in pursuing other species. Muskies can top 60 pounds, but a fish that big may eat only once every other day. Be there at the right time with the right bait or lure or strike out. When a giant muskie does decide to feed, it usually wants a big meal. Many anglers consider live suckers the No. 1 live bait, but some swear by huge spinnerbaits, crankbaits, wooden jerkbaits, and monster jigs that can measure up to 14 inches.

183 BUMP THOSE BLUES

River fishing can be daunting for a catfish angler. Anchoring and setting baits in heavy current is tricky, and posting up in just one or two spots throughout the day may not put you in the prime holes. Enter catfish "bumping." It's not a new concept, but the method of trolling a river with chunk baits is making a big comeback. It definitely takes some practice, but the payoff is huge. B'n'M Poles pro staffer Jason Aycock is a true master of the bump, and his knowledge will get you on more big blue cats than you ever thought possible.

GO HEAVY Aycock stresses the need for a light, sensitive rod with a fast tip and lots of backbone. A lighter rod is less taxing as you probe the bottom all day. Bass swimbait rods and muskie rods are perfectly suited for this application. Aycock also makes sure his reels aren't too heavy but have plenty of line capacity. His go-to is the Okuma Cold Water 350 Low-Profile Line Counter, with 65-pound PowerPro. This braid's strength and zero stretch is essential to feel the bottom, maintain control of your bait, and land big fish.

DRIVE A BIG RIG The rig begins with a heavy-duty 1/0 three-way swivel. One ring attaches to the main line. Another goes to a 2-foot dropper line of 20-pound mono ending with a 3- to 6-ounce bank sinker. Don't use more than 20-pound line for this sinker dropper, as you want it to break off easily if you snag so you don't lose the whole rig. The last ring of the three-way swivel attaches to the heavier end of the main leader, which Aycock constructs by tying 18 inches of 80-pound mono to a big barrel swivel and the

same length of 50-pound mono to the other side. The mid-leader swivel prevents line twist and makes the presentation look more natural. Finally, Aycock finishes the 50-pound leader with a 7/0 Daiichi Circle Chunk hook. As for bait, Aycock likes chunked skipjack herring, but gizzard shad is a close second.

BREAK THE CURRENT There are countless areas to target cats on any given river, but Aycock mainly focuses on big bends in the channel. From the bend and immediately downstream, the current is slower. In the perfect scenario, Aycock prefers the current at 2.5 to 3 mph; catfish will hold in the slower water, and the brush piles and logjams that accumulate there provide excellent cover for big cats to use as ambush locations and resting spots out of the flow. Wherever there is wood, he says, there will be blue cats. The most important piece of equipment for catfish bumping is a quality trolling motor. Aycock points the trolling motor straight into the current to slow down his boat by half the current speed. After a test drift, he'll power the motor to slow the boat to 1.5 mph in a 3-mph current. If it's 4 mph, he fishes at 2 mph, and so on. While drifting a rig, Aycock constantly bounces it up and down with a long, steady jigging motion. If you drag the weight across the bottom, you'll just get hung up. Watch your line, as the catfish often make it go slack as they push up off the bottom to attack the bait from below. When that happens, it can be very tricky to take up your slack and nail a solid hook-set, Aycock says, but often, the cats just try to rip the rod from your hands. Slack off for a second, and you could lose your entire outfit.

184 USE YOUR NOODLE

Your kids have finally outgrown the swim noodles gathering dust in the basement? Good. Here's how to recycle those noodles for jugging catfish.

STEP 1 Cut one 5-foot pool noodle into five 1-foot sections. (You'll be able to store five noodle-jugs upright in a 5-gallon bucket—enough to keep you plenty busy.) Wrap one end of each with three overlapping wraps of duct tape; this will protect against line cuts. Use a large darning needle or crochet hook to string a 4-foot length of stout mono (60- to 100-pound) or trotline cord through the tape wrap. Tie off one end to a washer or bead, pull it snug, and tie a three-way swivel to the other end.

STEP 2 To the swivel's lower ring, attach a length of 20- to 40-pound mono that's long enough to reach the bottom. Anchor the rig with sufficient weight for the current—any old chunk of iron or even something like half a brick will do. To reduce line twist while wrapping line around the noodle for storage, use a barrel swivel near the weight. To the third ring, tie in a 4-foot dropper line of 20-pound fluorocarbon and a circle hook.

STEP 3 If you fish at night, run a strip of reflective tape around the noodle on the opposite end from the line. Try a 4-ounce weight on the bottom and free-float the noodles as you monitor the action from the boat.

185

WATCH THE SPINES

There are three bullhead species—yellow, brown, and black. It's hard for nonscientists to tell them apart, though brown bullheads tend to be larger, averaging 12 to 15 inches long and reaching 6 or 7 pounds. All of the species have three sharp, mildly venomous spines, one at the front of the dorsal fin and one on each of the two pectoral fins. To avoid injury, grab a bullhead by its jaw as you would a bass or around the body behind the dorsal spine. If you do get pricked, rub ammonia on the wound for relief.

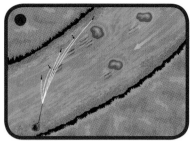

186 SPOON A TROUT

Like fins on a Chevy or a ball game broadcast over a scratchy transistor radio, trout fishing with spoons seems like something from a bygone era. Truth is, this method is as lethal now as it was in the old days. In April, chubs and shiners are spawning in streams across the country, and the biggest trout in the system are gobbling them up.

FLUTTER AWAY Spoons shine in stretches where dead wood or boulders create mid-river hiding places. Cast quartering upstream and retrieve slightly faster than the flow (A). This will get the lure riding just above the bottom where the big fish hold. Pause the retrieve any time the spoon knocks off a rock or moves into a slack spot. The fluttering stop-and-go motion mimics an injured baitfish trying to right itself.

MAKE THE CUT Trophy brown trout love to tuck beneath undercut banks, and a spoon is perfect for pulling them out. Creep into position over the deepest part of the undercut pool, and vertically jig a spoon as close to the bank's edge as possible (B). Make sure you don't cast a shadow on the water. Big trout often slam the spoon on the drop, so you should have one hand ready to flip the bail closed as the lure falls.

GET SOME HANG TIME If you can't get a good position downstream of a hole, set up directly upstream, disengage your reel's anti-reverse, and backreel the spoon into the current, letting it flutter down into the sweet spot (C). This is a deadly tactic if the hole has a ceiling, such as a logjam or root sweeper. Once the spoon reaches depth, keep your tip low and hang in the current for a minute before retrieving.

187 COMPUTE FOR CATS

Do you want to catch bigger blue cats from shore? A combination of online resources and maps can provide you with all the information you need to get it done. Start with an online depth chart, or, if you have $15, the Navionics app on your smartphone will pay dividends. Many shore-bound anglers don't think to rely on electronics, but being able to cross-reference between a depth chart and Google Earth will help you find the holes in casting range of the bank and then narrow down which ones are most accessible. This inside track on depth can provide the motivation you need to make that 10-mile hike that leads to the biggest blue of your life.

188 GO BULLISH ON BULLHEADS

These small catfish are usually easy to catch and also make for superb eating, which accounts for their huge popularity, especially in the Midwest. Rigging for bullheads is simple. Cover a size 4 to 1/0 hook tied to 6- to 8-pound-test monofilament with a gob of small worms or a single nightcrawler. Add enough split shot about 18 inches above the hook to give adequate casting weight. Because bullheads are most active after dark, the action should increase after the sun goes down. Prop the rod in a forked stick and pay attention to your tackle so it doesn't get dragged in by a night-biting fish.

Bullheads have extraordinary senses of smell and taste, and those can help you catch them. Here's one way:

STEP 1 When you make your first cast into a bullhead pond, you'll want to toss your line out at about a 60-degree angle to shore and then reel your weighted worm back slowly along the bottom.

STEP 2 Walk about 30 feet along the shoreline and make another angled cast on a trajectory that would intersect your first, creating an imaginary X out in the water. Drag your worm back slowly once again.

STEP 3 Cast your bait to the X-spot intersection, sit down, and watch your line. The scent trails that you've created should lead bullheads to your worm more quickly. I've caught plenty of them by doing this, whenever bottom snags or weeds don't interfere.

189 CATCH A RESERVOIR CAT

The blue catfish, weighing in at 30 to 40 pounds, can meet your monster-fish needs. Here's how to fish a reservoir and land a trophy that will bring tears to the eyes of any pro:

Flat

Creek channel

BOTTOM FEEDING This technique works well on a shallow flat that maintains a depth of 6 to 8 feet for 50 yards or more offshore before dropping sharply down to a creek or river channel. The biggest cats hover at the lip of the drop. Anchor your boat from the bow about 60 feet upwind of your target area and cast bottom rigs out over the transom. Set the rods in holders, put the reels in free spool, flip on the clickers, and wait. The bite is hottest when the wind blows baitfish up onto the flat.

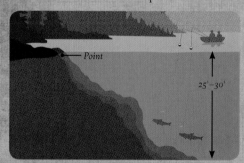

Point

25'–30'

SUSPENDED ANIMATION Mark suspended catfish with a depthfinder. (At 20- to 35-foot depths, they often hold 5 to 10 feet off the bottom.) Next, set your slip bobbers to keep the live baits 1 to 2 feet above the blues. Put your rigs out 25 to 75 yards behind the boat. Place the rods in holders and drift over the fish. If there's little wind or current, use the electric trolling motor to get your bobbers the proper distance away from the boat. Once they hit the right distance, lock the reel and slowly cruise around the area where the fish are holding.

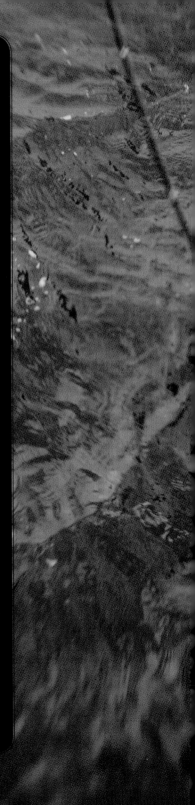

190 SEE THE SIGNS

Nothing is sweeter than sight fishing on a calm summer day in crystal-clear water. It's even better when the fish are feeding a short cast away. But when a storm rolls in, the wind picks up, or a cold front pushes your targets out of the skinny stuff, sight casting can turn sour. However, it can be done if you're willing to plan carefully, put in your time, and lean on the tips from these expert sight-fishing guides from across the United States.

SUDDEN STORM
Pro: Asher Koles
Home Water: Provo River, Utah
Target: Trout rising to a hatch

Even if spotting big fish in clear water has been the game all day, Koles doesn't panic when a storm looms. "A storm coming means there's a drop in pressure," he says. "This usually triggers a hatch, and cloud cover also diffuses the water's surface. The fish feel safer and it's more difficult for them to spot an angler."

Of course, it's harder for you to fully see the fish, too, so the key now is to read the rise forms, Koles advises. Splashy rises typically mean small fish. Soft rises or swirls are usually the bigger ones. In low light, it can be easier to pick out rise forms up- or downstream than directly across.

COLD FRONT
Pro: Kevin Morlock
Home Water: Lake Michigan
Target: Carp moving to deeper waters

"In a cold snap, carp move off the flats fast to look for warmer waters," Morlock says. "If that happens, I go where they were yesterday first and look for lingering fish. If there's no life whatsoever, I start working the flats edges."

The problem with fishing the edges, however, is that they're deeper. Add in some cloud cover and mud from rooting fish, and getting a good line of sight on your targets becomes tricky.

"Look for little mud tornadoes," Morlock says. "The tighter the spiral, the more recently it was made. Sometimes that's all you have to go on to lead a fish when conditions are poor."

STRONG WINDS
Pro: Justin Price
Home Water: Mosquito Lagoon, Fla.
Target: Redfish feeding in the shallows

"When wind kicks up, try to get out of wide-open water," Price says. "Find the lee side of an island and work the shoreline. The water under the mangroves won't have as much wind ripple, and it's easier to spot fish in the shade."

If you simply can't escape open flats, put your boat in the skinniest water you can find. According to Price, the shallower you get, the slower the boat will blow in the wind. As you ride the gusts, look for fish in downwind holes or channels where baitfish may get blown to waiting reds. Weighted lures and flies will get into the strike zone faster when it's windy.

191 SKIN A CAT

Here's an old-school way to skin an eating-size cat—say, 4 pounds or less.

SCORE IT Place a 3-foot-long 2x6 board on a level, waist-high surface. A truck tailgate works well. Using a knife, score the skin all the way around the head, just in front of the cat's gill plates. Make another slit down the back.

NAIL IT Drive a 16-penny nail through the fish's skull to secure it to the board. Cut off its dorsal fin. Brace the board against your waist, with the tail pointing toward you. Grasp the skin with fish-skinning pliers and pull it down to the tail and off.

GUT IT Remove the fish from the board. Grasping the head in one hand and the body in the other, bend the head sharply downward, breaking the spine. Now bend the body up and twist to separate head from body. Open the belly with your knife, remove the remaining viscera from the body cavity, and rinse well.

192 CATCH THE DRIFT

You may be able to paddle a rowboat around a pond, but maneuvering on a swift, boulder-strewn river is a different game, one worth learning if you're serious about reaching more trout. Besides steering safely downriver, you've got to put your anglers in the best position to catch fish.

PUT SOME BACK INTO IT Point the bow downstream and row backward, says Ben Scribner, owner of Flycraft USA. "My oars are always in the water; I'm constantly applying pressure against the current to stabilize the boat." A stable platform helps casters make the best presentations, but you should also look at what's ahead downstream of your position, read the water, and anticipate where the boat needs to be. "I try to give my anglers a downstream reach cast at a 45-degree angle. It gives them longer drifts and a better angle for a hookset," Scribner says.

MAKE THE BANK SHOTS Matt Kelley of ClackaCraft tries to keep his drift boat 20 to 40 feet from the bank. This gets most casters within easy reach of the soft spots where big trout hold. "It helps to focus on two points along the bank, such as a bush and a rock or a big tree," says Kelley. One should be close, the other a little farther downstream. "Use these points of reference to keep a consistent distance from the bank." (The actual objects change, of course, as you drift.) "And watch the anglers' casts to be sure you stay in their range. If they struggle to hit prime spots, readjust."

BRING UP THE REAR "The angler in the back has to deal with more obstacles—like oars and anchor davits—than the caster in the front," says Dan Leavens of Montana's Stonefly Inn & Outfitters. "That and the fact that he has to hit water already worked by the bow angler makes me try a little harder to get him in as good a position as I can." Many rowers point the bow into shore, making the rear angler cast farther. "I keep the better angler in the bow," says Leavens. "The team will put up more fish this way; the stern angler learns by watching good casts, drifts, and hooksets."

193 BREAK BREAD

Fly fishing for carp has a different appeal for different anglers. Many enjoy the challenge of stalking feeding fish in shallow water and trying to perfectly present a nymph or streamer to these snobby fish. For others, the appeal of carp on the fly is just that they're big and they pull hard. If you're one of the anglers less interested in the stalk and more interested in the fight, you can save yourself a lot of frustration by fishing bread flies.

A bread fly is white foam pierced on a nymph hook, thick enough that it won't get waterlogged and sink. It's a deadly tactic in park ponds and other areas where fish and local ducks are used to being fed bread.

Is a bread fly cheating? I love hunting lone carp grubbing crayfish on small streams. But if I'm short on time or in the mood to hear a reel scream, I've been known to cast a bread fly now and again.

194 SIGHT-CAST TO SUCKERMOUTHS

Got no respect for carp? Try stalking them in shallow water. These ugly fish are wary and smart and frequently hit 20 to 30 pounds. The key to fishing for carp in 2 to 4 feet of water is to go slow and easy. If you splash or stumble, they'll spook. Here's how to do it:

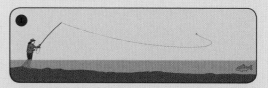

STEP 1 Pick a loner fish or choose just one in a group and cast in front of it.

STEP 2 Twitch the fly just a little as it sinks. Let the fly touch the bottom, and the carp will follow it down.

STEP 3 When the fish sucks up the fly, the take will be hard to feel. Hold your rod tip right down on the water and keep a straight line to the fly. That way you'll feel a little tug when the carp eats, and you can set the hook.

195

SHOOT A CARP IN THE AIR

There are plenty of reasons why you should spend a few summer days bowfishing for silver carp. For one thing, these invasive fish have now grossly overpopulated and are systematically destroying some of our best Midwestern river fisheries. And believe it or not, they're not bad to eat. They also grow to 40 pounds and leap 6 feet out of the water—often by the hundreds—when startled by the sound of an outboard. Who wouldn't want to shoot at that?

GET A JUMP-START Silver carp leap at the sound of boat motors, but if you want to really get them going en masse, run your boat in shallow water—10 feet deep or less.

Trim your outboard up and give it just enough gas to plow a good wake. If there are fish present, they'll be jumping in seconds.

GET IN POSITION Stand or sit at the transom of the boat. Any bow-fishing rig will work, but a reel that allows you to retrieve arrows quickly is a good idea.

PICK YOUR SHOTS On a good run, fish will be everywhere, but wait for one to jump near the boat. When it does, hit your anchor point, track the fish over the end of the arrow, focusing on a spot just underneath it, and let fly as the fish falls back toward the water.

196 WARM UP AFTER A SPILL IN FRIGID WATERS

Even before the waters ice over, a great late-season fishing trip can become dicey in an instant if your boat should capsize, if you get knocked overboard, or if you slip while wading out in open waters. Hypothermia, or dangerously low body temperature, is possible anytime the air temperature is below 50 degrees, and immersion in cold water can accelerate the process from hours to mere minutes. So, you're soaking wet after your dunk—what now?

The basics of fending off hypothermia are always the same: Get out of the wind, which saps warmth fast when it hits wet clothing, then get dry, get moving, and introduce a heat source. But different scenarios will present you with different challenges depending on where you are and whether you are alone. Here are the right steps to take in three key situations.

DRY OFF ON LAND If you should happen to have a slip while wading, the best-case scenario will be that you're within eyesight of your vehicle, where you will have left an extra set of dry clothes to change into with the heat pumping from the vents. Do not waste time wondering whether you can continue to fish; just get out of the water and get going. If you're within a mile of your car or campsite, hiking back will warm you, but you won't be out of the wind, so you have to get dry first. Remove all your wet clothes, and replace with any extra layers that you have or a buddy can spare. At the

very least, remove what you're wearing, wring out the water, and then put it all back on.

HANDLE GOING OVERBOARD If you're out on the water with other anglers and you should happen to fall off a boat, seek shelter below decks or behind a windshield, or get low and then change your clothes lying on your back while someone else drives or paddles the craft back to the launch. If you're alone, then you're better off getting to the nearest piece of land and sheltering behind the boat or a natural barrier while you work to get dry before you start your return trip back to the put-in.

ADDRESS EXTREME ELEMENTS Are you too far from the ramp or your truck to get there safely? Then you should start to gather firewood—even if a buddy is there to do it for you. The movement will help increase your internal heat production and will preserve dexterity in the short term. Pick out a natural backdrop, such as a big rock or hillside, to cut off the wind, and then build a fire in front of that backdrop in order to reflect heat onto your back as you face the blaze. Boil some water and pour it into a bottle, if you have one. Then place it against your body over your base layer. As the water cools off, drink it, and then boil more. Repeat these steps until help arrives or until you are well enough to be on your way back to (warmer and drier) civilization.

197 ADD FLAVOR TO YOUR SALMON LURE

No angler in the know would dream of casting or trolling a banana wobbler for king salmon without first adding a sardine or anchovy belly strip. But the effectiveness of bait wrapping a lure to add scent isn't limited to the Pacific Northwest. To wrap a lure, you'll need a fillet knife, scissors, and self-binding clear thread.

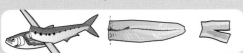

STEP 1 Fit the bait to the plug by filleting an anchovy and then cutting it into a section that's about three-eighths as long as the plug and two-thirds as wide. Using scissors, cut lengthwise through the strip so that it resembles a pair of pants.

STEP 2 Slide the "crotch" over the belly hook eye with the skin side down. Center the strip on the belly of the plug and secure one end of the thread by pinning it

under the first few wraps. Wrap thread from front to back, working around the hook. The wraps should be taut enough to indent the flesh. Finish off at the rear with several half hitches.

STEP 3 After adding a belly strip, you may have to tune the lure by turning the eyelet to the right or left to make it run true. Belly

strips stop emitting scent after 20 to 30 minutes. You can prolong their effectiveness by squeezing on a liquid attractant.

GET A CAT OUT FROM UNDER THE ICE

Dog days and catfish nights are a hallmark of summer, but the whiskered fish don't just bite when it's balmy. They feed all winter long under the ice and, when hooked on a light jigging rod, put up a much better fight than trout or walleyes. The trick to catching a mess of them is getting the first one on the line. After that, the action should be drop-and-reel.

GO DEEP A catfish's metabolism slows down considerably in winter. As a result, they seek out the warmest water, which is often found in the deepest hole in the lake. If you find one catfish, you'll commonly find a dozen or more, all lying close to the bottom, tucked tight against humps, rock piles, or wood structure.

GLOW FOR IT Just like summertime cats, wintertime whisker fish are most active at night. Dawn and dusk are good, but if you can stick it out until well past sundown, you're likely to be rewarded. Cats under the ice also respond well to glow-in-the-dark baits and jigs, and the later it gets, the more effective these become.

MAKE A STIR Even for bigger cats, smaller baits are more productive, so stick with fathead minnows, juvenile chubs, and my favorite catfish bait: three or four waxworms threaded onto a tiny teardrop-style jig. Drop your baited jig down to the bottom and work it aggressively. This action stirs up sediment and starts a feeding frenzy.

199 SCORE A MIDSUMMER STRIPER

The paradox of landlocked stripers is that they are big, brawling fish that can reach 60 pounds and pull like a plow horse—but they are also delicate, sensitive, and fussy. They function well in a very narrow temperature range: 55 to 65 degrees is ideal. When temperatures soar, these fish are forced to go deep to find cooler water—but the deeper they go, the less dissolved oxygen becomes available to them. This causes a slow bite at best and a striper kill at worst. To score a midsummer striper, you need to target river-run reservoirs and the churning tailraces of power dams, where the water is cool, oxygen-rich, and loaded with big baitfish.

When a lake's temperature is in the 70s, stripers will suspend 20 to 30 feet deep off main lake points, steep rock bluffs, and submerged standing timber along cavernous river channels. They'll bite best at sunup and sundown. Use stout baitcasting or spinning outfits to fish deep and vertical. Bait up with large gizzard shad (catch these in a cast net) or, where legal, 6- to 8-inch rainbow trout. Watch your bow-mounted sonar for suspending stripers and baitfish schools, and then lower your baits to just above the level of the fish, moving slowly around the area with your trolling motor until you contact active stripers.

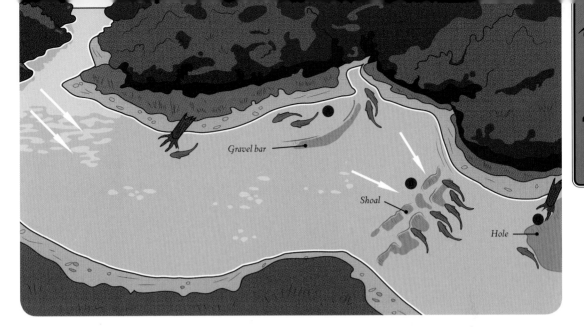

Gravel bar

Shoal

Hole

200 GIVE A DAM

When summer temperatures soar, it's time to move to the fast water found below a dam, where the temperature is frigid and the stripers get aggressive. Be there at first light, armed with beefy 7- to 8-foot baitcasting outfits with wide-spool reels sporting heavy line (30- to 40-pound mono or heavier braided line). Wolf packs of stripers will cruise shallow shoals and gravel bars at daybreak (A), hitting schools of baitfish with percussive surface strikes. Start with a big, noisy muskie prop bait, retrieving it with loud rips and tranquil pauses. As the fog burns off, switch to a quieter topwater glide bait, retrieving it slowly across the surface so the tail sashays back and forth, leaving a wake behind it. By midmorning, move to 5- to 10-foot holes adjacent to those shallow shoals and bars (B), casting a 10-inch soft jerkbait rigged with a treble stinger hook. Stripers shun bright sunlight, holding tight to undercut banks and submerged trees (C); cast the bait around these spots and skate it rapidly across the surface.

201 PULL BIG LIVE BAITS

In really hot weather, stripers will pack into the upper reaches of cold-flowing rivers. Topwaters work early and late in the day, but in the mid-afternoon a better approach is to pull big live baits—gizzard shad, skipjack herring, or rainbow trout—behind planer boards. You'll need an aerated circular shad tank to keep your bait frisky. Use 8-foot-long medium-heavy baitcasting rods and big reels spooled with 40- to 50-pound mono or up to 30-pound braided line. Start upstream of your target and rig your bait no more than 6 to 8 feet behind the board to keep it from constantly swimming into snaggy cover. Then, proceed slowly downstream under trolling-motor power, staying just ahead of the current so the board planes toward the shoreline. When your bait gets nervous, keep calm—a 40-pounder plastering a big shad on the surface sounds like a Buick falling off a bridge.

Planer board

Big live bait

202 WORK THE INSHORE HIT LIST

The areas in and around inlets and bay systems are prime territory for predatory gamefish. No matter where you live (unless you happen to be in the middle of a desert), these 10 spots are going to hold gamefish in your local waters.

1. BEACH TROUGH Deep troughs close to the beach are gamefish magnets. Stripers, weakfish, tarpon, redfish, and pompano are just a few species that cruise through these depressions looking for a meal. The easiest way to find troughs is to watch waves on the beach. If one breaks offshore and then flattens suddenly, it often means the wave encountered a deep spot.

2. ISLAND CUT Tidal flow that gets squeezed between small islands will generally create a deep cut as it scours out the bottom. These cuts can create tremendous ambushing spots for all kinds of gamefish, though fish such as flounder, redfish, seatrout, and snook are some of the species known to use them most frequently.

3. CHANNEL CONFLUENCE Anywhere two deep channels come together in a bay system is a great place to look for fish, particularly bottom feeders such as flounder and black drum. As the tide moves, smaller forage species skirt along channel edges; Colliding currents where channels meet can disorient them, making them easy targets for gamefish.

4. INLET RIP In inlets you'll often notice bulges, ripples, or standing waves on the surface, especially when tidal flow is at its peak speed. These disturbances are known as rips and are caused by structure or high spots on the bottom that force moving water to push up toward the surface. Gamefish stack up on the down-current side of whatever creates the rip, waiting for food to pass overhead.

5. INLET MOUTH When the tide is rushing out of a bay system, gamefish know to patrol the mouth of an inlet for a shot at an easy meal, as baitfish, shrimp, and other forage will be getting pulled into the ocean. Everything from tarpon to

stripers, tuna to grouper, will congregate here, and live baits or jigs worked near the bottom often produce best.

6. BUOYS It's always worth making a few casts around buoys and channel markers. These man-made structures provide a current break, and gamefish like seatrout and striped bass sometimes use that break to ambush bait. In the South, tripletail are notorious for hanging near markers and buoys. Cast a live or dead shrimp to the structure, and you'll know in short order if a tripletail is home.

7. JETTY TIP Whether the tide is pushing into an inlet or pulling out, jetty tips provide a current break where gamefish will wait for bait to get flushed past with the water flow. This is an excellent place to throw topwater lures that make lots of noise.

8. JETTY POCKET Incoming waves often scoop a deep depression along the beach right at the point where an inlet

jetty meets the sand. These pockets make terrific ambush points for everything from snook to sheepshead to striped bass. Gamefish will also work together to push a school of baitfish into a pocket so the food source can't escape.

9. TIDAL CREEK Even tidal creeks so small they are dry at low tide are worth fishing when the water's up. Small forage species know to use tidal creeks to get out of main channels at high tide. As the water falls, redfish, seatrout, flounder, and striped bass flock to the mouths of these creeks. Cast lures up into the creek and work them back into open water.

10. SHALLOW FLAT In Southern and Gulf states, species such as redfish, bonefish, tarpon, and permit are frequently found in skinny water, where they hunt for baitfish seeking refuge in the shallows and root for crabs and shrimp in the soft bottom. In the Northeast, striped bass and weakfish also hunt sand and mudflats during certain tidal stages, especially during marine worm hatches.

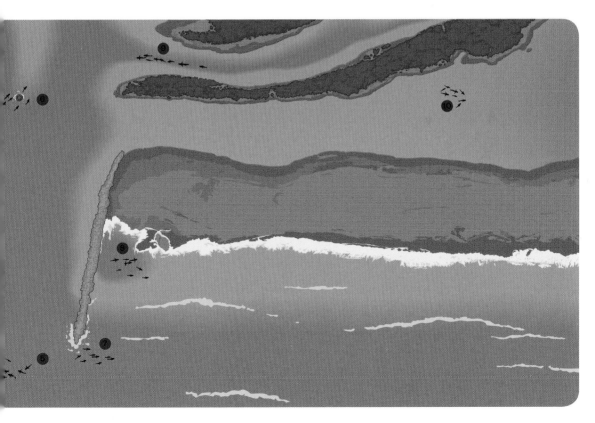

203 DANCE THE JIG

Diamond jigs are one of the most simple, yet effective, lures for catching bluefish and striped bass. They're inexpensive and mimic a wide variety of forage, from sand eels to herring. But a diamond jig requires a little more finesse than simply dropping to the bottom and moving the rod tip up and down. These three methods will get you hooked up.

TOP SPEED Blues and stripers often react best to baitfish fleeing quickly. When fish marks show up on your sounder in the middle of the water column, drop the jig all the way to the bottom and reel up as fast as you can. You don't actually have to jig the rod at all. When fish are keyed in to fast-moving bait, the hit will be more of a slam when they strike.

YO-YO When bait schools are really thick, below the surface baitfish will be zipping in all directions, while injured baitfish will

flutter and fall to the bottom. To mimic a baitfish both fleeing and dying, drop to the bottom and lift the rod high into the air in a sharp stroke. As you lower the rod to jig again, quickly reel up the slack. This gives the jig a dart/fall action, and since you keep picking up slack, you'll work the entire water column until the jig is back on the surface.

SLOW DRAG When sand eels are the primary food source available to them, bass and bluefish often hug the bottom, since this bait species burrows in the sand and mud down there. If you're marking patches of sand eels on the bottom in any location, let your jig touch down, pay out 20 extra feet of line, and lock up the reel. Don't jig or crank; just let the lure drag across the bottom. It'll kick up sand or mud as it moves with the drifting boat, mimicking a fleeing sand eel. Bass and blues will slurp it right up.

204 BOB AN EEL

Live eels are one of the most effective baits for striped bass throughout their Eastern saltwater range of Maine to North Carolina. Though eels are traditionally fished weighted along the bottom, anglers in the Chesapeake Bay have perfected a different technique. Using an oversize, round slip bobber, they'll suspend live eels at various depths throughout the water column, keeping one just off the bottom, one at midrange, and one just below the surface. Even in deeper water, a big bass will often rise to the shallowest eels, as their wiggle and dark silhouette stand out well against the back-lit surface and are irresistible to a cow striper. Though the method may have been developed in the Chesapeake, it works along any channel edge, hump, or rock pile that bass frequent.

Loop

Egg sinker

Swivel

205 RIG AN EEL FOR STRIPERS

In August 2011, Connecticut angler Greg Myerson caught an 81.8-pound striped bass that trumped the former all-tackle world-record striper by nearly 3 pounds. Myerson's fish ate a live eel, which is arguably one of the best striper baits ever. The problem with eels is they're expensive—about four bucks a pop. To be sure you get the maximum bang for those bucks, hook your eel through the top jaw and out one eye. This lets the bait breathe better—and lets you return any uneaten eels to the live well.

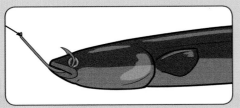

206 GET LOADED FOR STRIPERS

Diving plugs, such as Bomber Long As and Red Fins, have been staples in the surf-casting scene since they were invented. Though they produce lots of stripers out of the box, these lures are hollow, so when the wind is whipping, they can be a chore to cast. That's why surf anglers took to "loading" such plugs, and it's a practice that continues to put more bass on the beach even today.

STEP 1 Start by drilling a small hole in the belly of the lure.

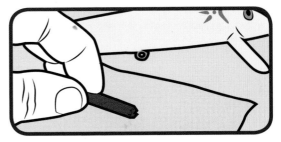

STEP 2 Next, cut a piece of wooden dowel to about 1 1/2 inches, making sure the dowel is slightly wider in diameter than the hole. Hone one end of the dowel piece to a slight point with sandpaper to create a cork.

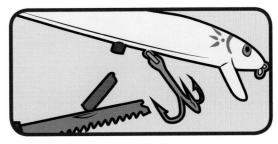

STEP 3 Use the dowel to plug the lure. When you're ready to fish, remove the cork to fill the plug with water, adding weight for casting while also allowing the plug to sink a little deeper. You can also drop in BBs to add weight before fishing. This also amps up the sound, as the BBs rattle.

207 GO FROM POND TO BAYOU

Redfish and largemouth bass have a lot in common. They both live in fairly shallow water that's loaded with vegetation, they feed on a wide variety of prey, and they rely less on vision and more on sound and vibration when hunting for their next meal. With that in mind, it stands to reason that a lot of the lures designed to catch largemouth on lakes and farm ponds will put a serious hurt on redfish cruising through salty lagoons, backwaters, and marshes. Here are three bass lures you should never go on a redfish hunt without.

▶ **SPINNERBAIT** These are great for redfish because their design allows them to run through weeds and grass without getting hung up, and the blade gives off flash and makes a thump reds can easily track, even when the water is murky. Since they  don't hang up easily, you can throw them into flooded reeds and marsh grass and drag them into open water. That's important because reds often hunt close to vegetation on shorelines.

▶ **CRANKBAIT** One method that works well for bass anglers is bumping a crankbait off stumps and rocks. This creates a knocking sound that gets the fish's attention and often prompts a strike. The same technique works for redfish whenever they are orienting to hard structure, such as  oyster bars or rock jetties. Depending on the water depth, a shallow- or deep-diving crankbait might be in order.

▶ **CREATURE BAIT** Creature baits look like aliens, and instead of resembling any specific forage species, they are designed to look like a combination of many and simply get a bass's attention. Because they can imitate everything from a crayfish to a lizard, they're bass killers.  Put them in saltwater and they look just like a crab or shrimp. Fished either on a jighead or a Carolina rig, these baits are deadly on reds that are grubbing the bottom.

208 LOSE THE SPIN

When anglers target large species—namely striped bass and bull redfish—in the surf, large baits and heavy weights are often in order to entice these brutes and deliver offerings to distant troughs. The problem with casting a whole menhaden head or live mullet along with a 5- to 10-ounce weight is that the rig tends to spin or "helicopter" in the air, causing tangles and hurting distance. One way surf casters have overcome this challenge is by building compact bait rigs. Whereas a common bait rig features a three-way swivel to connect the main line and hold the weight, plus a long length of leader for the hook, compact rigs use only a 3- or 4-inch length of leader tied to a single barrel swivel. Before that swivel is connected to the main line, a second barrel swivel is slid up the line. A weight clip is then connected to the sliding swivel. When cast, the weight and bait stay close together in a neat package that won't spin, but once they hit the bottom, the free-floating swivel holding the weight allows the bait to be pulled away by the current, or by a fish when it hits.

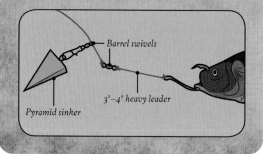

Barrel swivels

3"–4" heavy leader

Pyramid sinker

209 POP A TUNA

One of the most thrilling experiences in saltwater is watching a tuna smash a popper on the surface. Their speed and power is unmatched, and when that vacuum opens around your lure, followed by a plume of water, all you can do is hang on for dear life after you set the hook. Of course, the first part of the challenge is getting that lure in front of the fish; it's not easy.

Tuna are incredibly fast fish, often moving in packs as they herd and attack baitfish. With that in mind, it's critical that you position the boat well ahead of a moving school and let them come to you, as opposed to trying to chase them down. Tuna move so quickly that they're not likely to turn around if a popper lands behind them. Calculate their speed, and how frequently they surface along their path, and set up a good 80 to 100 yards ahead of them. It may take time to get your shot, but there's a better chance you'll connect when it happens.

210
GET READY
FOR SQUID SEASON

Longfin squid, which live from Newfoundland to Venezuela, form an essential building block in the ocean food web and are an important commercial fishery. When dense masses of them venture within easy reach of small-craft anglers, an underappreciated sport fishery unfolds.

Jigging for squid resembles ordinary vertical jigging, save for the peculiarities of squid jigs, which are hookless. They come in many types and sizes. Some glow in the dark, some are solid metal, others are plastic-bodied and float or sink at a slow rate, and a few have small integral lights. They all work, and they share a trait: rows of spiky pins built to take advantage of the feeding habits of squid, which seize prey with their tentacles and pull it toward their beaklike mouth.

When a squid reaches for a jig, the angler will usually sense its weight. Pulling back drives the pins into the tentacles. From there the angler simply reels in steadily,

being sure to give the squid no slack, which can allow the barbless pins to slip loose. The trick is to keep the squid moving smoothly and vertically, dragged along by the jig, and to continue the motion fluidly as it clears the water via a gentle lift and swing that carries the squid into the air and onto the deck or, even better, to a waiting hand.

The last steps can be elusive for new squidders. Gawking at a pinned squid boatside is almost impossible for many to resist, and also a good way to lose a squid. Still, this is not a difficult sport. Once a squid comes aboard, it goes immediately into a high-sided bucket of seawater-and-ice slurry. Squid decompose swiftly; on a warm night, your delicacy can turn foul in a flash. The slurry bucket has another function, too—it becomes a reservoir of squid ink, which makes cleanup easier later. When the squidding hits lulls, we transfer the squid into bags and bury them in a cooler with fresh ice, to await cleaning on land at sunrise.

211 SKIP
SOME METAL

Classic metal lures like a Kastmaster or a Hopkins are often reserved for deep jigging or working the bottom; their flash can be seen in low light and their weight gets them down fast. But don't rule out these metals as surface lures. In situations where species like bluefish,

striped bass, or redfish have schools of bait pinned at the surface, a weighty metal lets you reach the fish without getting on top of the action. Reel quickly with the rod tip high to get the lure erratically skipping and jumping across the surface, and hang on tight.

212 GET THE GAFF!

Knowing how to gaff a yellowfin tuna or albacore ranks next to opening a beer bottle with a knife blade on the manliness scale. Should you ever need to know, here's how to wield the gaff like a salty pro. Just make sure your gaff is sharpened. That's rule No. 1.

DEATH CIRCLE As the tuna tires, it will swim in circles (1) below the boat. The captain should keep the engines in gear so that the fish swims parallel with the stern. Position yourself just ahead of the angler.

HEAD GAMES Hold the gaff at the rear and mid grips, and never take a wild swing. Keep the gaff point turned down and wait for a clear shot at the head (2) as the fish moves toward you.

POINT TAKEN Calmly but sharply pull the gaff into the fish's head (3) using both hands. Body shots will ruin the meat. Aim for the eyes. The ocular area is tough and offers a better hold for lifting the fish.

HIT THE DECK In one smooth motion, drag the fish over the gunwale (4). The boat's forward momentum should make this easier.

213

VIBE OUT YOUR LIVE BAIT

When saltwater species get cued into a large school of baitfish, sometimes it can be harder than you'd think to get them to eat. When striped bass are feeding on menhaden, for instance, or tarpon are chasing mullet, there can be so much bait in the water that your livie doesn't get noticed. To fix the problem, all you need is a pair of scissors. Simply snip the lower part of the tail fin off your live baitfish and send it back out. It may seem like an insignificant change, but remember that all the other bait in the school is giving off the same vibrations underwater. A baitfish minus the lower part of its tail is going to swim differently, sink deeper because it won't be able to push as much water, and emit a completely different vibration from the rest of the school. Nine times out of 10, a livie with a cut tail won't last a minute, even if the bait schools are superthick.

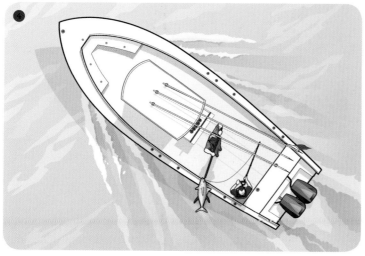

214 WORK A PENCIL POPPER

Pencil poppers are one of the most effective lures at imitating large baitfish splashing on the surface. Unlike standard short-body poppers, pencils take more than just a nudge of the rod tip to make a joyful noise. Follow these steps to whip a pencil like a pro.

RIP IT Pencil poppers are rear-weighted and will travel a mile. Using a 10- to 12-foot soft-action surf rod, cast the popper as far as it will go (1). The greater the cast distance, the more time there is for the popper's loud splashing sound to draw in fish.

GRIP IT Bend your knees slightly and tuck the butt of the surf rod between your thighs. With your non-reeling hand, grab the rod blank 6 to 10 inches above the first guide (2). This might feel awkward at first, but you'll get used to it.

WHIP IT Reel quickly as you whip the rod (3). The harder the rod flexes, the more forcefully the lure smacks and spits water. If a fish strikes, this position also puts the power at the center of your body for a solid hookset.

215 NAIL A WEAKFISH

Weakfish, as well as striped bass and sea trout, respond very well to soft-plastic baitfish-imitating lures. Most of the time, these lures are fished on weighted jigheads or single unweighted hooks to create a natural forward-swimming motion on the retrieve. But if you want to throw weakies, trout, and stripers a curveball, hit them with a nail. In lieu of traditional soft-plastic rigging, stick a finishing nail in the head of the bait and run your hook straight up through the tail. When the lure hits the water, it'll fall nosedown because of the nail's weight, but when you twitch, the bait will jerk backward. Pause and it'll flutter back to the bottom nosefirst again. It might not seem to make sense, but if you've ever watched a dying live baitfish struggling for life, they often twitch erratically and fall facefirst back to the bottom... and no predator species can pass up such an easy target.

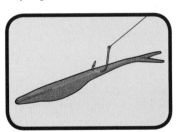

216 SNAP SOME RUBBER

Whether you're trolling for tuna in blue water or striped bass in the bay, rubber bands can catch you more fish and save you money. Send your trolling lure or bait out to the desired distance, loop a thick rubber band around the line (A), then loop the rubber band around the reel handle (B). This can get baits and lures a hair deeper, as your line will enter the water at a lower angle than it would coming straight off the rod tip. When a fish strikes, the rubber band snaps free of the reel handle and line, and you're clear to fight the fish.

217 STING A FLATTIE

Fluke and flounder can be finicky and often need extra enticement to hit a jig or bait. One method that's grown popular with the advent of artificial baits is a bucktail stinger rig. Start by tying a three-way swivel to your main line. Using 6 inches of flourocarbon, add a heavy bucktail jig (heavier than

you think you need) to one eye of the swivel. Next, tie a 20-inch length of fluorocarbon to the other eye, with a 2/0 octopus hook on the trailing end. Thread a soft-plastic shrimp or mud

minnow on the hook, drop the rig over a sandy or muddy bottom and let it drag. It'll look like forage making a cloud, and when fish investigate, the trailing bait will be right in their face.

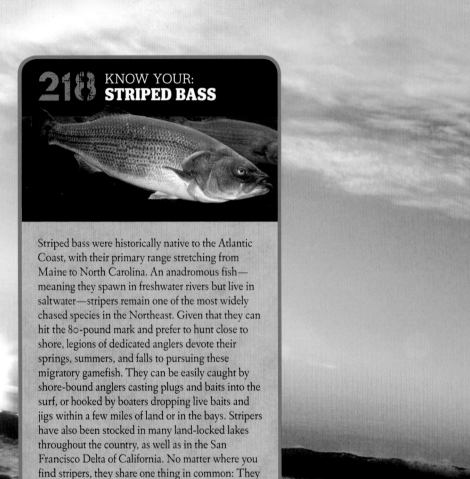

218 KNOW YOUR: STRIPED BASS

Striped bass were historically native to the Atlantic Coast, with their primary range stretching from Maine to North Carolina. An anadromous fish—meaning they spawn in freshwater rivers but live in saltwater—stripers remain one of the most widely chased species in the Northeast. Given that they can hit the 80-pound mark and prefer to hunt close to shore, legions of dedicated anglers devote their springs, summers, and falls to pursuing these migratory gamefish. They can be easily caught by shore-bound anglers casting plugs and baits into the surf, or hooked by boaters dropping live baits and jigs within a few miles of land or in the bays. Stripers have also been stocked in many land-locked lakes throughout the country, as well as in the San Francisco Delta of California. No matter where you find stripers, they share one thing in common: They strike lures and flies with a blow unlike any other species, and rip plenty of drag during the fight.

TACTICS

BY AUGUST, THE WEST BRANCH OF THE DELAWARE RIVER CAN

drive an angler to madness. Since April, the wild trout here have been barraged by every dry fly under the sun. The running joke is that by late summer, the fish have seen so many flies, they can tell you which shop your bug is from as it floats overhead. Despite the water boiling this time of year with rising trout, refusals are so common that you may want to rip your hair out in frustration. That's why a few years ago, my friend and guide, Joe Demalderis, and I tried a new tactic.

Instead of pounding the trout with the same patterns they'd been seeing for months by day, we started fishing in the dark and trading our bug-imitating flies for mouse-imitating flies. A funny thing happened: It worked. Darkness, it seemed, gave the hard-pressed trout some respite, which subsequently meant they let their guard down. After daytime anglers had struggled for one or two sips in an afternoon, we were hooking a good amount of 20-plus-inch browns as the day shift drowned their sorrows at the bar.

The moral is that you can never get complacent with fishing tactics; what has worked in the past can and will change by the season, the day, or even the hour. That's why the best anglers keep detailed mental notes on how they've adapted their approach based on the most drastic—and most minute—changes in weather, water conditions, and fish behavior. While it takes time to gain this knowledge on your home waters, this chapter will jump-start your thinking about some new ways to fool your favorite species.

219 BEAT THE WEEDS FOR FALL TROUT

Autumn can be a fabulous time to fish for trout, but to be successful you've got to learn to deal with the vegetation and change your tactics. After a summer's worth of growth, beds of aquatic plants spread in thick mats on the surface. Fish holding alongside or between islands of weeds or in shallow channels through the salad are supernaturally wary. Avoid wading if at all possible and stalk from the bank. Crouch. Creep. Crawl. Slither on your belly like a reptile. Do whatever it takes to get directly across from, or slightly below, the fish. Cast from a kneeling or sitting position.

Long, drag-free drifts are neither feasible nor necessary over shallow-lying fish holding around the weeds. A trout sees the surface of the water in a circular window centered above its head; the radius of the circle is roughly equal to the depth of the fish. A trout holding a foot down won't see your dry fly until it's 12 inches away. Drop the fly at the upstream edge of this window, laying your line directly atop any intervening vegetation. Let the fly float past the downstream edge of the window before picking it up—very quietly. If a hatch is in progress, it's likely bluewing olives. Fish a size 18 Parachute BWO or emerger pattern. When nothing's hatching, choose a Parachute Adams or Crowe

Beetle in the same size; small hook gaps are less likely to end up snagging on vegetation when you pick up the fly for another cast.

Bankside weeds and grasses reach their maximum height and droop low to the water, forming archlike tunnels that give trout shade and cover. To fish these prime runs, look for an entrance to the tunnel. Stay as far downstream from the opening as you can while still being able to pinpoint it with a cast. Drop a size 14 Elk Hair Caddis or ant pattern a few inches from the bank and let it snake down the tunnel. Your view may be screened, so strike at any disturbance.

If the overhanging vegetation is mostly long strands of grasses, you can take a brute-force approach: Use a pattern that is compact and bulletlike—a Dave's Hopper is good. Cast a tight loop to drive the fly through a thin spot in the curtain of grass. You may snag up a few times, but this tasty water is worth the trouble

Fall is terrestrial time on spring creeks, and the bugs are most active on warm, sunny days. Wherever you find open water or unobstructed banks that allow for a longer drift, flying-ant, beetle, and hopper patterns make excellent prospectors.

220 FIND A SECRET FISHING SPOT

Those little ponds in manicured neighborhoods and tucked behind strip malls can surprise you with bass, pickerel, crappies, and bluegills that are bigger and less pressured than those in the closest reservoir. You may never see such spots from main roads, so begin with some online sleuthing.

GO ONLINE Thanks to Google Maps, finding small bodies of water is easy. Start by entering your address into the search box and then zoom in or out until the scale in the bottom left corner of the map reads 1 inch = 500 feet. Look for water, searching a mile or two at a time in all directions. For hidden gems, focus on housing developments, shopping centers, and office complexes.

GO LOCAL Neighborhood ponds often existed long before the homes were built. Ponds in new developments are frequently stocked with gamefish to control mosquito populations and lily pads or milfoil to aerate the water. Heavy-commerce areas often have runoff retention basins (look by the back parking lots) or decorative ponds that hold fish. Of course, you can also find ponds hidden in the woods or a farmer's field, but fishing those may require knocking on doors. Not all of them will be accessible, of course, but that's all part of the hunt.

INVESTIGATE One pond, just 2 miles from my home and ringed by backyards except at one corner, produced a 3-pound bass and a few of its smaller cousins the first time I visited. I was treated to a real surprise while scoping out a fountain-filled pond on the property of a local community college. So many big carp were sipping in the film that the pond has since become my favorite place to flyfish for this species.

221 KNOW YOUR CRAPPIE

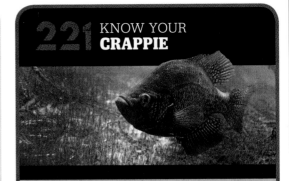

Prized as excellent table fare—especially when deep-fried—both black and white crappies can be found throughout the country and are one of the more scrappy members of the panfish family. With a larger mouth than sunfish and bluegills, crappies are more prone to attacking larger lures and baits, such as stickbaits and shiners. One of the most effective lures, however, is a small tube jig. Most anglers simply cast and retrieve tube jigs, but they can also be fished under a float or trolled. Crappies gravitate to areas with plenty of structure, with rockpiles, brushpiles, and weedlines being some of their favorites. Though during spring spawning crappies can be found in relatively shallow water, most of the time fishing around deeper structure is a better bet. Hook into a 3-pounder, and you've got a giant, but the current world-record black and white crappies top the 4- and 5-pound mark.

222 FISH CLOSE FIRST

Wading anglers always think the grass is greener on the other side of the river. But even if the water in front of you doesn't look as juicy as that bank on the other side, you should always fish your way across instead of just trudging toward what you think will be the best spot. I've caught loads of trout right at my feet in water that looked less than amazing. You never know what's between you and that honey hole in the distance.

223

HOLD YOUR BREATH

A good rule of thumb that will help you release fish with less stress is to hold your breath as soon as you take the fish out of the water. When you start feeling like you need to breathe, assume the fish does, too. This will help you learn to unhook fish quickly and not spend too much time taking pictures of the catch.

224

FEEL FREE TO VENT

Saltwater species that live in deep water, such as grouper and snapper, can embolize as you reel them to the surface, meaning the change in water pressure can cause gases in their swim bladders to rapidly expand. When targeting these species, carry a venting tool, which can be used to puncture the body cavity and release these gases. Without venting, the fish will not be able to dive and in most cases will die.

225 AVOID DOUBLE-HAUL MISTAKES

Like most aspects of fly casting, the double haul is more about feel and timing than it is about power. Simply put, to double haul you use your noncasting hand to pull the fly line away from the rod tip in an abrupt, well-timed burst—thus increasing the resistance and flex in the rod—first on the back cast and then on the forward cast. By increasing that flex, you boost line speed. And if you maintain a well-formed loop during your cast, that added energy translates to distance. The trick is to avoid these three common mistakes:

TOO MUCH LINE You need to feel what you're doing in order to to get your timing down, and that's hard to do with 60 feet of line flying overhead. Start short, with maybe 20 feet of line. Pull the line on your back cast, feel the resistance, and let the line spring back through the guides (sliding through your fingers so you can pinch it again). Give it another tug on the forward cast, release, and shoot the cast. Don't try long casts until you get the groove with short ones.

NOT GIVING THE LINE BACK TO THE ROD You're sunk if your cast ends up with your line hand down by your hip pocket, 3 feet away from your casting hand, with dead line flapping in between. All the energy is lost. You want your hands to spring apart and come together, like you're playing an accordion. If you're stuck on this, tie your wrists together with a 20-inch piece of string.

HOLDING ON When it's time to let fly with that cast, let go of the line! Haul on the back cast, haul on the forward cast, feel the flex, and when your loop gets ahead of your rod tip, let go of the line as if you're shooting a slingshot through the guides on your rod. Hanging on kills the cast. You'll soon learn how to gently release and regather the line with your fingertips as you're double hauling.

226 UNSTICK YOURSELF

If you find yourself stuck against a rock (1), the worst thing you can do is recoil. Leaning away from the rock shifts weight upstream, forcing that side of the boat or raft to dip deeper in the current (2) and upping your odds of sliding up onto the rock and getting pinned there. If you hit a rock, it's typically best to lean into the rock (3), so water pressure can buoy the boat and help spin you off to the side. The oarsman can help spin the boat free by pulling back on the upstream oar if the rock is in front of the center point of the boat (4) or by pushing forward if the rock is behind the center point.

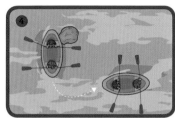

227 GET UPSTREAM

To move upriver, take the boat from the main current into an eddy and then backstroke in slack current (1). Moving from fast water to slow, and vice versa, can be very dangerous. Enter an eddy with the bow angled only very slightly into or out of the current. Never position your boat broadside to a strong current transition, or you risk turning over.

To move to one side of the river, position the boat at a 45-degree angle to the current by pulling on the oar that's opposite the side you want to reach (2 and 3). Then row backward with both oars; the boat will ferry toward shore.

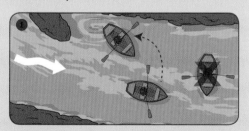

228 KNOW YOUR CUTTHROAT TROUT

Though cutthroat trout are stocked in some areas of the country, they are, by and large, found only in their native range in the Rocky Mountains from Washington to parts of Arizona and New Mexico. They get their name from the distinct red or orange slash mark below their bottom jaw. Unlike brown and rainbow trout, cutthroat trout are broken up into several subspecies, with Yellowstone cutthroats and West Slope cutthroats being the most widespread and available. Stunningly beautiful, cutthroats inhabit everything from high mountain lakes to tiny mountain trickles to major river systems. They are willing eaters that will hit many small lures and natural baits, but they are arguably most prized by flyfishermen who prefer dry flies. Even when an insect hatch is not occurring, cutthroats are quick to rise to attractor patterns, such as a Stimulator.

229 MASTER 8 MINNOW TRICKS FOR TROUT

If you want to hook a trout with spots as big as dimes, you have to give it a meal, not a snack. Try these eight natural and artificial approaches to matching live minnows and hook the biggest fish in the pool.

Slip sinker

Shiner

Split shot

1. LIVE MINNOW For a shore-fishing rig, thread a ¾-ounce slip sinker on the line above a swivel. On the bottom of the swivel, tie a 2-foot section of 6-pound-test fluorocarbon and a No. 4 hook. Add a 3- to 4-inch shiner hooked through the lips. Tie a rubber band in an overhand knot around the base of the rod. After casting, open the bail and tuck a loop of line beneath the rubber band. You can prop your rod in a forked stick, because the minnow isn't strong enough to pull out the loop, and such little resistance won't cause a trout to drop the bait as it runs with it. If snags litter the bottom, a shiner beneath a bobber is a better choice. Unlike warmwater fish that cruise just off the bottom, salmonids often swim through the mid-depths. Use the smallest float that will support the shiner and a single split shot. Hook the 3- to 4-inch minnow lightly through the back. To fish live shiners from a boat, replace the slip sinker with split shot. Drift the shore in an area where you can see the bottom on one side of the boat but not on the other.

2. SEWN MINNOW Push a No. 4 hook down through the nasal vent of the shiner and out the bottom of the throat. Then bring the hook down through the upper back all the way through the bottom of the fish. Slip the hook beneath the skin on its side and slowly tighten. The body should curve enough to make the bait turn and flip in the water (too much of a curve will make it spin). A very slow stop-and-start retrieve with the occasional twitch is often the best. Fish a sewn minnow in a stream's deep, slow water. Cast upstream and roll the bait along the bottom; add whatever split shot you need to get it down. In a boat, drift and cast toward the shore, working from the shallow into the deep. When the bait reaches the dropoff, stop the retrieve, and let it flip and flop and glide to the bottom.

3. RIGGED MINNOW This setup retains the natural form of the baitfish and benefits from a quicker, more aggressive retrieve. It works particularly well once the water begins to warm. Keep the minnow alive as long as possible by hooking the single main No. 6 hook through the nasal vent and then the stinger hook through the skin just below and slightly behind the dorsal fin. Make the rig by tying the stinger hook to the tag end of a clinch knot in a 2-foot, 6-pound fluorocarbon leader. Two inches between the main hook and a size 12 to 14 treble is the proper distance. Cast above obstructions such as logjams and midstream boulders and twitch it back with the flow, working crosscurrent, pausing when the minnow is within striking

distance of the hideout. Here is where the wriggle of a live shiner pays off.

4. CUTBAIT Cutbait can be still-fished on the bottom in pools, but an even better method is to hook it to a small jighead and drop it over a steep bank, jiggling and twitching it as it falls to the bottom, where you let it rest. Old-timers used a chub tail when there were so many creek chubs that they gobbled down the worm before the brook trout could get to it. The chub tail also tended to attract the biggest trout in a pool. The same strategy can be effective today. A good spot in the high water of spring is the first big pool of a feeder creek upstream from the main river.

5. STICKBAIT Minnow imitators seem best as the water starts to drop. They can run through very shallow water, and you can control the depth by the retrieval speed or model choice, which makes them ideal for river fishing. The smaller suspending lures are excellent big-river stickbaits because they hold at a depth rather than popping up to the surface once you stop reeling. Cast upstream and work the stickbait crosscurrent. You want your stickbait wobbling slowly when it gets to the target zone. Slow-water pockets surrounded by fast water are prime spots.

6. SPINNER The trick to catching big trout with spinners is to turn and face the flow, so the lure simulates a minnow moving along the bottom. Cast a spinner as far upstream as possible and reel just fast enough to keep ahead of the current. The long, heavy blade will tick off the rocks. Try to match the blade to the stain of the water—silver in clear, gold in tannin. As the waters recede, fish the transition line along the dropoff to the main river channel.

7. STREAMER The key to presenting a streamer is to work it crosswise to the current so that its full profile is visible to trout. Try to cast farther upstream than you think you should, giving the streamer time to sink. Use a floating line, which makes mending possible and lets you keep the streamer broadside. Match the material to the current—a bucktail in the fastest water, feathers in a moderate current, and a marabou in slow water.

8. SPOON Spoons give trout presentations they don't see as often. Flutter along dropoffs in lakes, making the spoon imitate a baitfish trying to right itself. In early-season rivers, stand over deep pools and jig a Little Cleo along undercut banks. Later in spring, cast upstream and work back with the current, letting it flutter into the head of the pool.

230 STAY WITH YOUR TROUT RIVER THIS FALL

On moderate-gradient rivers, fall brings fewer hatches and smaller flies, mainly bluewing olives and midges. These insects demand small imitations, from size 18 down into the 20s, as far as you have the courage and eyesight to go. You need 6X to 8X tippet, and on glassy water with spooky fish, leaders of 12 feet or longer.

Trout won't move far for tiny bugs; you must place your fly precisely in the feeding lane, a move best made with a downstream presentation. Station yourself upstream and slightly to one side of a rising fish. Aim about 3 feet above the fish and 3 feet beyond the far side of its feeding lane. Stop the rod tip high on the forward delivery so the line falls to the water with some slack. Quickly lift the rod and skate the fly toward you, directly into the drift line. Then drop the tip to give slack and float your fly right down the pipe.

Always check out bankside eddies, especially after a hatch. Drifting insects collect in these backwaters and circulate on conveyer-belt currents past hungry mouths— like you see in some sushi bars. Look closely for trout snouts dimpling the surface film. Don't let the tiny rise forms fool you; the fish could be huge.

On many autumn rivers, browns moving upstream to spawn offer a shot at your best catch of the year, provided you change tactics. These fish must be provoked into striking, and it's hard to pick a fight with a fly the size of an eyelash. You've got to invade their personal space, and nothing serves like a streamer. The key is to keep moving and cover some real estate.

Migrating browns stick primarily to the main channel, intermittently holding up in the slow current behind submerged obstructions and along deeper or rocky banks. Holding fish are scattered, and you can search the most water by casting upstream, parallel to the shoreline. Drop a streamer a few inches from the bank. Alternate dead-drifting the fly with twitches imparted by the rod tip, stripping in line to control the slack. Make five or six casts and move on. Browns in the channel are traveling upriver, and the best way to intercept them is by working down-stream, swinging a streamer. Begin at the head of a deeper run, off to one side of the channel. Cast across the current, and take an upstream mend to let the fly sink. Let your streamer swing on a tight line, following it with the rod tip until it's directly below you. Take a couple of steps downstream and cast again, continuing through the run.

Bigger rivers hold the potential for double-digit fish (as in pounds, not inches), so don't go lighter than 1X tippet. In fall, you'll want every edge you can get.

231 PLAY TO A SURFACE-FEEDING TROUT

Watching trout rise from a vantage point on the riverbank will tell you where to cast. But by taking an even closer look and noting how those trout are rising, you can also glean exactly what type of fly to throw at them—especially when many different bugs are flying in the air. Here's what to look for.

▶**THE SIP** A very subtle dimple appears in the water, and only the nose of the trout surfaces. This means the fish are either sipping midges or eating spent mayfly spinners.

◀**THE SLURP** If you see more pronounced "beaks" on the surface, fish are dialed in on a hatch—likely mayfly duns. When the fish are really chopping, try a crippled fly variation.

▶**THE SPLASH** A sudden, explosive pop with some splash says that the trout are on moving targets, like skittering caddisflies. Tie on a caddis pattern and don't be afraid to give it a twitch.

◀**THE BOIL** When you see disturbed water but no faces—only a dorsal fin and maybe a tail—that's the sign that fish are eating emergers before they reach the surface.

232 KNOW YOUR BROWN TROUT

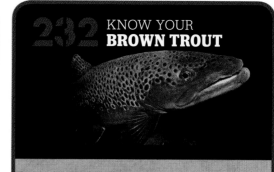

While brown trout can be found in almost every state in the Union, many anglers don't realize that this common species is not native to the United States. All brown trout, from the wild stream-bred fish in the American West to those grown in East Coast hatcheries, are descendants of either the Loch Levin strain from Scotland or those originally native to the forests of Germany. Smaller brown trout in streams, rivers, and lakes can be quite ravenous, readily attacking stickbaits, spinners, and a wide variety of flies. Jumbo browns in the 24- to 30-inch range, particularly those that live in rivers, are often considered "wise" and wary, holing up under gnarly logjams and in the deepest pools, where they feed only once or twice a day. Browns this size will eat anything from a mouse swimming across the surface to a trout half their own body length.

233 CATCH TROUT WITH M&MS

When faced with stubborn coldwater trout, the M&M—that's "mealworm and marshmallow"—may turn things around. Start with a simple slip-sinker rig, and finish it with a size #8 Gamakatsu baitholder hook. Next, slip a Kraft Jet-Puffed Mini Marshmallow onto the hook and slide it up the shank until the hook eye is covered, leaving the bend of the hook and point exposed, and tip the business end of the hook with a juicy mealworm. The marshmallow not only provides extra visual attraction, scent, and flavor but also keeps your mealworm floating right at the fish's eye level.

234 FISH HEADWATERS FOR AUTUMN TROUT

On higher-gradient, boulder-strewn headwaters, the trout are concentrated into fewer spots by a flow volume at or near the annual minimum and warm, clear water that's low in dissolved oxygen. On summerlike days, head straight to the pockets. The turbulence produced by in-stream boulders gives the trout fresh air in the water. Fish the froth with a high-floating, buggy dry: a size 14 or 16 deer hair caddis or small Stimulator. Approach the water directly downstream and use short, precise drifts to cover the riffled apron of water behind the boulders, as well as the bubble lines and the foamy water alongside chutes.

When autumn days feel more like winter, go subsurface. Nymphs such as Hare's Ears, Pheasant Tails, and Princes—beadhead or weighted—do well. In fall's shrunken currents, fishing without a strike indicator gives more precise control in the narrow drift lanes. But this requires that you get close to the fish. Look for pocket-water seams, slots, and current tongues that run knee-deep or better. The surface chop will help mask your approach, but keep low, move slowly, and use the cover of boulders and brush for concealment.

Rig a pair of nymphs about 8 to 12 inches apart and position yourself about a rod length across from the target water and slightly downstream. Flip the flies upstream at a 45-degree angle and raise the rod to remove any slack. With the rod tip high, lead the flies downstream on a barely taut line. Focus on the leader where it enters the water; if it pauses or twitches, strike instantly.

Years ago on an autumn trip, an expert fly angler gave me a bit of advice: Instead of concentrating on the head and gut of the pool—prime summer water—look to the edges and tailouts. Aquatic forage is skimpy in fall, and the trout rely more on insects that fall to the water from surrounding vegetation. Fish will feed along shady banks or take up stations at the tail, where the narrowing current funnels food to them. A flying-ant or beetle imitation is a good choice, but on these smooth, clear waters, stealth means more than pattern. Prespawn brook trout will congregate in these same tailouts and attack a streamer swung down and across in front of them. In this shallow water, you're best off with an unweighted feather-wing or bucktail pattern.

235 DROP RIGHT IN

Fishing two flies—an old method that has enjoyed a renaissance in recent years—lets you turn fluctuating water levels into an opportunity. The following fly rigs allow you to adjust your presentation to any level. With both rigs, strikes often come at the end of the drift. Drag causes the dropper to rise, simulating a hatching nymph and triggering a strike. When you're about to give up on the drift, be ready.

HIGH-WATER RIG In more torrential waters, attach an indicator at the butt of a 3X leader. Tie a size 8 weighted stonefly nymph to the end of the leader. On the hook bend, tie 2 feet of 4X tippet with an improved clinch knot. At the terminal end, tie on a size 12 Hare's Ear or a size 12 Sparkle Pupa. The leader should be 1 to 2 feet longer than the water is deep, depending on the current speed. Then, cast upstream and present the nymphs drag-free. When a fish takes, the indicator will twitch, lurch, or sometimes just stop.

LOW-WATER RIG After water levels fall, begin with a size 12 elk hair caddis. On the hook bend, tie 3 feet of 4X or 5X tippet with an improved clinch knot. At the other end, tie on a size 14 Caddis Pupa or a size 16 or 18 Beadhead Pheasant Tail. Cast upstream and present the flies drag-free. Set the hook if the dry fly twitches or disappears.

236 CUT SOME SLACK

In early spring, you may encounter high, murky water. In these conditions, big trout will often hole up in slow-spiraling eddies. Contrary to popular belief, these fish will frequently face downstream in the slack water created behind boulders and other current-breaking structure. Nymphs that incorporate some purple material or have flashbacks are highly visible to trout in dirty water. Fish them on a 10-foot leader, starting at the outside edge of the eddy and gradually working toward its center. Cast upstream and allow the fly to dead-drift. Take up the slack as the fly drifts back toward you, watching the line for subtle bumps and stops.

237 FISH WITH BACK-POCKET PLASTICS

Soft plastics are right at home on smallmouth rivers, but on trout streams they've taken a backseat to Mepps spinners, Rooster Tails, and Panther Martins. But if you can embrace some of the more modern baits and tactics, you'll put up not only bigger numbers of fish but also bigger fish, and will do so in situations where classic spinners often come up short.

GRAB HOLD To reduce snags, rig your drop-shot hook in line, not on a trailing leader. Keep adding lead-free split shot to the bottom of the rig until it's heavy enough to stay in place during the drift (A), moving only when you make it advance by popping the rod. Crimp the split shot loosely to help it slide off if it gets hung up.

HOLE SHOT Drop-shot rigs are just as effective for trout as they are for bass, particularly in those deep, dark holes with bottom-dwelling monsters (B). Those fish may let 10,000 spinners pass overhead, but a drop-shot can keep a soft-plastic minnow in place on the bottom, wiggling away until a brute can't help but strike.

JIGGLE A LITTLE As you slowly work the drop-shot through the pool, impart action to the plastic by gently—but rapidly—shaking the tip of the rod. It doesn't take much movement to get the bait dancing in place.

SLIP ONE PAST Small slip indicators designed for flyfishing let you stay stealthy while drifting soft plastics through seams (C). Set the float stop so the plastic can fall three-quarters of the way to the bottom during the drift.

WORK THOSE LEGS Soft-plastic crayfish, hellgrammites, and leeches rigged on a tiny jighead work best for slip-floating pocket water (D). Their wider profiles allow them to fall more slowly, and their fluttering legs make them look appealing without the need to create action with the rod tip.

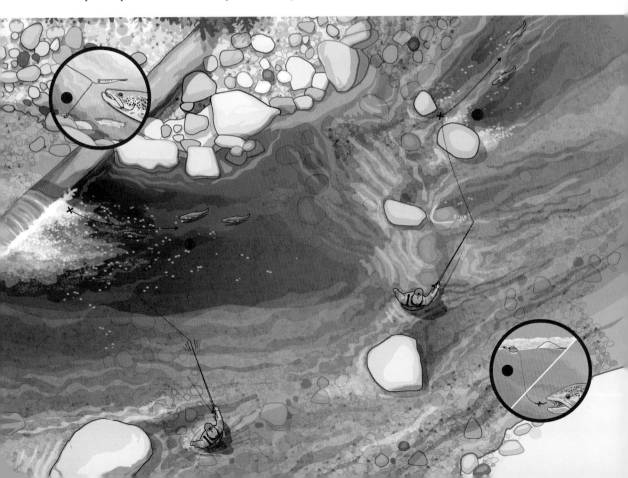

238 NAIL THE NET SHOT

When chasing big fish like salmon or steelhead on foot, it never hurts to have a dedicated net man, as these fish don't make it easy for you to bring them close enough to scoop yourself. If you end up being the guy holding the net for a buddy, here are a few pointers: Always stay positioned downstream of the angler. Even if the fish is running upstream, 99 percent of the time it will turn around, and the net shot will happen downcurrent of the rod man. Once the fish is in net range, never try to scoop from upstream. Always keep the bag half submerged downstream of the fish, and always scoop the catch headfirst.

239

LIFT AND LOWER

Never overlook shallow runs between deep runs in early spring for big trout, especially when water levels come up and increase the depth of those shallow runs a bit. In these spots, try an in-line double fly rig, consisting of a Finnish raccoon shad streamer 18 inches below a size 10 Beadhead Pheasant Tail nymph. Cast upstream (1) and allow the flies to sink but don't strip the line. Instead, gently lift the rod (2) and then lower it (3) to give the flies an enticing crippled action. Trout often strike just as the flies begin to rise in the water column or immediately after they begin to fall.

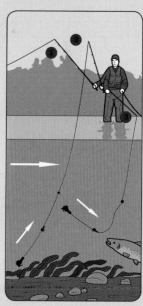

Winter steelheading in Great Lakes tributaries involves icy flows, sluggish feeding, small flies, and big crowds. Spring fishing means big bugs and voracious hits.

Success with fish dropping back into the lake now is all about effectively covering a run—which you should have all to yourself this quiet time of year.

USE HEAVY METAL In the fly department, bigger is better come spring. My favorite streamer is an olive-and-white Zonker with a silver body tied on a 4X long hook (A). This fly has a meaty baitfish profile that steelies rarely ignore. If you have to go to the bullpen, try a black leech or a conehead Woolly Bugger in olive, brown, or black.

With nymphs, it's tough to beat black or brown stoneflies in sizes 6 through 2 (B). A 6- to 8-weight rod and reel with a smooth drag loaded with floating line will cover just about any situation you will face. Add split shot to sink flies in runs with shallow to medium depth; loop on a sink tip in the deep stuff.

GET A HEAD START Begin at the head of a run and fish the seams between the fast center and slower edges (C), where steelhead can intercept food without fighting the teeth of the current. Drift a stonefly nymph or conehead Woolly Bugger under an indicator.

One simple and sneaky trick you can try is to clip the hackle off the Bugger in order to make it look more like a baitfish.

MEAT IN THE MIDDLE At mid-run, switch to a Zonker. Cast long and slightly upstream, and then strip the streamer back so it swims across the run, showing its full profile to any fish that may be looking for a mouth-watering snack (D).

If you move a steelhead and it misses, remember its exact location. Come back later and drift the same lane with a nymph-and-indicator rig.

SWING LOW Take a few steps and make your way downstream. Cast across the run with a dark-colored Intruder (E) and let it swing through the tailout, stripping the fly upstream as the swing ends (F).

This fly has a weighted head that helps it get down fast. Keep a death grip on your rod, because a drop-back that hits on the swing can yank it from your hand.

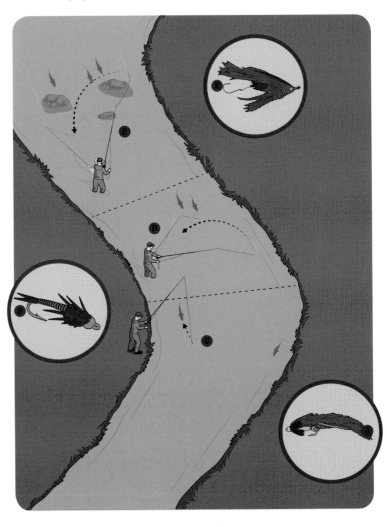

2-41 PADDLE TROLL

Why waste all that paddle power simply getting from point A to point B? You can catch a world of fish by trolling streamers and plugs behind canoes. A canoe's typical pace seems designed for imitating baitfish, and the inconsistent rate of speed keeps your lure moving up and down in the water column—a strike-inducing action.

To troll a floating or floater-diver plug, attach a few split shots to the line 2 feet ahead of the lure. Or work a shallow-running crankbait over beds of submerged vegetation. Run 100 to 150 feet of line behind the canoe and vary your paddle strokes to lend a stop-and-start action to the plug.

Trolling streamers and wet flies for rainbow and brook trout is a classic lake tactic, but you can also apply it to rivers. Use an intermediate or sinking fly line to put a Muddler Minnow or Woolly Bugger down deep. Trolling through long, apparently unproductive stretches will ensure that you leave no structure unfished. Paddle bank to bank and back again to find where fish are holding.

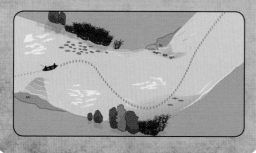

2-42 EXECUTE A POWER PIVOT

At times you'll have to turn a boat abruptly—you may have to dodge a rock you didn't see, or maybe your buddy hung his fly on the bank. A scissor stroke will alter your course quickly. To cock the bow sharply to the right, pull back on the right hand and push forward on the left. To go left, reverse the moves. The side you pull back on is the direction the bow will turn.

2-43 RIDE THE CURRENT IN A CANOE

Often the fishiest place in a river is along a current seam or eddy line where the flow is broken by a boulder or island and reverses course. Holding the boat in such spots is tricky, but fish stack up in the slack and wait for prey to wash down the swifter water. Work it right, and you can fill the cooler.

FISH AN EDDY Paddle past the obstacle in the current and cross the eddy line two boat lengths beyond it. Now turn upstream. This puts you in a good position to fish the head of the slack. Cast into the slack just below the blockage, and work the current seams diligently. You can now also paddle upstream to the head of the eddy and make down-and-across casts. Work your lures or flies downstream to the tail of the eddy and make sure they swing across the current.

HANG TIGHT To stay along a current seam or eddy, rig a combination quick-release system so you can either toss the anchor overboard or tie off to an overhanging tree. Secure a 75-foot length of ⅜-inch anchor line to the canoe bow. Tie the running end to a carabiner and clip it to an anchor. You'll be able to unclip the anchor, slip the line around a midstream branch, and fasten the carabiner to the line itself for a no-fuss hold. Make anchoring even easier by screwing an eyebolt or eye strap to your bow deck. Run the anchor line through the eye and tie it off at your seat. Now you can weigh anchor from there, with no more leaning over the end of the canoe.

244 CATCH SUNDOWN BROWNS

If your lake holds any type of brown trout—wild, holdover, or stocked—these fish will be on the move in the fall, looking for the perfect spawning habitat. They're after a creek to run up, but even if none exists, they'll still cruise near the shore, feeding heavily as they search. Most of this activity takes place in the dead of night, but if you're willing to play in the dark, a well-presented stickbait can land you the monster brown you've been dreaming about. Here's the routine.

CRASH THE CREEK Searching browns gravitate to mud bottoms and shoreline cover, but they really concentrate on where creeks enter a lake. Visit these areas after a rain, which increases the flow, and you'll be casting to more fish.

WAKE THEM UP Nothing gets nighttime browns fired up like a stickbait waking across the surface. If a steady retrieve fails to draw explosive surface strikes, an occasional pause can turn an unseen follower into a biter. You'll hear the bite before you feel it, so let the rod load before swinging. Browns often have lousy aim after dark and may miss a lure once or twice before connecting.

BE IN THE DARK Big browns are less likely to enter the shallows and feed on the surface under the bright light of the harvest moon. Concentrate your efforts on cloudy nights, or nights surrounding the new moon.

DRAW PARALLELS Cast parallel to the shoreline or angling toward it. The trout follow the contour of the bank, and casts made at an angle (as opposed to straight out from the bank) will keep your bait in productive water for longer.

GO ALL THE WAY After-dark browns have a habit of swiping at a lure just as it's about to be pulled from the water. Be sure to fish each retrieve all the way to the rod tip.

BANK ON IT Brown trout will venture into inches of water at night. If the bank is clear, you won't even need to get your feet wet. I've spooked enough fish on my first step into the lake that I now make it a habit to take a cast or two before even dipping a toe.

245 KNOW YOUR FLATHEAD CATFISH

When you hear about a noodler wiggling his fingers in a submerged rockpile and ripping out a 100-pound catfish with his bare hands, that catfish is most likely a flathead. Native to the lakes and rivers stretching north and south from Mexico to North Dakota and east and west from the Appalachian Mountains to Arizona, flatheads are voracious predators and highly territorial. For those not brave enough to let a big flathead clamp down on their extremities, live bluegills or shad are preferred baits, and nighttime is often the right time to connect with these brutes. Flatheads thrive in murky, muddy water—look for them in soft-bottom channels, around rocky ledges, and in backwater holes and eddies that create a good spot for a big cat to lie in ambush, waiting for its next meal.

~~~

246 SNAG THE BEST CASTING POSITION

Fish in large, swift rivers typically hold close to the bank, so try to set a course that keeps you 30 to 60 feet off the shoreline. It's the oarsman's job to position a drift boat or raft so anglers in both the bow and stern can cast freely to the bank. This can be accomplished by keeping the bow of the boat at a 45-degree angle away from the bank, toward the middle of the river (A). The angler in the bow will have the first, but farther, cast. The stern fisherman will also have a clear range of fire. If the bow is angled toward shore (B), the stern angler won't have a clear casting angle downstream.

247 BUILD A BETTER DROP-SHOT

Even during the hottest fishing months, there are times when bass will not respond to anything but the most subtle finesse presentation so you had better know how to use a drop-shot and a finesse worm if you want to catch them.

A drop-shot rig is easy to tie and will score largemouths and smallmouths by any structure at any depth. Use lighter spinning tackle spooled with 6- or 8-pound fluorocarbon line. To tie a drop-shot, attach a #1 or #2 Gamakatsu hook to your line with a Palomar knot, leaving a 4- to 30-inch tag end, depending on how far off the bottom you want to fish your worm. After tying the hook on, pass the tag end through the eye of the hook again and pull tight so the hook sticks out perpendicular to the line, facing up. Finish the rig by tying a drop-shot weight to the bottom of the tag and threading a Zoom Finesse Worm on the hook. Once this rig hits bottom, shake the rod tip to get it wiggling in place.

248 GET THE DROP ON BASS

Done right, a drop-shot rig can be irresistible to even picky fish. The key is the rate at which it sinks; soft-plastic bait should fall flat through the water, not dive nose-down. To accomplish this, try a $\frac{1}{32}$-ounce split shot. During the spawn and postspawn, shorten the space between the bait and the tag end, where you hang the split shot, to 4 inches or less (A). By cutting the tag end down, you minimize the problem of tangling around structures. Bass will often attack the soft plastic as it falls through the water. If the bait hits the bottom without a strike, shake the rod to give the worm some enticing action. After a few shakes, gently retrieve the bait and then cast to your next target.

Concentrate on tempting shallow-water largemouths around docks, near deadfall, and adjacent to vegetation (B). Also, try to intercept postspawn lunkers on shelves adjacent to flats (C).

Try fishing a 7-foot medium-action spinning rod and a spinning reel spooled with green fluorocarbon line. In open water, you'll want to use 6-pound line; near structure, use an 8- to 10-pound line. For the rig, use a 7-inch worm in triple margarita, a 4/0 Gamakatsu EWG hook, and one $\frac{1}{32}$-ounce split shot. Work at close range, pitching around tree limbs, docks, and so forth.

Because this rig requires light line, target a spot close to where you think bass are and entice them away from cover. The natural action of the gliding drop-shot bait will make this possible.

249 KNOW YOUR SMALLMOUTH BASS

Much like largemouth bass, smallmouths can be fooled into eating anything from live bait to flies to just about every style of artificial lure available. What sets them apart, however, is their scrappy nature. Smallmouths are known for the bulldog fighting abilities that trump their largemouth cousins. Hook a smallmouth in a deep lake, and it's going to make every effort to swim to the bottom and snap your line. Hook one in a swift, rocky river, and it will try to find a boulder to wrap around and bust you off. Though these fish can be found throughout the United States in many types of water, their preferred habitat includes a combination of cooler water, rocky structure, and current, making them much more prevalent in rivers, particularly in the Northeast and Northwest, than largemouth bass.

250 PULL BASS FROM BENEATH THE BOARDS

Bass like docks because they provide shelter and a steady supply of bluegills, shad, and other baitfish. But how largemouths relate to docks in spring depends on the spawning stage. This time of year, on any given lake, you'll find bass in all three modes: prespawn, spawn, and postspawn. Here's how to fish docks no matter which stage the fish are in.

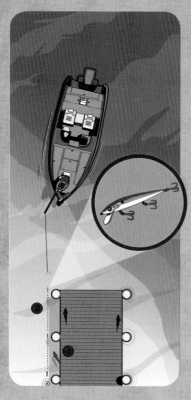

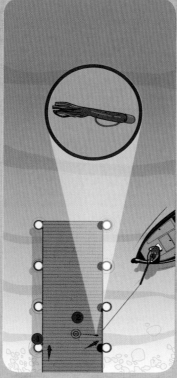

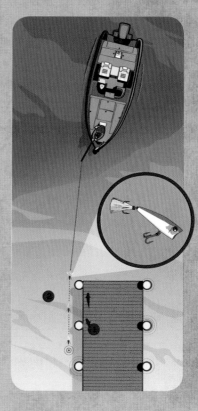

PRESPAWN Concentrate on docks off spawning areas where there is quick access to deeper water, such as those near main-lake points, secondary points, and steep banks. Work a shad-colored suspending jerkbait parallel to the outer edges of the docks, where prespawn bass tend to hold (1). Let the bait hover for 3 seconds or more between twitches (2). Another excellent choice is a $^1/_4$- to $^1/_2$-ounce black-and-blue skirted jig matched with a pork-rind trailer. Swim it a few feet beneath the surface along the dock's edges to imitate a bluegill. Or hop it along the bottom to mimic a crayfish.

SPAWN Spawning bass will gravitate to docks in shallow water, typically to the pilings at the nearshore end (1). They also frequently spawn directly beneath the walkway connecting floating docks to shore. Here, use a 4- or 4$^1/_2$-inch Texas-rigged tube, and peg a $^3/_{16}$- to $^5/_{16}$-ounce bullet sinker against the lure to keep it from sliding up the line. Flipping, pitching, or skipping the lure far under the dock will produce the most strikes (2). Though it takes time to master the flip, the cleaner the presentation, the more strikes you'll draw, as the first drop often counts most.

POSTSPAWN As the spawning period wanes, you can find excellent topwater action around docks. Before heading back toward deep water, postspawn bass may continue to hold near shallow docks for a few days. They tend to suspend under a dock's outside edges (1) and will nail a topwater popper worked past them (2). The window of opportunity can be relatively short for postspawn stragglers, as their willingness to stay will depend largely on the amount of forage species around the dock. However, these bass can offer some of the most exciting fishing of the year.

251 SHAKE THE BED FOR GIANT BASS

Look for the first big breeders to spawn in coves, bays, and boat canals. Wear polarized sunglasses to inspect the areas near boat docks, flooded bushes, blowdowns, and grass edges. Any of these could reveal a giant bass. Keep searching until you find one. Remember that it often takes a big bait to rouse a bedded superbass. An exceptionally lifelike swimbait is the ticket. It can mimic a bream feeding on bass eggs. Cast beyond the bass and swim the lure into the bed, working it there until you find the spot that aggravates the fish. Then twitch your rod tip on a slack line to make the bait bounce up and down like a feeding bluegill. Hold on tight.

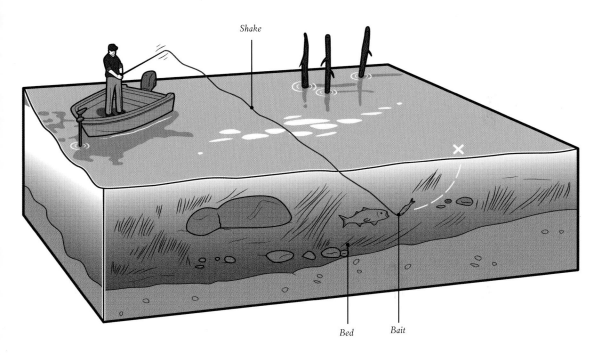

Shake

Bed   *Bait*

252 SHAKE A TAIL FEATHER

In the late summer, smallmouth bass have a habit of keying in on bug hatches much like trout do. In many parts of the country, caddis and mayflies become a staple part of their diet this time of year. Flyfishermen can easily match these food sources, but if you're not a fly guy, a simple way to catch more bug-focused bass is to use poppers that include feathers on the rear hook. When paused, the tail feathers hang just below the surface film. Smallmouths often mistake these dangling morsels for the bugs they crave. Hits can be subtle, so keep a sharp eye for dips in your lure. Don't expect a big bang.

253 SEND FROGS UNDER COVER

When water in the shallows climbs to over 63 degrees, lunkers gravitate to the heaviest cover available in a spawning flat, including bulrushes, windfalls, cattails, brushpiles, and docks. To deal with this, you need a snagless frog lure. Black is always good, but try white and the basic frog pattern as well.

Skip the frog into dense cover, let it rest briefly, twitch it once, and let it rest again. Then work it back with quick twitches and short pauses. Use a 7-foot medium-heavy baitcasting rod with 50-pound braided line, and set the hook hard when a big bass boils.

254 RIP A RATTLEBAIT

The rule of thumb for prespawn cold-water bass is to fish slow. But like every other rule, this one is made to be broken, which you can do with a lipless rattling crankbait. Concentrate on points and submerged grassbeds, as well as 45-degree banks and flats adjacent to creek-channel bends. Early in the season, try crayfish patterns, particularly those that are bright orange-and-red in stained water and green-and-brown in clear water. According to bass pro Kevin VanDam, Strike King's ½-ounce Diamond Shad runs deeper than other lipless rattlers,

which is an advantage in cold water during the prespawn. With 8-pound monofilament, you're able to run an unmodified lure down about 7 feet. Rather than using a deliberate stop-and-go retrieve, which many anglers employ now, try keeping the nose of your bait quickly tapdancing over the bottom. This faster retrieve covers more water, increasing the odds of running the rattler through the strike zone of a bass. In the cold water, the fish's strike zone is going to be significantly smaller. If you get the lure in its face, the bass is going to bite.

256 USE MONSTER TUBES IN THE SHALLOWS

Once they begin spawning, the trick to catching giant bass is spotting them on or near their beds. Wear polarized sunglasses and slowly cruise sheltered shallows, looking for nests on firm bottoms such as sand or gravel—especially along sunny banks and near stumps, docks, windfalls, or other cover.

Go with a 6-inch tube in pearl, rigged Texas-style with a 6/0 worm hook and ¼-ounce bullet sinker. This oversize tube rouses extra-large fish. Slip to within casting range of the bed, and when that big female faces away, pitch the tube softly into her nest with a stout flipping rod matched with 20-pound fluorocarbon line. Lightly twitch the bait in place. Experiment until you find an action that aggravates the bass. Then keep it up until she inhales it.

255 JIG A WORM

Tournament pros like a plastic worm on a jighead—but not just any worm or jighead. The worm, 4 to 6 inches, must be very skinny. The round-ball jighead usually weighs ⅛ or ¼ ounce and has a size 1/0 hook. This setup is used with 8-pound-test line in shallow or deep water, depending on the cover. Let it sink but keep it off the bottom. Once the lure is in the

zone, give it a shake, and the skinny worm will respond with a shimmy. Effective depths range from 10 to 30 feet at deep points, bluffs, and boathouses.

PLOT A FALL PIKE ATTACK

The slightest difference in barometric pressure, brightness of the sky, surface chop, or water temperature has a significant impact on where fall fish hold and feed. And being prepared for those subtle variations can be the difference between getting skunked and enjoying some of the most exciting freshwater predator fishing of the season. Focus your attention on a shallow bay where pike can lurk near points, submerged structures, drop-offs, and weedbeds, keep an eye on the weather, and follow these season-specific tips to experience the absolute peak of the pike.

THE WEEDBED (A)

As a rule of thumb, the worse the weather, the deeper pike will dive into the vegetation. Except in the brightest, calmest conditions, be prepared to go deep into the cabbage. Unfortunately, you're almost guaranteed to snag and break off, but that's the price you must pay for the pike experience.

IDEAL WEATHER Steady rain, cool temperatures (lower than 60 degrees), and a calm wind

BEST LURE Dardevle Clicker Spoon

BEST FLY Black-and-white squirrel Sculpzilla with a weed guard on a T3 sink-tip fly line

PRESENTATION You want to flutter baits and flies just above the vegetation, have them fall into the weeds, and pull them out. Don't be afraid to get down into the greenery.

Most strikes will happen on the fall. Pinch down the barbs on your hooks and flies to stay untangled more often while plowing the fields.

WEATHER ADJUSTMENT On brighter days, cast a shallow-diving crankbait across the vegetation, and retrieve so the lure skims the top of the cabbage.

THE DROP-OFF (B)

This is the best spot to concentrate your attention during fall. Pike like to lie in the transition zones between shallow, warmer water and deep, cooler water, particularly where there is cabbage that holds baitfish.

IDEAL WEATHER Solid overcast and a wind of 5 to 10 mph that creates a light surface chop

BEST LURE Chartreuse Rat-L-Trap

BEST FLY Chartreuse-and-white Clouser Minnow

PRESENTATION Pull a shallow-diving crankbait 1 to 3 feet beneath the surface, and pike will attack it from below. Cast toward the lip of the drop-off and let your bait fall along the slope above the pike's holding spot.

With flies, follow a similar tact: Let them sink a foot or two, then retrieve with quick strips. In clearer water conditions, lighter lines and leaders are in order.

WEATHER ADJUSTMENT If the wind picks up and rain starts to fall, switch to darker-colored lures—like blacks and purples—to turn on the bite.

POINTS (C)

On most fall mornings, you can find pike near points that break the current blown in from the main lake. Cast across the flow to lure a pike out of holding cover and into open water, where it will attack your bait.

IDEAL WEATHER Partly sunny, high winds after recent rainfall

BEST LURE Lil' Hustler Double-Willow Pike Spinnerbait

BEST FLY White Zonker

PRESENTATION Pike aren't accustomed to baitfish approaching them, so don't cast over the target zone. Land your baits off the point, near the edge of the current, within sight (or earshot) of pike.

If weeds prevent you from making a subsurface presentation, try working a popper from the edge of the vegetation toward open water.

WEATHER ADJUSTMENT When pike slow down on cold mornings, size up on lures and flies by about 20 percent and slow down your retrieve.

SUBMERGED STRUCTURE (D)

When you find a rock pile, downed tree, or other submerged structure near the main lake, concentrate your casts on the windward sides of the structure, reeling or stripping flies toward open water.

IDEAL WEATHER High pressure, bright skies, and a light breeze

BEST LURE Mepps Syclops Spoon No. 2

BEST FLY Black-and-purple Pike Bunny on clear sinking line

PRESENTATION Work your lure so it tracks about halfway between the surface and the structure—close enough to get the pike's attention, but far enough to let the predator attack. With flies, use long, steady strips, or even a two-handed barracuda strip.

When you have a pike on your tail, keep your rate of retrieve exactly the same. If you stop a bait dead in its tracks, you may as well throw a rock at the pike and shoo it away.

WEATHER ADJUSTMENT In nasty weather, use lures that plod along more deeply. Now you can slow down that retrieve rate. Add longer pauses between shorter strips with a fly.

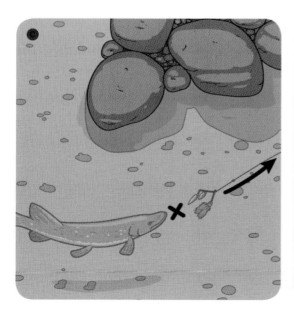

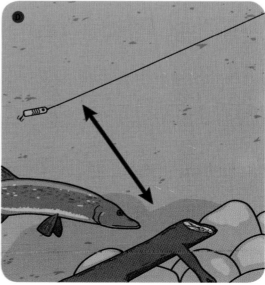

258 ENGAGE IN A COLOR SCHEME

Wherever you fish crankbaits for fall walleyes, subtle variations in flash, finish, or size may score more strikes, but there's probably only one best base lure color. These remain consistent from region to region where primary forage and water clarity are similar. Based on my observations from chasing 'eyes across the Midwest and Great Lakes, here are the perfect walleye hues for your home waters and when you're on the road.

WHITE The rivers and giant reservoirs in the Dakotas are loaded with shad and smelt, which are white and gray. A white or pearl lure (A) matches perfectly and shows up well in clean or dingy water.

GOLD The tannin-stained waters common in northern Minnesota actually highlight a gold lure (B). Here, and anywhere else where the walleyes themselves have golden sides and dark backs, gold seems to score well.

PERCH Yellow perch are the top prey in much of the walleye's range from the eastern Dakotas to Lake Ontario's shores. Opt for natural perch colors in clear water and vibrant fire-tiger patterns (C) in dirtier water.

ORANGE In muddy rivers, like the Mississippi and the Illinois, most lures disappear just inches below the surface. But orange(D), a murky-water staple, seems to always put fish in the boat despite the chocolate milk.

PURPLE The Great Lakes are loaded with emerald shiners, which have pinkish and purplish hues on their flanks (E). With that in mind, I never fish any of the Great Lakes without a solid stock of purple lures.

259 SKIP A JIG IN TIGHT QUARTERS

Underneath docks and overhanging trees are likely spots to find unpressured, hard-to-reach bass. The best way to introduce those bass to your lures is with this skipping trick.

Holding the rod sidearm, start your cast with the rod pointed at the water (not at your target). Moving to the left (right if you're a lefty), rotate your arms and the rod above your head and back down your right side. You're making a complete, vertical circle with the rod and accelerating as you complete the cast. Finish with the rod tip pointed directly at your target as the line shoots off the reel. So, if you're aiming at a spot tucked behind two dock posts, your eyes and your rod tip should be pointed right between the posts as you accelerate and stop the cast. It's harder to skip at short range than at a distance of 30 feet, where momentum works in your favor. Don't overpower the cast. Your accuracy and the distance of the skip, as in skipping stones, are all about angles—and that comes with practice.

You'll want to focus on shady spots that are tight to the bank. Overhanging limbs make good target zones, but working underneath docks is best. Look for signs of recent spawning activity in the near vicinity—barren patches of sand and gravel in water 4 feet deep or shallower. Then concentrate your casts in areas from the edge of the dock to bulkheads or natural shoreline.

Try casting a medium-heavy rod with a baitcast reel and 17- to 20-pound fluorocarbon line. For a lure, try a ⅜-ounce jig in green pumpkin, brown, or black. Modify jigs for "skipping season" by trimming the skirt.

260 KEEP ON THE GRASS

Although smallmouth bass often hang out near rocks and gravel, they also feel at home in aquatic vegetation, especially right after the spawn, when smallies gravitate to prey-rich weedbeds to fatten up before migrating to their summer haunts. Look for productive greenery on points, humps, and the edges of dropoffs in 3 to 8 feet of water (or a little deeper in clear lakes). The bass will relate to the outside edges of the weeds, as well as the lanes and pockets that make ideal ambush zones. Use any of these tactics to pluck bass from the grass.

DANCE A TOPWATER BAIT, a proven winner for this kind of fishing. Make long casts with a 7-foot medium-heavy baitcasting rod, a high-speed reel, and 15-pound line. Work that popper or spook all the way back to the boat and steel yourself for some explosive strikes.

BURN A SPINNERBAIT over the grass to trigger jolting reflex strikes. Use the same baitcasting outfit as above and tie on a ½- to ¾-ounce chartreuse spinnerbait rigged with slightly undersize double-willow chartreuse blades, which will keep the bait from rolling.

SWIM A TUBE on 10-pound line with a 6½-foot medium-heavy spinning outfit. Slide a 1/16-ounce, exposed-hook jig into a 3½-inch root beer–green flake tube. Cast out and work the bait in very slowly. Done right, the lure seems to almost hover over the grass and coaxes bites even from tentative bass.

261 | TAKE IT TO THE SLOPES

Steep structures allow sluggish early-spring bass to make major depth changes without swimming long distances. It's a simple matter of conserving energy. A bass on a main-lake flat, for example, might have to swim 200 yards or more to go from 3 to 12 feet of water, but on a vertical rock bluff that fish can reach the same depths by swimming only 9 feet.

ROCK BLUFFS These structures consistently produce prespawn bass, and because the rock walls are typically apparent above the shoreline, they're easy to locate. Look for bass to suspend along the face of bluffs, where they'll make quick vertical movements to pick off baitfish.

STANDING TIMBER In spring, target emergent timber that lines the edges of major creek runs, rather than submerged timber along very deep river channels. Bass will suspend around the trees, warming themselves in the sun, and then move into the shade to ambush prey.

SUBMERGED HUMPS Avoid the tops of these structures in spring. Instead, use your graph to pinpoint the side or end with the sharpest slope. That's where the biggest bass will hang out. Drop a jig or a drop-shot-rigged worm almost straight down to the fish.

RETAINING WALLS In lakes that have a good deal of residential development on or around them, wood pilings or concrete blocks often line the banks to prevent erosion. Bass readily cruise these vertical walls looking for shad and crayfish. When they're not feeding, they'll drop back and suspend off the structure.

45-DEGREE BANKS Technically, these banks are far from vertical, but they slope into deep water fairly quickly and often have small, steep ledges on them that hold bass. A suspending jerkbait will work here and in all of these places if the water is clear; fish it with slow twitches.

262 CAST THE CRANKS OF SPRING

When it comes to hooking coldwater bass in early spring, you can't beat crankbaits. These lures swim with a tight wiggle that appeals to lethargic bass in water below 50 degrees. Here are four varieties to keep in your tackle box.

COFFIN BILLS A crankbait with a coffin bill fends off snags. A ¹/₂-ounce lure is heavy enough to cast accurately to windfalls and other snaggy cover. Crank slowly as it comes through the structure, and pause every time it pops over a limb.

LIPLESS RATTLERS Most of these sinking, hard-vibrating crankbaits have noisy rattles. Slow-roll them over submerged grass 5 to 10 feet deep. Most strikes are going to happen after you snap the rattler through a strand of the grass.

FLAT DIVERS These will descend to 8 feet and have nearly neutral buoyancy. They're ideal for cranking banks that slope into the water at a 45-degree angle. Target pea gravel to basketball-size chunk rock at the mouths of spawning coves. Tick the bottom with a slow to medium-slow retrieve. Go with a shad or crawfish color.

THIN MINNOWS The subtle roll and twitch tempts bites when sluggish bass shun more active lures. Run it over 45-degree-angle banks and secondary points. Also, slowly retrieve the lure parallel to each side of a dock to pull bass from beneath. An occasional stop-and-go cadence can make a huge difference.

263 CATCH A BIG, FAT PERCH

Schools of big yellow perch hug the bottom in open water, usually between 10 and 30 feet deep. Use a lake map and electronics to locate gradually sloping bottoms and mid-lake reefs with scattered submerged weeds.

With your boat positioned perpendicular to the wind, cast a baited perch rig off the bow and stern. Make repeated drifts with the wind, slowly dragging the rig along the bottom through likely areas, until you get a hit. When you catch one, toss out a marker buoy. Then circle upwind within easy casting range and drop anchor. By staying upwind of the school, you will be able to readjust your position by shortening or lengthening your anchor rope. It also allows for easier bite detection.

If you're fishing bait, toss a baited tandem rig past the buoy, let it sink to the bottom, and drag the rig slowly over bottom structure and through weeds. Keep a fingertip on your line, plus an eye on your rod tip. If you're fishing with a jig, cast out and let the lure sink to the bottom first. Then jig, but don't pop it up and down like a yo-yo. Instead, slowly lift it off the bottom and drop it back down.

Most fishermen going after big perch choose a 5- to 6¹/₂-foot ultralight spinning outfit. For casting jigs, go with a medium-action graphite rod. If you'll be tossing perch rigs, a slow graphite or even fiberglass stick is better. Either way, a sensitive or soft rod tip is a must for detecting subtle bites. You want light, low-stretch line. A quality 4-pound mono is standard, but many big-perch fanatics use a superbraid matched with a fluorocarbon leader.

264 KNOCK ON WOOD

Stumps may be a great place to lose lures, but they're also baitfish magnets, and hungry bass traveling to and from spawning beds pause beneath their gnarled roots to rest and feed. Don't cast randomly at any stump you stumble across. Pay attention to the spawning cycle to hit the stumps most likely to hold big bass.

TRANSITION As bass move into tributaries on their way to spawning grounds, they often pause to rest and feed. Bump stumps with a jig-and-pig, a crawdad-colored crankbait, or a 6-inch junebug-colored lizard Carolina-rigged.

PRESPAWN Stumps along channel bends and junctures in the main lake hold bass before they start for spawning areas. Probe with a 1/2-ounce black-and-blue jig-and-pig. In clear water, hover a jerkbait or slowly retrieve a subtle-action crankbait over them.

STAGECRAFT Before the spawn, bass stage in stump rows along the edges of shallow channels high in the arms of tributaries. Tap a jig-and-pig or the lip of a fat, shallow-running crankbait in a crawdad color off the tops.

BEDTIME In old reservoirs, where upstream shallows are covered in soft silt, spawning bass will lay their eggs on the hard surfaces of stumps and their roots. Flip a black neon and junebug–colored Texas-rigged tube or lizard on top of a stump and let it lie there, twitching. Don't retrieve too quickly.

STUMPING FOR STRIKES A good way to attract bass that may not otherwise see your bait is to cast close enough to a stump for your lure or sinker to bang against it. If you're using a heavy jig or plastic bait, don't retrieve it too quickly.

THE MORNING AFTER If you found stumps holding bass during the prespawn, try them again once the fish leave their beds.

265 MAKE A BOWFIN CONNECTION

Bowfin won't win any beauty contests, and they'll wreak havoc on your favorite bass lure. But they're aggressive and will outfight any bass or trout around. Here's how to find and catch them if you want to give it a shot.

GRASS ROOTS Bowfins thrive in grassy areas both in pristine lakes and rivers, as well as in backwater swamps and oxbows. So locating the salad is step one.

BEEF UP Bowfins have strong jaws and strong wills. Chase them with a heavier rod designed for frogging or swimbaiting, and opt for 50- to 65-pound-test braided line.

WHITE OUT Bowfins love to eat cut bait on the bottom, but if you want to target them with artificials, it's tough to go wrong with white. Spinnerbaits and soft-plastic finesse baits like the Zoom Fluke are prime picks.

266 KNOW YOUR YELLOW PERCH

With the exception of the Great Lakes, where recreational anglers and large charter boats that hold more than 30 people target perch year-round, open-water fishing is not the primary way people around America catch perch; ice fishing for perch is much more popular. Yellow perch remain highly aggressive all winter long and are often easier to coax into feeding during the cold season than species such as crappies and bluegills. The short rods necessary for ice fishing are also perfectly suited to getting the maximum fight out of a scrappy perch. Tiny soft-plastic jigs, little spoons, and small live minnows or maggots are popular baits and lures for targeting perch through the ice. In open water, these fish will take a swing at a number of lures, including small in-line spinners and small, slender stickbaits.

267 ENJOY A CAROLINA EGG ROLL

Here's a pro tactic to tweak a classic rig to swim baits across rocky bottoms. Fish using a big, soft-plastic bait on a Carolina rig. Use a 7-foot, heavy-action casting rod, a low-profile baitcasting reel, and 20-pound fluorocarbon line, with a full 1-ounce egg sinker (A). Shape trumps mass, as the fast-falling, easy-rolling character of the egg results in a freer-swimming bait—and more hookups. Look for points and rocky ledges—any marker in a migration path that connects deep and shallow water. You'll also find some current (B) in this area and a fairly clean, rocky bottom. Cast all around the boat, feeling your way as you retrieve the bait and the

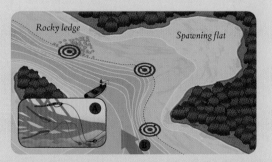

Rocky ledge *Spawning flat*

sinker rolls over the structure. When you feel resistance, set the hook. Once you start consistently hooking up at a certain depth and find the right speed to move your bait, stick to that pattern.

268 LEARN DEEP SECRETS

Two places where you can consistently find active bass when it's hot out are long, sloping points that reach far offshore before dropping off and the lips of creek and river channels, called ledges, especially on outside bends and channel junctures.

Start by idling around the main lake while viewing your depthfinder. Normally, you'll see suspended fish, which are typically inactive at a certain depth, often about 14 feet or so. Remember that number once you determine it, because that's where you're going to find feeding bass on points and ledges throughout the lake.

DEEP CRANKING Comb the points and ledges with a $1/2$- to 1-ounce, long-billed, shad-pattern crankbait that will run deep enough to tap the bottom at the depth you're fishing. Use a 7-foot medium-action baitcasting rod and 8-pound line, and make long casts to get your bait to its maximum depth. These crankbaits work best at 18 feet or less.

CAROLINA RIGGING For fishing in waters down to 30 feet or more, it's hard to beat a Carolina rig, which casts far, sinks fast, and stays in the strike zone throughout the retrieve. Casting these rigs calls for a heavy-action 7- to $7^{1}/2$-foot baitcasting outfit. Use a 4-inch french-fry worm Texas-rigged on a 3/0 worm hook. Watermelon and pumpkinseed are proven summertime colors.

HEAVY JIGGING If you're after big bass in particular, cast a $1/2$- to $3/4$-ounce weedless jig dressed with a plastic craw, using a 7-foot medium-heavy baitcasting rod and 12-pound line. Go with crawdad colors in clear water and black-and-blue in stained water. After casting, jump the jig off the bottom with long sweeps of the rod and then let it swing back to the bottom while you hold the rod tip high. This bait isn't apt to catch as many fish as the subtler Carolina rig, but the jig's big profile will trigger strikes from some of the lake's heftiest bass.

269 DREDGE A BRONZEBACK

Just because you're fishing a tube doesn't mean you need to jig it up and down. Prespawn smallmouths can be sluggish in colder water and are sometimes more interested in slurping a sculpin or crayfish off the bottom than in chasing fast-moving forage up into the water column.

This dragging technique has scored some of my heaviest smallies, especially in deeper water with soft bottom where these fish often stage before moving shallow to spawn.

Green, brown, and gray tubes work particularly well, as they most closely match the forage species that like to hang out in areas of soft bottom. Squirt some liquid attractant into the tube to make it doubly deadly.

PLAY THE LONG GAME Position the boat so it will drift over the slope or deep flat you want to target. Make a long cast and let out an extra 20 to 30 feet of line once the tube hits bottom. If there's no wind, use the trolling motor to create a drift.

KICK-START THE BITE Keep the rod tip low to the water and let the tube drag along the bottom as the boat moves. As the tube bumps across the bottom, it'll kick up sand and mud like a fleeing crayfish or sculpin.

KEEP IT TIGHT When a fish eats, don't expect a hard slam, but rather a soft bump, and then resistance as if you're snagged. Keeping your line as straight and tight as possible will make strike detection easier.

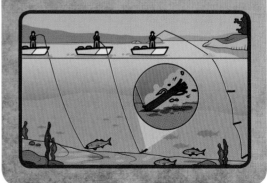

270 TAKE THE LONG SHOT

THE SPOT Black crappies begin spawning when the water hits 60 degrees, usually in 3 to 10 feet of water over a sand or gravel bottom. Points near creek channels at the mouths of bays are excellent places to start the hunt. The fish may hold anywhere from the end of the point to just inside the bay, and the more points you hit, the more fish you'll catch.

THE LURES A 2-inch curly-tailed grub on a $\frac{1}{8}$-ounce jighead is a traditional search bait, but small swimbaits and tiny diving crankbaits are equally effective and have actions that the fish may not see as often. Keep one of each rigged on your boat deck for quick presentation changes without retying. In clear water, light colors like chartreuse and white are usually the top producers.

THE GEAR Light-action spinning rods measuring $6\frac{1}{2}$ to 7 feet are ideal for making long casts with small lures. A crappie's mouth is soft, so choose a rod with a slow tip to keep hooks from pulling free during the set and fight. Small-diameter braided line helps lengthen your cast and is sensitive enough to detect subtle crappie bites at a distance.

THE METHOD Keep your boat at least 15 to 20 yards away from the point. Breezy days tend to be more productive, as a chop on the water generally makes fish more active and helps break up your shadow and reflection. Stay upwind of the point and fan cast across it, working the lure with a slow, steady retrieve. In clear, cool water, a crappie's strike may be quick and light, so set the hook immediately on even the

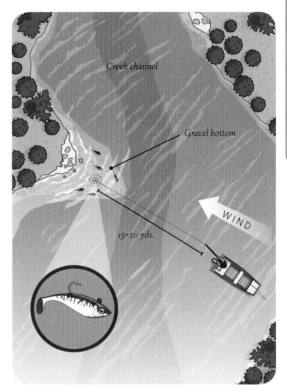

Creek channel

Gravel bottom

WIND

15–20 yds.

slightest bump. When you catch one fish, drop the anchor and spend at least a half hour covering the point with casts. It's common for the action to ebb and flow, but rest assured: In spring, if you've found one crappie, more are probably holding in the same location.

271 CRUSH SKINNY-WATER CRAPPIES

As lakes ice out in the North and water temperatures start to rise in the Midwest and the South, crappies flood into the skinniest water they can find to spawn. Unlike other species, they won't shut down during this time, and the catching can be fast and furious if you know exactly where to cast.

FEEL THE HEAT A temperature gauge will help you find warmer water, but look on the northern ends of lakes, which get more sunlight during this time of the year. Mud bottoms that hold the sun's heat are an added bonus.

POP THE CORK It's essential to fish shallow in no more than 5 feet of water, and nothing will work better than a fixed float with a crappie jig underneath. The Thill Crappie Cork can be used in a fixed position or as a slip float. Attach the float 1 to 4 feet above a $\frac{1}{16}$- to $\frac{1}{8}$-ounce jighead, depending on depth. Jigheads can be tipped with artificials like a Southern Pro Crappie tube or baits like a live fathead minnow.

STAY PUT Target structures like brush piles, stumps, and even boat docks. When you start getting bites, don't move there's bound to be plenty more.

272 CATCH WALLEYES SIX WAYS

Take to the lake in your boat and try one or all of these walleye pro techniques.

STAY BOLD After a cold front shuts down the bite, most anglers go to lighter tackle and slower presentations. Try a contrary approach, using bigger lures and erratic retrieves to provoke reaction strikes. Rip a jigging spoon, as this classic ice-fishing lure can fire up lethargic open-water walleyes. Choose a $1/4$- to $1/2$-ounce model and cast to the edges of weedbeds, timber, or rocky structure. Wait for the lure to flutter to the bottom and then jerk the rod tip to rip the spoon toward the boat. Let it sink and repeat.

GET ON BOARD For eliciting bites from walleyes, the use of planer boards is unparalleled, but they don't do you any good if you miss those strikes. When you troll a crawler harness beneath a board, add a flag strike indicator. The flag signals any slight change of the planer's action. Also, because short-striking walleyes often nip the bait below the terminal hook on a standard harness, use a No. 10 light-wire treble at the very end of the crawler to nab sneaky bait stealers.

DO THE SLIDE Add slider rigs to your trolling setup. These are basically droppers attached to the main trolling line via a sliding snap about halfway between the planer board and the boat. Where legal, sliders let you cover a wider swath of water and try a variety of baits to pinpoint what walleyes want on a given day. Use a heavier dropper line than your main line to help prevent tangling. The key is to vary the depth (by adding more weight or longer line) and spinners and crankbaits until you start getting hit.

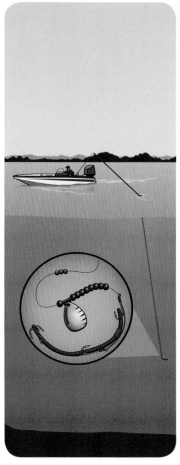

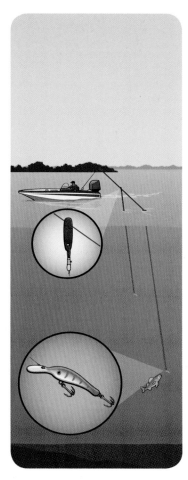

LIGHTEN UP A Roach rig is a classic setup for slowly trolling or drifting bait along promising bottom structure that employs a special walking stinger; it's a great tactic when the bite turns tough. First, lighten things up with a 6-pound mono main line, a $3/8$-ounce sinker, and a 4- to 8-foot-long 4-pound leader. Anchor directly above marked fish and present the rig vertically. With your finger on the line, you'll feel the minnow start to get livelier when a walleye is on its tail. That's when you open the bail to let the bait swim free.

CRANK A CRAWLER The crawler harness isn't just for bottom fishing anymore. When walleyes suspend high in the water column (and where multiple lines are legal), pair this traditional favorite with a deep-diving crankbait. Here's how to rig it: A 3-way swivel goes on the end of your main line. To the top ring, tie a 5-foot leader and connect a crawler harness with a quick-change clevis. On the remaining ring, tie a 10-foot leader and attach a snap and a crankbait. This lets you change baits easily until you hit gold.

BE A JERK Aggressive postspawn walleyes are just as quick as bass to clobber what appears to them to be a wounded baitfish. Take advantage of this tendency by casting longer jerkbaits to shorelines, rockpiles, or submerged weeds in 2 to 6 feet of water. Point the rod tip toward the water and be sure to snap it sharply back three or four times while reeling in slowly to create an erratic, rolling action. Pause several seconds and resume snapping. Be ready for walleyes to strike on the pause.

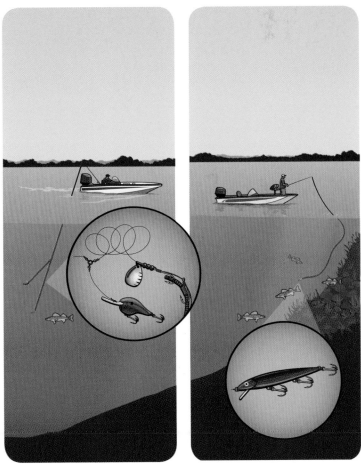

273 FIND LATE-SUMMER LARGEMOUTHS

By late summer, bass fishing is not for the faint of heart. Largemouths are often deep and lethargic, and they're also frequently starting to relocate and suspend at mid-depth ranges as forage begins to move. This is when professional anglers start following the ABCs of summer fishing: aquatic vegetation, bridges, and current, the three shortcuts to finding fish.

LOCATION	 Aquatic Vegetation	 Bridges	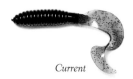 Current
WHY BASS LIKE IT	Hydrilla, lily pads, hyacinths, and other greenery hold forage and provide cover, shade, and higher oxygen.	Cover, shade, and abrupt depth changes are always present; nearby rocks often hold forage.	Moving water produces higher oxygen, washes in food, and usually creates cooler temperatures.
WHAT TO LOOK FOR	Edge irregularities, especially depth changes; brush, logs, or rocks with the vegetation; isolated patches of greenery.	Brush lodged on the upstream side of pilings; current breaks behind pilings; baitfish around pilings.	Eddies and protected calmer water; rocks, small islands, other visible cover like stumps or logjams.
TECHNIQUES AND TACKLE	Skitter floating frogs over the top and through openings; flip tubes and jigs into open holes; run shallow crankbaits along the outside edge. Use 50- to 65-pound braided line for frogs and tubes; 12- to 20-pound fluorocarbon for square-bill crankbaits.	Bulge a fast spinnerbait parallel to abutments and pilings near the channel first. Cover the brush at upstream pilings with a crankbait; hit the downstream side of abutments with a drop-shot rig. Use 8- to 16-pound fluorocarbon line (it sinks).	Cast light jigs, plastic grubs, or Texas-rigged worms upstream and let current carry them into quiet eddies. Work small buzzbaits across calmer areas, especially in early morning. Use 12- to 16-pound fluorocarbon for strength and low visibility.

274 GET A JUMBO ON THE ROCKS

In late August and early September, wolf packs of jumbo yellow perch in many lakes snap up hatching insect larvae on mudflats 12 to 30 feet deep near rocky reefs. A ⅟₁₆- or ⅛-ounce Lindy Slick Jig dressed with a 2-inch fathead minnow dupes perch best; choose the shinier colors. Vertically snap the jig up 18 inches and let it fall on a slack line. Quiver the jig just above the bottom to induce a strike.

When your graph marks a school of roaming perch, idle upwind (1) and let the breeze push you over the fish. Hold the boat directly above the school when it's calm (2). If you don't get a bite quickly, move on.

275 WRESTLE WITH A GAR

Alligator gar are one of the most misunderstood freshwater species in the U.S. Capable of growing longer than 8 feet, and sporting a mouth full of needle-like teeth, these brutes have been scorned for decades, blamed falsely for everything from attacking humans to decimating gamefish populations. In reality, these living dinosaurs should be put on a pedestal by any angler that enjoys a truly arm-wrenching fight.

Texas's Trinity River is arguably the most famous gar water in the country, and guide Dawson Hefner has been plying its waters for years. His method of setting baits—usually chunks of common carp—can be used to hook these behemoths anywhere they live.

Hefner explains that gar prefer to sit in areas with little or no flow at the

bottom of runs or tight to the banks, out of the current. To get his baits in the sweet spots, he rigs them below a large slip float and casts directly into the main flow. Hefner will let the bait

ride the current naturally while paying out line. Wherever the chunk settles on its own should also be the soft spot where any gar in the hole will be laid up.

276 CAST A CAN'T-MISS SMALLMOUTH LURE

A serious smallmouth fisherman often has a deck full of rods and lure compartments filled to the brim when he leaves the boat ramp in spring. This time of year, it's easy to overthink things and get caught up in bait choices. It's true that a wide array of lures can produce now, but if you want to do more catching than thinking, never leave home without these three baits.

JERKBAITS Jerkbaits are fun to fish and highly effective. They're also the perfect tools for locating fish, as they'll draw active feeders in from a distance. In the early season, I prefer suspending jerkbaits, which stay in the zone when paused. Crushing blows that come on a fast jerk are exciting, but don't be afraid to pause for more than 10 seconds between twitches if the fish aren't committing. I've learned that downsizing your baits can greatly increase the number of strikes you draw in spring, so head out armed with lures in the 3- to 6-inch range.

DROP-SHOTS The ability to twitch a bait in place is a huge advantage. Even if the fish aren't actively feeding, keeping a bait dancing at eye level will often annoy a smallmouth into striking. Pay close attention to your line diameter; downsizing from 8- to 6-pound-test can make a huge difference in the number of bites you'll get. Small baitfish-imitating soft plastics with plenty of tail wiggle produce best.

SWIMBAITS Soft-plastic swimbaits have become smallmouth staples across the country, even outshining classic lures like the spinnerbait on many bodies of water. Much like jerkbaits, swimbaits attract fish from a distance, but they have a lot more versatility. When fish are aggressive, you can increase the retrieve speed and work in some quick pumps of the rod tip to trigger bites. For fish that are slow to strike, you can crawl a swimbait across the bottom while imparting short hops. These baits fish best on a jighead.

277 BE A NIGHT STALKER

Just because the sun goes down doesn't mean the species you love to catch go to bed. In fact, sometimes the biggest fish in the pond, lake, or river don't eat at all until nightfall. Catching them past sunset requires some minor tweaks to your daytime tactics.

BASS Both largemouths and smallmouths stay active all night, especially when there's a full moon to shed some light. Fishing after dark is a prime time to bust a heavy bucketmouth or bronzeback on the surface. Opt for lures like the Jitterbug, which makes a lot of noise as it's slowly retrieved. The slower the retrieve, the more time a bass has to track and smack the lure. Be sure to give the fish a chance to turn and dive before setting the hook.

TROUT Big brown trout will hunker down all day and go on the feed after sundown. Now is the time to throw large streamers and stickbaits in dark colors. Remember that at night, fish see lure profiles, not colors, and dark colors produce better silhouettes. Stickbaits that rattle, and streamers with bulkier hair heads, will produce more vibration underwater, making it easier for big trout to home in. Work in slow twitches and strips, and set on any tap.

PANFISH Bluegills and crappies will happily chow down in the dark, especially near a light source. Light attracts small baitfish and bugs, providing a late-night feast for panfish. Fixed dock lights are magnets, but if you can't find one, pick up a portable floating light designed specifically for nighttime crappie fishing. Once you attract some bait to the light, work jigs from outside the range of the glow to inside. The biggest panfish often hang out just beyond the light's reach.

278 DO THE WORM

Come summer, Alabama bass pro Russ Lane goes big. "I catch more and bigger bass by supersizing my plastic worms in hot water," he says. "The body temperature of the bass is always the same as the lake temperature, and once lake water hits the mid-80s to low 90s, the fish's metabolism is cranking in high gear and it'll gulp the biggest prey it can find." Just how big does Lane go? At least 10 inches—and up to 14.

PEA SOUP In low-visibility conditions, Lane targets isolated submerged stumps, logs, and weed patches with a Texas-rigged worm—one in a dark color with an oversize ribbon or paddle tail that emits maximum vibrations (A). "I'll peg the sinker with a toothpick to prevent it from sliding up the line," he says. "This keeps the sinker tucked up tight against the worm's head, which lets me detect light bites more easily in heavy cover." Lane casts a few feet past his target, then hops it along the bottom, using the rod to steer it into the cover where a bass is holding. "The instant I detect a tap," he adds, "I'll lower the rod tip, reel up slack, then hammer the fish with a hard upward hookset."

ALL CLEAR In clear highland lakes, bass often lurk offshore on deep points and ledges during summer. Here, Lane drags a big worm on a Carolina rig so he can cover large pieces of deep structure quickly. He casts the rig, lets the sinker hit bottom, then drags it along with slow sideways rod sweeps, pausing to reel up any slack (B). "Visibility is usually good in these lakes, so I'll use a long, slender, translucent metalflake worm with a ribbon tail," he says. "As the heavy sinker bumps along the irregular bottom, the worm trailing behind it floats up and settles back down enticingly. When I detect resistance, I'll quickly reel up slack line, then set the hook low and to the side."

279 KNOW YOUR CARP

Common carp, mirror carp, and grass carp are all technically invasive species, brought to the United States from Europe and Asia and released in American waters. And they certainly have flourished. All carp species are very hardy, and adapt well to living in both warm and cold climates. They can be found in almost every state, but what's most interesting is that it wasn't long ago when many U.S. anglers considered carp a "trash fish" not worth serious pursuit. That's changed in recent years, thanks to both an interest in fishing methods adopted from Europe, where carp fishing has always been extremely popular, and the discovery that carp can be caught on the fly. Today major U.S. fly tackle manufactures offer special rods, flies, and line just for carp. The appeal is that carp are big—hitting the 50-pound range frequently—giving avid fly guys a much harder fight than the average trout. Carp are omnivores, so you can get them to eat a berry fly on the surface or a crawfish fly stripped along the bottom. For the non-fly angler, European bite alarms, boilie baits, and other specialty carp tackle are quickly becoming more available stateside.

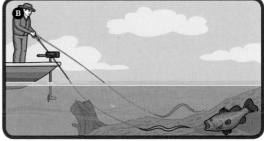

280 SLOW DOWN FOR NIGHTTIME MUSKIES

In summer, when fishing pressure ramps up in many lakes, your best shot at a 50-plus-inch 'skie will come in the small hours of the morning. That's when expert guides break out the dual-blade Double Cowgirl bucktails and give lessons in speed control. Muskies don't react to visual cues in the dark. They use their lateral lines to feel vibration, and slow-turning blades give off more of a thump.

Because you want the blades on these giant spinners to just barely turn, fishing with them at night is less strenuous than it is during the day, when a fast burn is in order. Target the edges of weedy flats, as muskies lying near the bottom in deeper water move shallow by night. Most strikes come at boatside, and the trick to sticking the fish here is

forgetting the figure 8 that daytime fishermen execute with a short line before picking up the lure to recast.

A fast figure 8 during the day makes the fish think the prey is getting away, so they'll attack. At night they can't see the lure as well, so you want to execute a long, slow L turn along the boat instead, just to keep the blades moving.

Don't expect a strong take from your fish. Most muskies strike and keep moving forward with the lure, putting slack in your line, so a subtle tap is worth a hard set. It's also important to know that muskies often hunt in packs after dark. It's not unknown to hook as many as four fish on back-to-back casts, so don't spend too much time taking photos of your first one.

281 SEE A CAT IN THE DARK

Hooking a 60-pound flathead in the dark isn't the hard part of this hint—it's working the fish out of the submerged tree where you likely found it that's going to present the real challenge. To win this tree-hopping night game, you'll want both a specialized rig and an application of brute force.

Live bluegills are a great bait, but you don't want them swimming around, tangling in the trees. So instead of a single hook and leader, rig the bait on a 1-ounce jighead, passing the hook through the bottom jaw and out one eye. The jighead is tied directly to a 30-pound mono main line.

Using a 7-foot heavy-action conventional rod, drop the bait straight down, working all around a submerged tree, starting on the deep side and moving to the shallow side. The heavy jighead provides better contact with and control of the bluegill in the sticky stuff. As the cats may be on the bottom or suspended among the limbs, it's important to work the entire water column.

Each drop should last only about 20 seconds. Basically, just give the bait a twitch or two and then move on. If the fish is there, it'll bite pretty fast. You just have to keep that

line tight and walk up and down the boat to get the fish away from the tree. You may want to do as some guides do and use a brush anchor—a metal clamp with teeth tied to a nylon cord—to tether your boat directly to the above-surface branches of the trees that you're fishing. If one tree doesn't produce a fish or a strike, move on to the next, but consider returning to a tree that was unproductive earlier. You never know—a big cat may have dropped by in the interim.

282

BEAT THOSE SHALLOWS BLUES

Catching blue catfish usually involves probing the deepest holes in a river system. However, like many other species, they take note of the rising water temperatures in the spring. Blue cats will move toward warmer water and at the same time will gorge in preparation for the ensuing spawn.

Instead of anchoring over deep water in the spring, employ drift tactics that allow you to probe the bank and skinny water, anywhere from 2 to 10 feet deep. First, use your temperature gauge and electronics to identify shallow mudflats with the warmest water possible. Structures like downed

trees and brush are a huge bonus. After you've chosen a stretch of river you want to fish, head upstream and begin your drift, keeping the boat at casting distance from the shore.

A slip-float rig is the best way to fish shallow water effectively. Tie a 4/0 circle hook on stout leader and adjust the float according to depth. Fresh-cut bait like gizzard shad will

always get the most bites. Cast your rig upstream, because it will drift faster than the boat. Pay particular attention to structure, as the slip float will allow your bait to remain free of snags. After the float drifts a short distance past the boat, retrieve and repeat. When you see it go down, reel tight, refrain from setting the hook, and get ready for battle.

283 TROLL WITH DOWNRIGGERS

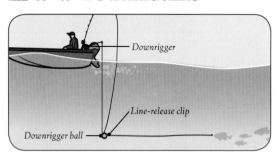

A downrigger consists of a large reel holding a thin wire cable that passes through a pulley at the end of a short boom. The cable end is fastened to a 4- to 12-pound ball that usually has a fin or vane to keep it tracking straight. The whole assembly is permanently mounted on a boat's rear deck corner. Some small portable units are designed as clamp-ons. Use one or more on powered boats 16 feet or larger.

Downrigging can run your lures deeper than any other method. In extreme cases, depths can be as much as several hundred feet, but 30 to 60 feet is most common. It's a great light-tackle method, too, because when a fish strikes, the line pops out of a release clip next to the trolling weight so the battle proceeds unencumbered by heavy gear. In most summer trout and salmon fishing, your sonar will show larger fish and schools of baitfish at or near the thermocline, that narrow band 30 to 70 feet deep where water temperatures drop radically. It's very simple to run your downrigger weights and lures at that depth all day long.

With the ball at the surface and the boat moving at about 2 mph, let your lure out 30 to 60 feet behind the boat. The Acme Super Smelt is a fine choice among the slim, so-called "flutter" spoons that are trout-and-salmon favorites. Fasten the line to the release clip and put the rod in the adjacent rod holder. Make sure the reel drag is set extremely light so line will pay out as you lower the trolling ball. Once the ball is at the desired depth, tighten the reel drag back to a normal setting and reel in enough line so your flexible rod tip is bowed down slightly. When a fish strikes, the tip will pop up and pick up the slack.

Downrigger weights are heavy and can swing wildly in the air when you're trying to rig a lure in a wave-tossed boat. The ball can damage your boat's hull unless you control it. When rigging, keep the weight just under the water's surface, where it'll remain stable.

284 GET A WALLEYE ON BOARD

Planer boards are very effective for trolling walleyes, but they are a bit complicated to use. These 7- to 12-inch floating "boards" hold your line 50 to 100 feet off to the side of the boat. Setting a pair of planers, one on each side, means you're covering a swath of water up to 200 feet wide and are thus more likely to encounter fish. And because the lines and lures are far away from your droning outboard, you're less likely to spook fish. They can be used in any water conditions from any boat, but work best in calmer water with a powerboat, usually 16 feet or longer.

The most common walleye setup includes a 6-foot-high mast mounted in the boat's bow. This mast holds two large take-up reels with cord that attaches to left- and right-side planers. The planer boards are tapered or ballasted to run at the surface.

As the boat moves slowly, pay out a board on its cord until the desired distance from the boat is reached. Then release line from your reel so your lure is running about 60 feet behind the boat and attach a release clip to your line and also to a "quick clip" that you slip onto the planer-board cord. Line tension from the trolled lure makes the clip slide along the cord all the way out to the planer board. Reel up slightly so there's a little line tension between your rod and the board, and put the rod in a rod holder.

For the ultimate in walleye trolling, you can run two planer-board lines out on the sides and run downriggers or flat lines straight off the back of the boat. You'll be presenting a range of lures at a variety of depths and places, and you'll be so busy keeping track of it all that there won't be any time for lunch.

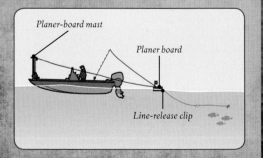

285 SPIN UP A STEELHEAD

In-line spinners can be lethal on steelhead if you know how to present them. Here's the plan.

STEP LIGHTLY Steelhead running a riffle won't always use the deepest part of the run, so don't wade in too far. Your swing should finish close to the bank.

AVOID A POOL PARTY Deeper, slower pools may be full of fish, but those steelies aren't likely to chase down a spinner. Instead, focus on riffles at the heads and tailouts of these pools. Steelhead holding in and moving through faster water are more likely to be game for a reaction strike. Such spots also tend to be shallower, so a spinner sweeps through at the

fish's eye level. Chromers that have just entered a river system from the lake or ocean are often the most aggressive, so target fast-moving stretches as close as possible to the big water.

CLEAN SWEEP Cast the spinner across or slightly downstream (A), and hold the rod parallel to the water as the line comes tight and the blade begins to thump. Don't reel, but lead the lure slightly with the rod tip as it swings until it is directly downcurrent (B). Now reel it back slowly; sometimes fish that have followed the spinner will strike just as the lure begins to move upstream. Reel up and repeat. Start with short casts, and go incrementally longer to cover the water across and downstream of your position.

286 GO SPINNERBAITING FOR COLDWATER BASS

You can catch big wintertime bass by slow-rolling a spinnerbait in water as cold as 47 degrees. After a sunny warm front has baked the surface water for a few days, bass come up from deeper water in feeding mode. Carefully casting to fallen trees is the key. You'll be able to pluck winter bass from main-lake windfalls on steep, rocky banks. Here, the bass can quickly move shallow or deep in response to the weather. When they swim up after a warm front, they typically suspend in the outer limbs of the fallen trees. They'll readily nab a spinnerbait swimming above them.

THE TACKLE In most situations, you'll do best slinging spinnerbaits with a 7-foot medium-heavy baitcasting rod matched with 50-pound braided line (A). The exception is in crystal-clear water, where pros suggest 14-pound fluorocarbon. Braided line is so sensitive that you'll know instantly when you bump a limb or get a strike. The bites can be light when the water's cold.

THE LURE A ¾-ounce chartreuse-and-white Booyah spinnerbait (B) is a winter workhorse. Try a small nickel Colorado blade ahead of a gold No. 7 willowleaf blade. The big willowleaf lets you crawl the spinnerbait at the slow speeds that appeal to sluggish bass hanging 5 to 12 feet deep.

THE TECHNIQUE Slow-roll the spinnerbait across the limbs at a 45-degree angle (C). Let the bait sink to the depth you want to fish before you start retrieving. If the bass are less than 5 feet deep, switch to a ½-ounce spinnerbait.

287 KNOW YOUR BROOK TROUT

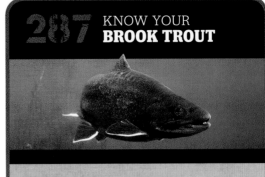

Technically a member of the char family, "brookies" are the only trout native to the northeastern United States, with their natural range extending down the Appalachian Mountains from Maine to Georgia. Today native brook trout populations suffer due to global warming and development throughout their range. Still, cults of anglers in the Northeast hunt the tiny natives on light fly and spinning tackle in hidden streams that flow clear and cold. Natural brook trout are hard to find, but this fish is raised in hatcheries throughout the country and makes up a number of stocked fish that end up in waterways every spring and fall. Whether they're native or hatchery-raised, you can count on them being aggressive; brook trout will often take a swipe at almost any lure or fly that gets in front of their face.

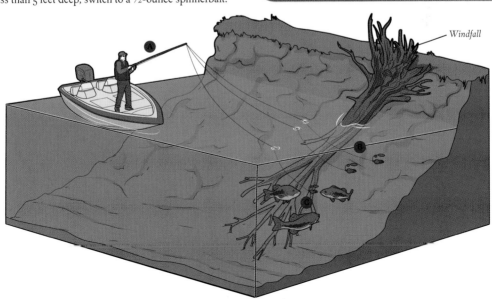

Windfall

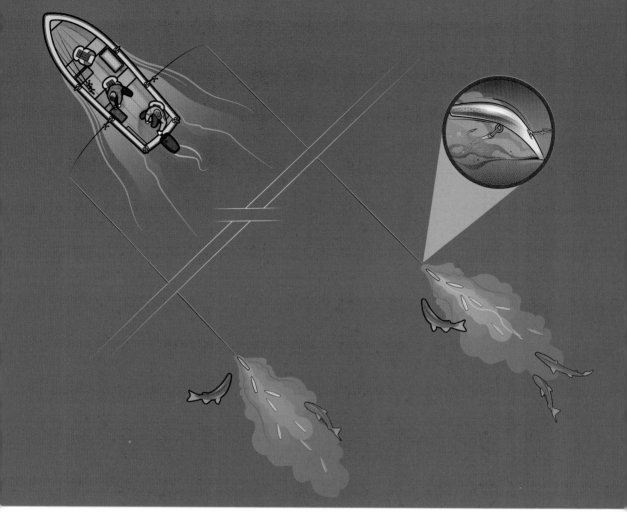

288 BUST AN ICE-OUT LAKE TROUT

After months of lurking in the deep beneath the ice, hungry lake trout invade shallow bays and flats in search of baitfish in spring. Your job: Watch your fishfinder to locate deep lake channels and pools that lead into the shallow bays. Typically, bays and flats with 15 to 30 feet of water will hold lots of big fish. Don't concern yourself with vegetation or bottom structure; instead, look for sandy bottoms where you can troll back and forth without worrying about snags.

Tie a Luhr-Jensen Kwikfish Xtreme 15X rattle lure onto each of two medium-action rods—secured in the middle-left-side and middle-right-side rod holders—matched with reels spooled with 8-pound mono. Yes, that is light line, but it sinks fast and is less visible. Set the lures 70 to 100 feet

back. The prey the fish are feeding on should dictate your lure color. My favorite lake is loaded with kokanee salmon and yellow perch, making silver/blue scale and Slammer my top patterns.

When trolled at 1 to 1.5 mph, these lures produce a slow, wide-action wiggle that drives lake trout crazy. Of course, you must take wind speed into account: Pay attention when pushing into the wind or going with it. You're at the right speed when the noses of the lures are stirring the sandy lake bottom, which kicks up debris—and appeals to the territorial nature of these fish. Troll the entire length of the flat before making a wide turn and heading back across it in the opposite direction.

289 CRANK THE CREEK

As the prespawn progresses and smaller male bass begin cruising the skinniest nearshore waters, the biggest mamas lurk nearby. But they stay hidden, gravitating to any slightly deeper water within flats and bays. This makes reservoir creek channels and ditches—which may bottom out at only 3 or 4 feet—the hottest mega-bass spots just prior to the spawn.

The tight wiggling produced by a flat-sided crankbait really triggers these fish to bite. Toss your crankbait across a creek channel or ditch and run it at medium speed over the edge of the drop. Keep the lure bumping bottom and bouncing off any cover. In clear water, retrieve a jerkbait over the wood. Pay special attention to tree stumps and logs along the edge.

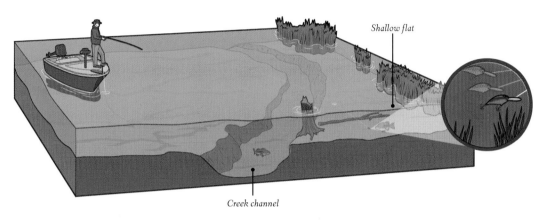

Shallow flat

Creek channel

290 STROKE UP A LUNKER

Countless lures and techniques used all over the country were born in the reservoirs of the Tennessee River. Stroking a jig is among the most unusual—as well as most productive in June for offshore bass. Here's how Kentucky Lake veteran angler Jason Sealock does it.

TACKLE Sealock recommends fishing with a 7-foot medium-heavy-action or heavy-action rod and a fast reel, such as an Abu Garcia Revo STX with an 8.0:1 gear ratio. Go with heavy line; Sealock prefers fluorocarbon, 15-pound-test minimum.

CONDITIONS Stroking a jig is a standout tactic in slack water, when bass spread out and suspend in the water column. The fish show up clearly on a side scan: The water may be 20 feet deep, and there'll be a huge school of fish stacked off the bottom.

TECHNIQUE Make a long cast and point your rod tip at the water. After the jig hits bottom, play out 5 or 6 feet of line, then jerk the rod back fast, bringing it all the way up until it hits your shoulder. The idea is to take up that slack line so that it tightens at the end of the stroke. The jig should pop up off the bottom but stay in the strike zone and move through the whole school of fish. There'll be a big bow in your line as the jig is falling, but that's when you'll get the bites. You'll see the line jump. Use that high-speed reel to take up slack and set the hook. If you miss the strike, just let the jig fall again because another fish will grab it—virtually guaranteed.

291 FIND THEM IN FALL

If you're looking for fish other than the fall mainstays, use this guide to locate five popular species when the temperatures start to drop.

① CRAPPIES Crappies follow baitfish schools into bays as summer turns to fall. Look for these fish to feed here until the water temp dips below 50.

> **BEST FALL TACTIC** Skip standard tube jigs and work small stickbaits and rattle baits. Crappies are aggressive now, and bigger lures equal bigger fish.

② CATFISH Catfish looking to pack on pounds before winter head to riprap, where they gorge on crayfish and baitfish attracted to the sun-warmed rocks.

> **BEST FALL TACTIC** It never hurts to be aggressive when going after fall catfish. Try hopping a big live shiner on a jighead on the bottom around the rocks.

③ BLUEGILLS Bluegills transition to ledges close to shallows in fall. This gives them access to both warmer water for feeding and deeper wintering holes.

> **BEST FALL TACTIC** It's tough to beat a slip bobber–and–nightcrawler combo, but if you want to target monsters, replace the worm with a fathead minnow.

④ LARGEMOUTHS As the temps fall, shad seek the remaining warm water in the backs of creeks. Bass are hot on their trail.

> **BEST FALL TACTIC** If the shad are holding shallow, throw a Spook-style topwater bait at them. Even in cooler water temperatures, bass will crush it.

⑤ YELLOW PERCH When perch leave summer weedbeds, they head to rock piles and humps in 10 to 30 feet of water to feed on crayfish and baitfish.

> **BEST FALL TACTIC** Small blade baits, such as the Heddon Sonar, get down fast and emit a lot of vibration when vertically jigged. Big perch can't resist.

292 ANGLE FOR AUTUMN CRAPPIES

For many crappie fishermen, the only good thing about autumn is hunting season. They use cold fronts, reservoir drawdowns, and lethargic fish as excuses to trade their rods for bows or rifles. But you can still catch plenty of slabs this time of year with a little planning and strategy, and veteran Tennessee guide Jim Duckworth can show you how. Here are his favorite fall tactics.

ROCK IT "Many Sunbelt reservoirs are lowered 5 to 15 feet in fall in anticipation of heavy winter and spring rains," Duckworth says. "The drawdown forces shallow baitfish to relocate to steep riprap banks, where they feed on algae that coats the rocks. Hungry crappies gorge on these minnows." He loads the boat by casting a 1½-inch Berkley PowerBait Atomic Tube, rigged on a ⅛-ounce Blakemore Road Runner jig spinner, to the rocks with a light spinning outfit.

GET THE DROP "A creek-channel drop-off bordering a shallow flat is also a likely place to find crappies now,"

Duckworth adds. "They'll scatter out over the channel after a cold front, then gang up along the drop to feed on passing bait schools." Duckworth suggests trolling a 200-series Bandit crankbait on a soft-action bass cranking rod with 20-pound braided line at 2 to 3 mph. "Motor tight to the drop-off in a lazy S route," he says, "so the lure ticks the outer edge of the shallow flat and then swims into the deeper channel."

SPOON FEED "By the time the leaves fall and the lake's surface temperature has dropped below 60 degrees, crappies will be fattening up on shad," says Duckworth. "Use your fishfinder to locate baitfish schools suspending off points at the mouths of reservoir creeks, then jig a ½-ounce Bass'n Bait Rattle Snakie spoon just above the school. Rig the spoon on a 6-foot medium-action spinning outfit with 20-pound braid and a 2-foot fluorocarbon leader." Follow this Tennessee veteran's sage advice and the bites will be anything but subtle.

293 RATTLE A MUSKIE

While muskies are famous for their stubbornness, the early season takes that trait to a whole new level as they move through spawning stages. Not too long ago, bass anglers on muskie-stocked southern lakes found themselves catching a fair share of these elusive fish in the spring. As hardened muskie fishermen using their typical year-round tactics struggled to boat fish, stories of 50-plus inchers would come somewhat consistently from the bass guys. There was always a common denominator: a rattlebait.

Fast-forward to the present day. Rattlebait fishing for muskies is now common not only in southern lakes but also everywhere else these fish swim. Keep in mind that some states have closures where they naturally reproduce, but if you can legally target them in the spring, keep reading. Although muskies may not be heavily feeding while they're spawning, there is something about a rattlebait burning through skinny water that they can't resist.

Having the right gear is essential. You'll need a medium-action or medium-heavy-action muskie rod that handles $1/3$ to 3-ounce lures. The baits you'll be throwing are small, so the muskie broomstick need not apply. Reels should be strong and fast, taking in a minimum of 30 inches per crank. Spool with 65-pound braid and no more and no less than 100-pound fluorocarbon leader. There are several choice rattlebait options, but the Bill Lewis Super-Trap is a killer. Focus on shallow, warm cover near deeper water. Make long casts, engage the reel the second the lure hits the water, and burn away. You'll know when you have a fish.

294 COVER THE COVER

Largemouths will charge spinnerbaits from any type of cover, but they tend to show a preference for various areas on any given day. Find out where the bass are currently holding and then focus your efforts accordingly. You need to probe shallow grassbeds, boat docks, stumps, flooded bushes, the limbs of fallen trees, and any other available cover until the bass tell you where to fish for them.

Take advantage of your lure's characteristics when searching for these bass. The spinnerbait is one of the most snag-resistant lures and efficiently combs vast amounts of water (even at low speeds). Cast beyond the cover when possible and then guide your spinnerbait close to it with your rod tip. Don't overlook riprap and rocky banks; bass often position themselves nearby in shallow water when it rains. Move your boat close to the bank, cast parallel to the shoreline, and keep your bait hard to the rocks throughout the retrieve. When a bass takes a shot, you'll know, because it won't be subtle.

295 PINPOINT A SPRING WALLEYE

Finding fish is the most essential part of catching them. When it comes to walleyes, there's no easier time to do that than early spring. Regardless of where you are in the lower 48, marble eyes will be in some phase of the spawn come April, and their spawning locations are very predictable. But check local regulations this time of year, especially if you plan on keeping any for dinner.

If the river is your game, look no further than the closest tributary. River walleyes will be in close proximity to incoming streams and creeks for the majority of early spring. They'll stage outside of virtually every available inlet before the spawn, pile into even the shallowest water to mate, and hold relatively close to trib mouths after the spawn.

The same rules apply for lake fishing, but with a few added options. If your impoundment has tributaries, target them. In addition to incoming streams and creeks, any canals, including those lined with houses and docks, will hold walleyes. If no such areas are available, shallow bays serve as prime spawning haunts. Walleyes in the skinniest water will most likely be mating, but those found in adjacent deeper water will be in prespawn and postspawn stages. All you have to do is get a stickbait, grub, or crawler harness in their faces.

296 GIVE IN TO BLIND AMBITION

A layer of ice and snow can make figuring out where to fish on a new lake or pond challenging—but not impossible. First, you need a depth chart. Look for areas that structurally match with the species you're targeting. For warmwater fish like bass and pike, look for weedy areas. For trout or salmon, dropoffs are productive. For all species—especially walleyes—look for offshore humps. Mark these places on the map. Once you have your map plotted, here's how to set your tip-ups in the strike zone.

STEP 1 Drill 11 holes in a U pattern across gradients. Set two rows of tip-ups—starting about 40 yards apart—at 5, 10, 15, 20, and 25 feet deep. Set the last tip-up in 30 feet of water between the two rows. If there is an offshore hump in the area, set a couple more tip-ups there at 5 and 10 feet. This spread puts bait in front of fish that are traveling along gradients and hunting in the area.

STEP 2 Rig the shallower tip-ups, those at 5 and 10 feet (and the hump set), with the biggest baits, like a shiner, because the fish at these depths will be hunting. The deeper sets get smaller baits, as these fish may be less active. Drill additional holes by the hump and the deepest sets where you and your buddy can work jigs. You'll put a few panfish in your bucket and draw the attention of a bigger predator fish. And if nothing else, the activity will help keep you warm as you wait for a bite.

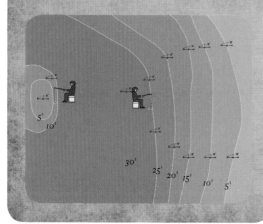

297 KNOW WHEN YOU'RE ON THIN ICE

Ice is generally said to be thick enough for walking and fishing at 4 inches. But not all ice is created equal. Clear ice that forms in December will be stronger and more elastic than the same depth of ice in March, when the bonds fusing the crystals have become stressed from spring sunlight, giving it a honeycombed appearance. Color also counts. Beware of black, gray, or milky ice, which lacks the strength of clear green or blue ice. Expect snowpack or standing water to weaken ice, and steer clear of exposed rocks and logs, which can conduct heat to the surrounding ice. Decaying vegetation also leads to unstable conditions. Seldom is ice uniformly distributed across a lake surface. Ice near shore, which is subject to both conductive heat from the land and reflected sunlight from the bottom, will be weaker than ice that forms over open water. Springs and inlets can prevent the formation of safe ice. Even waterfowl and schooling fish, such as carp, can slow ice formation by circulating the water.

The golden rule of walking on ice is "Probe as you go." Use an ice chisel or spud bar with a sharpened point to act as your "ear to the ground": Safe ice sounds solid and dull when you thump it. Rotting ice creaks or feels spongy. A single hard jab will usually break through ice that is less than 3 inches thick. If in doubt, test ice thickness with an auger or, more efficient, a cordless ¼-inch drill with a ⅝-inch wood auger bit. Carry a retractable tape measure for a precise measurement.

298 JIG BIG LAKERS IN SKINNY WATER

Fighting a jumbo lake trout through a hole in the ice is an intense experience, but to get a 20-plus-pounder on the line, you have to think outside the box when hunting on the hard water. One pro tip is to skip the deep water and go shallow. Legendary Colorado ice guide Bernie Keefe frequently jigs in as little as 3 feet of water, provided there is deeper water close by. Keefe says big lakers in deep water can often be finicky, but if a monster comes in shallow, it's there for one reason only: a fast meal. You won't have light taps and half-hearted strikes. A laker on shallow flats wants to grab a meal and get back to the nearby depths fast, so your jig won't get hit—it'll get slammed. Hang on tight.

299 DRILL DOWN ON IT

When fishing from a boat, most anglers move around the lake and try new spots all day, but in ice fishing, many just drill holes over spots that have been productive in the past and stay put. The thing is, making the effort to move on the ice and drill lots of holes will get you more fish. Since you can't cast in different directions on the ice to run your lure through new pieces of water, drilling holes even 20 feet apart can increase hookups significantly, especially when fishing species like lake trout, pike, and walleyes that tend to roam around an area. There could be fish all around your lure or bait that just don't get close enough to see it, but a redrill a short distance away will put the offering right in the zone. Some ice fishing guides will drill more than 100 holes a day and cover 3 miles of lake, and they usually catch the most fish. I also landed the biggest lake trout I've ever caught through the ice after three drops into a hole not 30 feet from one I'd been jigging for an hour.

300
BE A WALLEYE PUPPET MASTER

Swimming jigs are to walleyes what jelly donuts are to bears, but surprisingly few ice fishermen use them. The lure itself is nothing new, but a little puppet mastery will bring the jig to life. Here are the most effective motions:

LIFT AND DROP Try this basic action framed within the first 2 feet off the bottom. Use some finesse here—a light, smooth snap fares better than a sudden jerk. Add a circular motion to give the lure an erratic movement, which the walleye interprets as a bait in distress—in other words, dinner. Walleyes typically hit the lure on the drop. Subsequently, the next lift develops into a hookset.

SHIMMY AND SWIM Walleyes are known to be stingy biters. When that happens, reduce the range to 6 inches and soften the stroke. On a taut string, the lure continues making deliciously unpredictable moves, but without the octane. Do a shimmy—basically an in-place quiver—every half-dozen lifts. That kind of nervous behavior can propel a wary walleye to bite.

Try these tricks on a medium-action 28- to 30-inch rod and 10-pound braided line for improved feel, with a 2- to 4-foot-long 8-pound-test monofilament shock leader. The inherent stretch of mono line helps set the hook without pulling the lure from the walleye's mouth.

301
CHUNK UP A GIANT FLATHEAD

Flatheads are arguably the most aggressive of all American catfish species. These fish are active hunters, stalking prey such as suckers, bluegills, and even bass after the sun goes down.

Flathead fishermen in the know often seek out the biggest live baits they can catch, knowing that the bigger the meal, the bigger the catfish that's likely to eat it. However, many of these devout flatheaders will also tell you that when you first start fishing, you should always remember to make sure at least one of your lines is baited with cut bait.

While flatheads gorge on live baits, cut baits release more scent. Therefore, many wise catfishermen fire out a chunk of shad, bluegill, or sucker to simply draw flatheads to the area where their baited lines are sitting.

Sometimes it's the cut bait that gets eaten first; however, the cut bait may also entice a big flathead close enough to the spread to pick up the vibration of one of your live baits. If that flathead is hungry enough to be attracted by the cut bait's scent, you can bet it will be hungry enough to investigate the enticing offer on your line!

302 HIT THE FARM ICE

You don't need a fancy underwater camera, gas auger, or snowmobile to ice-fish that 1-acre pond up the road. Once the ice is at least 4 inches thick and safe to walk on, grab a rod, something that will chop a hole in the ice, and a bucket of live shiners. Here's where you'll find the fish:

SLOPES Those shallow, weedy areas that held bass in warmer times are not going to hold much now except baitfish trying to escape danger under the ice. But largemouths and crappies will often hug the slopes leading up to those shallows (1), where they can sneak in and grab a

meal. In this area, drop a live shiner on a single hook with a split shot 12 inches up the line. This rig allows the bait to swim freely, making it more likely to trigger a bite from fish that are inclined to roam and chase a moving target.

EMBANKMENTS Most farm ponds have one steep side, and this is typically where you find the deepest water (2). Perch, bass, and crappies will spend most of their time tight to the bottom, but a live shiner on a jighead dangled in front of them won't last long. Drop the bait all the way to the bottom and slowly reel up until you hit the school.

303 POWER UP

Power plants are often built along rivers so they can draw in necessary cooling water. Heated water flows back out into the river, drawing bait and gamefish like a magnet in winter. If the area is legally accessible, look for fish in these spots.

MOUTH Large predators, such as muskies and striped bass, will patrol the area where warm discharge water meets cold river water (A). They're less interested in small bait, so work a perch-colored twitchbait near the end of the chute or live-line big baits like suckers or shad.

BANK Walleyes and larger smallmouths tend to hang along the sides of the discharge chute out of the main current (B), waiting for forage to flush down to them. Hop a white grub on a jighead through the water below any current break.

HEAD Baitfish congregate near the head of the discharge, where the water is the warmest (C). Crappies, perch, and smallmouths hang in the calmer water next to the center flow, picking off bait that washes into the eddy.

304 KNOW YOUR CHINOOK SALMON

Also known as king salmon, this is the largest member of the salmon family and can weigh over 90 pounds. Native to the Pacific Coast from Northern California to Alaska, Chinooks are prized for their quality on the table and their brute fighting ability. In late spring through early summer (and in fall in the case of Great Lakes salmon), Chinooks return to the rivers of their birth from the ocean, where saltwater anglers wait to intercept them in bays with trolling spoons and jigs, and fly and conventional anglers line rivers to throw plugs and streamers as the fish migrate upstream. Once salmon enter rivers to spawn, they stop feeding. Striking at a lure or fly is purely an aggressive reaction. Popular salmon lure and fly colors are rarely natural but instead bright and flashy to essentially annoy a salmon into biting.

305 GET YOUR FLATS FOOTING

Rookie bonefish anglers have a tendency to look too far ahead and walk too fast when wading the flats. Focus on the water 40 to 60 feet around you in all directions and move very slowly. You're more likely to see the shadow below the fish instead of the fish itself. Look for the flash of a tail sticking out of the water or a color change on the bottom that's moving or irregular. Don't expect to see the whole fish.

Schools of bonefish like to travel through channels on the flats with a bit more depth. Depressions also offer a quick escape route as the tide falls. If you find a channel close to a vast muddy flat, it's worth standing and waiting a while. Often, bones will come to you as the tide drops and they return to the channel to head to deep water.

If you drop a fly directly into a school of fish, or on a loner fish's head, you're going to spook it. Make every effort to lead the fish by 8 or 10 feet. Bonefish like a moving target, so as the fish gets closer, make short strips to hop the fly. When you get hit, strip-strike hard before you lift your rod to fight the fish. Lift too early, and you'll pull the fly out of the fish's mouth.

306 PLAN A PARTY

Since I was a kid, I've been fishing on party boats—or head boats—for everything from walleyes to tuna. These walk-on charters offer an easy, affordable way to fish big, open waters. The downside, however, is that you can be sharing the rails with upwards of 100 people—some skilled, others not so much. So, how do you show everyone on board who's boss? Try these strategies.

BACK IT UP Whenever possible, post up along the stern railing. If chumming is involved, you'll have first crack at any fish moving up the slick. If you're bottom fishing, there's a good chance the sonar transducer is located in the rear or middle of the boat. So when the captain anchors to fish a wreck or reef, the structure usually ends up under the stern. The best way to secure a spot in the back is to not show up only 10 minutes before shove-off. Get aboard at least an hour early.

LOB THEM BLIND Overhead casting is typically frowned upon on party boats, but that doesn't mean you can't gain some distance. The trick is learning to lob rigs and lures underhand. Point the rod straight down along the side of the boat, get a pendulum action going with just a few feet of line dangling off the tip, and fling the rig sharply as you bring the rod back up to the rail. Just getting a few feet past everyone with lines dropped straight down can pay off huge.

MIND YOUR LINE Head-boat amateurs have a nasty habit of dropping their baits, then not paying attention to where their line is going. Keeping your rod pointed straight out away from the boat is critical, especially when drifting, because the lines move with the current. Being aware of your line's position, plus those of surrounding anglers, is the easiest way to avoid big tangles, which also gives you a fishing power play while others are knotted together.

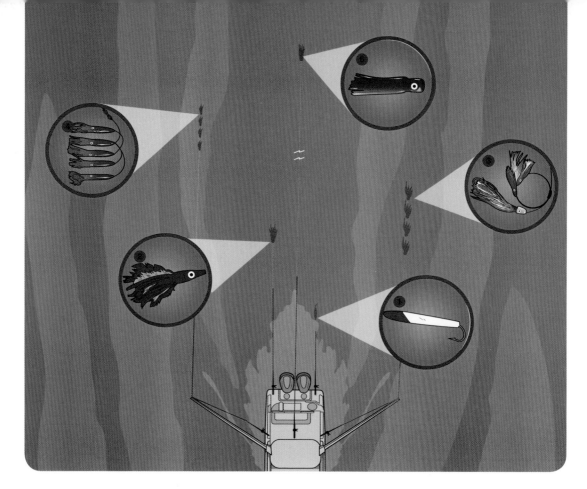

307 ASSUME THE TUNA POSITION

Offshore trolling can be intimidating to novice bluewater anglers, but you don't need a huge boat and the ability to troll 16 lines to catch yellowfin and bluefin tuna. If you've got a smaller boat with outriggers, five trolling combos, and some basic tuna lures, you're all set. Follow this simple plan for positioning the right lures in the right spots while running 5 to 7 mph, and you'll be eating sashimi in no time.

1. 15 TO 25 FEET Tuna like the bubble trail made by propellers. That's why you should always have a lure with lots of action, like a cedar plug, swimming right in the prop wash.

2. 35 TO 40 FEET Position a single tuna feather or skirted lure just beyond the prop wash. This lure will take fish that are interested in the bubble trail but not willing to come in close to the motors.

3. 55 TO 60 FEET From one outrigger, pull a daisy chain of skirted lures in the clean water past the prop wash. These lures should be weighted so that they keep dipping below the surface and rising back up.

4. 75 TO 80 FEET On the other outrigger, drag a daisy chain of hollow squid lures. These squids will dance and splash on the surface, not only enticing tuna in the spread but also attracting others in the area with sound.

5. 150 TO 300 FEET Always dump one of your lines way, way back behind the boat—in what's called the "shotgun" position. A lure with a chugging head that makes noise on the surface should pick off any shy fish that refuse to come into your main spread.

308 GET A JUMP ON STEALTHY SNOOK

A guide once told me that a snook is like a mugger in an alley—it hides in the shadows, waiting for prey to pass by. Then it bolts out and attacks. Snook are naturally nocturnal feeders, and many guides base a hunt around tidal flow. These fish prefer to let the tide bring a meal to them, and they'll use any structure that breaks the current—particularly dock pilings and bulkheads—as ambush points. A high outgoing tide is best; a slack tide hardly ever produces fish. If you find a lighted dock that creates a strong shadow in the water, you've hit big-snook pay dirt, but fooling a fish hiding under the boards boils down to proper presentation. Never pitch a bait directly to the spot the snook is likely holding in. You have to cast uptide and let the bait naturally move down into the light. If it doesn't get attacked in three or four casts, either the fish isn't there or it's not going to eat.

Opt for a live pinfish or finger mullet pinned through the nose with a 4/0 circle hook and rigged weightless on a 30-inch length of 40-pound fluorocarbon. The heavy leader will withstand abrasion on pilings and on a snook's sharp gill plate. When a snook does grab the bait, it's critical to fight it with the rod first and the reel second because low, severe rod angles are often necessary to get the fish away from the structure.

309 KNOW YOUR RED DRUM

Also known as redfish, this inshore saltwater species is one of the most widely distributed in the country. What makes these fish so popular is that you can adapt almost any fishing style to their pursuit. Flyfishermen can delicately present crab flies to tailing reds in shallow coastal marshes of the Florida Everglades. Surf-casters working the rough shores of North Carolina can fire chunks of fresh menhaden in hopes of scoring a giant "bull" red from the sand. Anglers working the dirty water at the mouth of the Mississippi River in Louisiana will get drags screaming by working a popping cork and soft-plastic shrimp. No matter where or how you hook a red, be ready for a fight. Big fish weighing 20 to 50 pounds will drain a spool of line and dog to the bitter end.

310 GET THE RED OUT

Stalking redfish in shallow marshes is one of angling's ultimate thrills, and when the water's clear, you can spot the lit-up copper and gold in a redfish from a mile away. So what happens when the water is murky or stained? Don't fret. If you know the telltale signs of a red, it's easier than you think to decipher what kind of fish are swimming close by without actually seeing them.

WHAT TO LOOK FOR

BROAD V-WAKES A guide I fished with once likened a redfish to a fire extinguisher being pulled underwater. There will be a distinct bulge in the surface made by the fish's broad, blunt head, followed by a long trailing V-shaped wake. Reds often swim very straight and deliberately, so if the wake is moving erratically, it's probably something else.

TAILS There's no surer sign of a redfish than spotting a gold tail with a black spot waving in the air. When reds grub in the muddy shallows for shrimp and crabs, they'll angle their bodies down and their tails will break the surface. Not many other fish in a marsh feed this way, but if you do see another tail, remember: No black spot, no cast.

MOVING GRASS Other marsh residents, such as sea-trout and jacks, will typically feed in open water and deeper channels, whereas reds often hug grassy shorelines and flooded cane banks. They also swim into flooded vegetation to chase bait, so if you see moving grass or cane, there's a good chance it's signalling a red out hunting for a meal.

WHAT TO AVOID

WISPY V-WAKES If you see V-wakes on the surface that pop up quickly, move fast, and then disappear, don't get excited. You're probably seeing mullet. Though these baitfish can grow quite large and push a sizable amount of water, they move much quicker and far more erratically than a redfish.

BIG, SUDDEN SPLASHES These could be from redfish, but if they are, you'll probably see another splash in the same area in short order. If there's one big splash and no more movement, you've probably just seen a gar. Gar lie still as logs just under the surface, bolting away suddenly and creating a big splash when they get spooked.

DIVING BIRDS Most of the time, a big flock of birds isn't going to point to redfish, at least not when you're in a backcountry marsh setting. Birds are typically drawn in when fish attack a school of baitfish from below and drive it to the surface. Sea-trout and jacks corral bait in this manner. Reds more often feed close to the bottom, so they're not as likely to be the initiators of a bird blitz on the surface.

311 SNEAK UP ON STRIPERS

Throughout the Northeast and the Mid-Atlantic, striped bass begin swimming up the coastal creeks, inlets, and rivers in May, where many will often remain for the summer to feed on the plentiful baitfish that get pushed with the tide in these high-current areas. Targeting these bass takes some stealth, as they can be highly pressured and wary. Step one is to attack at first and last light. Step two is using the current to time your approach and dictate your boat position. Stripers use the slack pockets on inside bends to ambush prey, and the best way to ensure that your topwater lure gets smashed is to cut the corners.

POWER DOWN When you approach a bend, position the boat so the current carries you toward the inside corner, and kill the engine (A). If you have a trolling motor, you'll be able to make adjustments once the big engine is shut down; if you don't, do your best to gauge the path of the current and keep the bow pointed downstream.

THROW LONG Just before the boat rounds the turn, make a long cast with a popper over the corner and into the slack pocket on the other side (B). Braided line helps cut through marsh grass if a section of your line ends up spanning dry land. Stripers often smash the lure within two pops.

LEAN IN When you get bit, set hard and move the rod away from the corner. As the boat is pushed around the turn, you want to keep side pressure on to steer the fish away from the bank (C). Getting a fish out of the hole quickly also ups your chances of scoring another bass from the same pocket on a repeat drift.

312 TAKE 'EM TO SCHOOL

A school of mahimahi can be downright ravenous, attacking any baits or lures pitched close by as soon as they hit the water. When one fish is hooked, the others often follow it during the fight, so you should never take a struggling mahi out of the water until someone else on the boat hooks the next one. Once there's another fish on, the first hooked fish can be reeled in. The second angler should keep his or her fish fighting in the water until the first angler recasts and hooks another. If you were to keep pulling each mahi into the boat, leaving no struggling fish in the water for the rest to follow, the school would disperse or lose interest, moving away from the boat or getting a sudden case of lockjaw.

313 POP ON OVER

Many saltwater anglers are married to the idea that if they don't see any gamefish feeding on the surface, there's no use in casting a topwater lure. But that's actually the opposite of the truth. Sometimes when the ocean just seems completely devoid of life and you can't get bit no matter what lures or jigs you try below the surface, a topwater lure can draw a strike, even from a fish holding at a considerable depth. Why? Because sound is a powerful thing, and sometimes the chugging and splashing of a popper on an otherwise quiet surface is the little trigger

that gets lockjawed fish chewing. Next time you're marking fish on your sounder but can't get them to eat, make a handful of casts with a loud popper or Spook-style lure with rattles. The monster striper, snook, redfish, or seatrout that rises to the occasion might shock you.

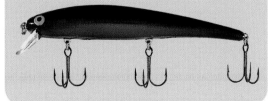
314 FIND STRIPERS IN THE DARK

Summer success with nighttime stripers often means moving away from the main beach and targeting areas with current where nonmigratory bass stake claims during the hot months. Inlets—especially those with bridges—are good spots, as a falling tide will draw forage from the bay to bass stationed near the inlet mouth or behind pilings.

If you can learn how to swing a plug, you'll catch a lot more bass than you would just by reeling. Try casting upcurrent at a 45-degree angle, then lock the reel and never turn the handle. As the line comes tight in the current, the lure will dig and start swimming across the current on its own. To a bass, this looks like a dead, floating baitfish that suddenly came to life. It's a real strike trigger.

Even after the line completely straightens out, give the lure at least 20 seconds of extra hang time to entice any reluctant bass before retrieving for another cast. The trick after catching one fish is to repeat the same swing again and again, as stripers will often congregate in a small area.

315 MOUNT YOUR CATCH AND EAT IT, TOO

Ever notice that you can gauge the size of a fish just by looking at the tail? If you don't want to pay for a replica mount or waste the meat by having a skin mount made, fillet your next whopper, save the tail, and make your own trophy.

STEP 1 Remove as much meat as possible from the base of the tail with a sharp knife or grapefruit spoon. With wire cutters, clip the spine as far back as possible. Don't damage the skin or lose any scales. What's left should be a hollow pocket.

STEP 2 Spread the tail out and press it between two pieces of cardboard covered in wax paper. Use binder clips to keep pressure on the cardboard.

STEP 3 Rub the inside of the pocket with borax laundry powder and then fill the pocket with expanding plumbing foam. Place the tail in a cool, dry spot to set for three weeks.

STEP 4 Once dry, remove the cardboard and paint the tail to revive the color. Spray paint and acrylic work well. Saw off any excess foam to create a level surface, and glue the tail to a plaque or wood base for display.

316 SCALE FISH WITH WATER

Here's an easy method for scaling fish: First, place the fish on a scaling board with its tail secured in the clamp (if you don't have a scaling board, just hold the fish down by its tail with your thumb). Next, attach an ordinary pressure nozzle to a garden hose and simply spray the scales off from tail to head. Flip the fish and do the other side. Scales come off easily with no damage to meat—it takes less than a minute to do a whole fish!

317 PRINT THAT FISH

Japanese anglers invented *gyotaku* (fish rubbing) more than a century ago to record their fish and prevent the rampant lying that goes on with fishermen everywhere. Today several American fish printers have elevated the form to fine art. Follow their instructions, and you can make a print arguably—and there will be an argument—worthy of the wall (in the bathroom, maybe). Here's how to make your artistically fishy statement.

CATCH IT Some fish print better than others. You'll want to start with one that has fairly large scales, like a sunfish, rock bass, crappie, perch, or bass.

DE-SLIME IT Using hand soap and paper towels, clean the slime off the fish, pat it dry, and place it on a layer of paper towels over a foam board. Prop the fins open with wadded paper towel and pins, and put small pieces of paper towel under the gill plate and in the mouth to keep moisture from seeping out. Then let it air dry for 10 minutes or so.

INK IT With even strokes, brush the ink onto the fish from the gills toward the tail. Starting with lighter shades of ink on the belly, gradually move to the darkest along the back. Next, ink the head, excluding the eye (you'll do that last), and then the fins. If the fish has spots or other distinctive markings, paint them in over the base coat with appropriate hues of block ink. Don't go for photorealism; simplify the color scheme and then paint in only enough to give the right impression.

RUB IT Put a clean paper towel under the fish, then carefully lay a sheet of rice paper down over the fish. Hold the paper in the middle with one hand and use the other to thoroughly rub over the fish, working from the center out.

FINISH IT Peel the paper off. If you didn't apply enough ink, wipe the fish clean, let it dry, and try again. After it dries, use water-colors to paint the eye.

318 FISH YOUR DREAM WATERS

While my travels have taken me to countless U.S. waters, as well as some tremendous fishing locations abroad, there are still plenty of dream destinations I've yet to fish. Reaching a few of these places is a lofty (and in some cases expensive) goal, but if I had my way, I'd chase these eight fish before I check out for good.

BALTIC SEA NORTHERN PIKE

I've traveled as far as the Canadian tundra to catch monster pike. However, some of the biggest pike in the world can be found in Sweden in the Baltic Sea. Yes, the Baltic is salty, which is why this fishery intrigues me so much. It's the only place in the world where pike not only thrive in brackish water but also grow massive in a salty setting.

ICELANDIC ATLANTIC SALMON

Not only is the landscape in Iceland gorgeous, the country's Atlantic salmon run is outstanding. While I've chased the species in Canada, there is something about doing it in the turquoise River Fossa. Knowing that in many cases only two anglers are allowed to fish a long stretch at a time, that sounds like heaven.

ARGENTINE GOLDEN DORADO

As a lover of salmon, bluefish, and striped bass, I'm determined to chase golden dorado in Argentina. These brutes combine the speed, power, and jaw force of all those aforementioned species. A big golden can literally turn a wooden topwater plug into sawdust and then melt your drag as it runs.

AFRICAN GOLIATH TIGERFISH

Goliath tigerfish can easily break the 100-pound mark in the Congo River, and in my opinion, they are one of the most fearsome fish in the world. If I ever get there, I'll take a goliath any way I can get it, but I'd be lying if I didn't say I really want one on a big muskie fly connected to a thick steel leader.

MONGOLIAN TAIMEN

It's a long, long journey to Mongolia, one filled with planes, Jeeps, and even horses. But that's what it takes to reach taimen in the country's northern rivers. Taimen are the largest member of the trout family, with the potential to reach 40 pounds or more. Someday, I hope to see one that size smash a giant rat fly on the surface in person.

KAMCHATKA RAINBOW TROUT

The rivers of Russia's Kamchatka Peninsula are known to produce some of the biggest wild rainbow trout in the world. More importantly, they are largely unpressured and the fish are highly aggressive. During the summer months, it's tough to swing a mouse fly or big streamer without it getting hammered.

VANUATU GIANT TREVALLY

I'm a junkie for topwater hits, and in the saltwater world, nothing makes a bigger splash than a giant trevally. Getting to them literally means flying to the other side of the world, but it'd be worth it just to see one 80-plus-pounder thrash a huge popper along the Vanuatu reefs. I'm not sure I'm strong enough to fight one, but I'd like to try.

NEW ZEALAND BROWN TROUT

The browns in New Zealand are almost as breathtaking as the country's mountains. They're massive and some of the most colorful browns on the planet. Problem is, they're also some of the most wary. Because New Zealand's rivers are so clear, getting a shot at one of these trophies is a real challenge, but one I'm dying to take on.

GLOSSARY

ATTRACTOR FLY A large, flashy dry fly designed to grab a trout's attention; does not mimic a specific insect.

BACK CAST Any point during fly casting when the line is in the air behind you.

BACKLASH When the line on the spool of a reel tangles or knots. This is usually caused by loose line on the spool, wind, or the spool revolving too quickly on the cast.

BANK SINKER A rounded weight designed to roll and move across the bottom instead of anchoring a rig or bait.

BEADHEAD A small brass or tungsten head used to add extra flash and weight to nymph and streamer flies.

BEDDED Refers to any fish that's positioned over or guarding a nest of eggs.

BELLY BOAT A tube with shoulder straps and a seat harness that allows an angler to float in a body of water; fins are worn on the feet to allow the angler to maneuver.

BOBBER STOP A knot of string or rubber bead threaded on the line that stops a slip bobber from sliding up the line. Placement of a bobber stop determines how deep the bait or jig below can sink before it suspends below the float.

BOTTOM BOUNCER A weight with a long wire arm that ticks along the bottom while drifting. The arm helps keep the weight from hanging in rocky bottoms.

BRAIDED LINE Any fishing line woven from strands or fibers of materials such as Dyneema, Dacron, or Spectra. Typically thinner and stronger than monofilament.

BUCKTAIL JIG A lure with a weighted lead head and a tail made from the hair of a deer's tail.

BULLET WEIGHT A bullet-shaped sliding sinker most often used to rig soft-plastic lures Texas or Carolina style.

BUTT The last section of a fishing rod, located behind the reel seat.

BUZZBAIT A skirted topwater lure with a wire arm that features a plastic propeller on the end. When retrieved, the propeller creates noise and a bubble trail on the surface.

CADDIS A classification of water-borne insects that consists of over 12,000 species found in rivers, streams, ponds, and lakes throughout the U.S. Many fly styles mimic caddis in various stages of their life cycle.

CANE POLE A fishing rod made from bamboo. There is no reel, but rather a fixed length of line tied to the end.

CAROLINA RIG A rig with a bullet weight slid up the main line, followed by a glass bead. A barrel swivel is then tied to the end of the main line to stop the weight and bead from sliding any lower. A leader is tied to the other end of the barrel swivel, and the hook that will hold the soft-plastic lure is tied to the opposite end of the leader. The bead and weight will bang together to make a clicking sound.

CIRCLE HOOK A round hook that is designed specifically to catch in the corner of a fish's mouth. Circle hooks are supposed to thwart gut hookings, thus improving the odds of healthy releases. These hooks are favored by anglers who chase large species that require giving the fish time to run off with the bait.

CLEVIS A piece of terminal tackle that holds a spinner blade to the wire arm of an in-line spinner or spinnerbait. The clevis rotates around the arm, giving the blade its action. Some clevises are designed to allow anglers to quickly change blade colors and styles.

CONEHEAD WEIGHT A conical metal head used to add weight to streamer flies.

CRANKBAIT A family of lures usually made of hard plastic that produce a tight wobble when reeled with a steady retrieve. Most crankbaits have lips that determine how deep they dive, though some lipless versions exist. Crankbaits are typically used to mimic baitfish or crayfish.

CREATURE (lure) Soft-plastic lures that do not mimic a particular species of forage, but rather incorporate unnatural tentacles, arms, ribs, fins, and claws into their designs to grab the attention of a bass by producing more action, visual stimulation, and vibration than standard soft-plastic styles.

CUTBANK A bank of a river or stream that's been gouged out by the current, creating an indented pocket underwater, and an overhanging lip above the water.

DEAD DRIFT This term refers to the drifting of fly down a section of river or stream when the objective is to make the presentation look as natural as possible by not imparting any movement with the rod and controlling your line so the current does not speed up or slow down the fly's drift.

DEADFALL A tangled cluster of dead trees, limbs, or brush in the water.

DEPTHFINDER An electronic device used on boats that measures water depth with sonar.

DORSAL FIN The fin on a fish's back closest to the head.

DOWNRIGGER A device used while trolling to place a lure or bait at the desired depth. It consists of a 3- to 6-foot horizontal pole, which supports a large cannonball weight by a steel cable. A release clip attaches a fishing line to the cannonball weight, which is lowered to the desired depth manually or electronically. When a fish strikes, the line is yanked free of the release clip.

DROPPER RIG A rig used in flyfishing that usually consists of a bulky dry fly and a small nymph. To rig it, a short piece of tippet is tied to the hook of the dry fly, while the nymph is tied to the other end of the tippet. The dry fly keeps the nymph, a.k.a. the "dropper," suspended in the water below it like a bobber during the drift. This allows you to entice fish on and below the surface simultaneously.

DROP-SHOT RIG A rig used with soft-plastic lures that keeps the lure suspended off the bottom. The hook that holds the lure is usually tied directly to the main line or a loop in the main line, and a 12- to 15-inch tag end is left below the hook or loop. A special drop-shot weight connects to the bottom of the tag end.

DRY FLY Any bug-imitating fly designed to float or drift on the water's surface.

DUBBING Any material—usually fine hair, fur, or synthetic fibers—used for creating the body of a fly.

EDDY Any point in the flow of moving water where the current moves in the opposite direction of the main current, often creating a small whirlpool or area of calmer slack water. Eddies form most often behind obstructions, such as deadfalls and boulders.

EMERGER Any fly tied to mimic an aquatic insect during the point in its life cycle when it has just hatched off the bottom of a lake or river and is swimming to the surface, where it will dry its wings and fly away.

FALSE CAST Any stroke in fly casting that is made while the line is in the air before it is laid down on the water. Used to work line through the guides to extend a cast's length or to build shooting momentum to give a cast more reach.

FISHFINDER An electronic device that uses sonar to draw a digital image of the water column, thereby showing the depth and position of gamefish or baitfish under the boat.

FLASHER An electronic device used to find gamefish and baitfish through ice. Flashers emit sonar beams, and fish or bait appear as bars of varying thickness on the screen.

FLIP A style of casting used most often in bass fishing to cast jigs or soft-plastic lures to small targets, such as dock pilings or submerged tree stumps only a short distance away from the end of the rod.

FLOATING LINE A fly line engineered to float on the surface. This is the most commonly used style of fly line.

FLUOROCARBON A material used to make fishing line and leader material that's praised for its abrasion resistance and near invisibility underwater.

FOOTBALL JIG A bass lure with a rubber skirt and a weighted head with an oblong shape.

FREE LINE A live bait presented with no weight on the line, allowing it to swim as naturally and freely as possible.

FRENCH-FRY WORM A style of soft-plastic worm, short in length, with a curled body shape.

GAFF A large hook mounted to the end of a pole used to land large fish once they're brought to the side of the boat.

GLIDER A style of muskie and pike lure that darts side to side in long strides underwater when a twitching action is imparted with the rod.

HACKLE Feathers used to create wispy collars or bodies on flies. The term can also refer to the collar of a dry fly.

HATCH Refers to a lot of aquatic insects leaving a body of water after their wings have formed and dried.

HOOK HANGER A U-shaped eyelet usually found above the reel seat on a rod that offers a place to attach a hook when the rod is not in use.

HYDROLOGICAL MAP Any map that specifically depicts the distribution of water on the Earth's surface.

INDICATOR A small float made specifically for flyfishing that allows the angler to detect strikes when drifting nymphs or wet flies; also called strike indicators.

IN-LINE SPINNER Any type of lure with a spinner blade that revolves around a single, straight wire post.

JERKBAIT A style of lure designed to dart erratically when the rod tip is twitched. Most hard jerkbaits have lips to control how deep they dive with each twitch, and longer, more slender bodies than crankbaits. Hard versions of these lures are also called twitchbaits or stickbaits.

JIG Any lure designed to work with a rise-and-fall motion directly below the boat or during the retrieve after casting a distance. Most jigs have a weighted head and tail made from hair, feathers, rubber, or soft-plastic material, though others, such as long, slender metal lures that imitate various baitfish, can also be considered jigs.

JIG-AND-PIG A rubber-skirted lure with a weighted head, coupled with a pork skin or soft-plastic trailer threaded onto the hook to give the lure more action in the water.

JIGHEAD A weight with a hook and eyelet molded directly into lead. Jigheads come in all shapes and sizes and are most commonly used with soft-plastic lures.

LEADER Any length of monofilament, fluorocarbon, or wire added by the angler to the end of the main line or fly line for purposes such as bite protection, shock absorption, or reducing the fish's ability to detect the line underwater.

LINDY RIG A bottom rig for live bait presentations that uses a flat sliding sinker that will "walk" over rocky bottoms without getting snagged.

LINE-COUNTER REEL Any reel with a built-in counter that's internally connected to the spool and tells the angler exactly how many feet of line is being let out or reeled in.

LINE-TIE EYE A term used to describe the eye on a lure to which the main line or leader is tied.

LIVIE An angling term that refers to any baitfish that's used in live form.

LOGJAM A group of logs, tree trunks, or limbs that has gotten stuck in one area of a moving piece of water and created an obstruction.

LUNKER A slang term that usually refers to a big largemouth bass.

MARKER BUOY Any man-made floating or stationary marker that aids in navigation on the water by denoting the edges of a channel, a shipping lane, the entrance to a harbor, or an underwater obstruction.

MAYFLY A classification of water-borne insects with very short life spans. Mayflies are found in rivers, streams, ponds, and lakes throughout the U.S. They are common trout forage in both larval and adult form. Many fly styles mimic mayflies in various stages of their life cycle.

MEND To lift any fly line between the rod tip and the fly off the water after the cast and place it upstream so that the fly always precedes the line during a drift. Mending allows a wet fly or nymph to sink deeper, and when you're dry fly fishing, mending helps attain a drag-free drift.

MONOFILAMENT Fishing line made from a single fiber of polymers that have been melted and extruded through holes of varying sizes that determine the line's thickness and breaking strength.

NOODLING The act of using your hands and feet as catfish bait by sticking them in underwater holes and rock-piles, wiggling them, allowing the catfish to clamp down, and wrestling it out of the hole.

NYMPH Any fly designed to fish below the surface that mimics an aquatic insect in the post-larval, but pre-adult, stage of its life cycle. In biology, *nymph* is also the general term for aquatic insects in their pre-adult life cycle stage.

PARTY BOAT Fishing vessels open to the public that can accommodate a large group of anglers. Most of the time, no prior reservations are needed, as anglers can simply walk onto the boat and pay the fare onboard. Mainly found near oceans and on big lakes.

PLANER BOARD Used for trolling, planer boards are made from plastic or wood and have a beveled edge. Some planer boards are pulled with special rods separate from the rod pulling your bait or lure or on thin ropes, and your fishing line attaches to the board via a tension release clip. Some lighter planer boards are attached directly to the main line and do not snap free after a strike. Both styles pull the line off to one side of the boat when deployed, widening your trolling spread and allowing you to fish more lines by keeping them separated.

PLUG Any long hardbait with a diving lip that mimics large baifish species, such as herring, suckers, or menhaden. Technically, there is no difference between a plug and a large, long crankbait, but the term is commonly used in saltwater fishing and by pike and muskie anglers.

POPPER Any topwater lure with a cupped mouth designed to chug and spit, and spray water as it's moved across the surface.

QUICK-STRIKE RIG A live-bait rig used in muskie fishing. It features two treble hooks connected with wire leader, one of which is placed in a baitfish's head and the other in the tail so that a hook ends up in a muskie's mouth no matter which end of the bait it decides to attack. Usually only one point of each treble hook is placed in the bait so upon the hookset, the hooks pull free of the bait quickly and stick in the muskie's hard mouth.

RATTLEBAIT A term used to refer to a lipless crankbait with internal rattles.

REEL RATIO A fraction that defines how many inches or feet of line are wound onto a reel spool with each revolution of the handle.

RIFFLE A choppy section of a river or stream caused by the water moving over a shallow rock-strewn area, sandbar, or gravel bar.

RIPRAP A term that refers to man-made underwater structure, such as old building foundations, old docks, or piles of concrete blocks.

SABIKI RIG A rig used for catching baitfish species such as herring that features 6 to 10 tiny feathered hooks on one leader with a weight on the bottom. Sabiki rigs mimic an entire school of very tiny baitfish or shrimp and are usually jigged straight up and down below the boat.

SAN JUAN WORM A simple fly pattern that mimics a mealworm or garden worm. They are available in a wide variety of colors; brown, pink, and red are top producers.

SEAM Any area in moving water where currents flowing at two different speeds meet as they run parallel to each other, forming a visible border.

SEINE A long net with fine mesh stretched between two stakes that's used to collect baitfish in streams and small ponds.

SHANK The section of a hook between the bend and eye.

SHINER Though there are some species of small fish that are scientifically referred to as shiners, such as the golden shiner, this term has come to refer to any species of small, shiny-scaled baitfish sold in a bait shop.

SINK TIP A length of heavy sinking line either added temporarily to the end of a fly line when casting streamers or nymphs to achieve more depth in certain situations, or permanently fused onto the end of a floating fly line for full-time use in deeper water.

SLAB A slang term for a large crappie.

SLINKY WEIGHT A weight cut from a coil of soft lead to form a long, cylindrical sinker. Also called a pencil weight. Cutting the lead from the coil allows the angler to determine exactly how much weight they want to use based on water depth and current speed. Most often used in moving water, slinky weights also hang up less frequently on rocky bottoms during the drift.

SLIP BOBBER/SLIP-FLOAT A float that slides freely on the main line or leader, and is stopped by a bobber stop. Slip bobbers slide down to the bottom of your line, making it easy to cast. Once they hit the water, the bait or jig sinks and the slip bobber will slide up to the stop, the placement of which determines how deep the jig or bait can sink.

SNAP Terminal tackle that's tied to the end of a line or leader that acts as a clasp, allowing you to quickly change lures or weights without having to cut and retie the line.

SNAP-WEIGHT A weight used in trolling that clips onto your line via a release clip. Snap weights aid in getting lures or bait rigs to the proper trolling depth, and are most commonly used in walleye fishing.

SOFT BAIT Any lure made from soft-plastic material.

SONAR An electronic system that uses transmitted and reflected underwater sound waves to detect and locate submerged objects or to measure the distance to the floor of a body of water. Depthfinders and fishfinders all use sonar.

SPEY CAST A style of flycasting that is used to cast a fly long distances when there is not enough backcast room behind the angler to execute a traditional overhand cast. Most popular on large rivers where one needs to cover a wide swath of water in one drift. Special rods are made just for this casting style.

SPIDER RIGGING A method of slow-trolling for crappies where 6 to 10 poles that can measure up to 16 feet in length are arranged in an arc around the front of the boat to present a lot of baits or small jigs at different depths simultaneously.

SPINNERBAIT Most often refers to a lure with a weighted head, a rubber skirt, and an L- or V-shaped arm extending over the back that holds the spinner blade. Popular because they can be run through thick cover without collecting weeds.

SPLIT RING A formed wire fastener shaped like a circle. Split rings are small versions of the rings commonly used on key chains. Split rings are used to attach hooks to eyelets on lures or as a line-tie on a lure.

SPLIT SHOT A small, round weight that is crimped directly onto a line or leader. Split shots are available in many sizes, and most are easily opened and closed with your fingers or pliers to allow weight to be added or removed quickly.

SPOOKY Referring to a fish or group of fish that is wary or easily startled by sounds, shadows, or movements.

SPOON A wobbling lure usually made from a single piece of curved metal.

STAGING Refers to the movements of a fish or to a larger group of fish prior to a change of location based on the season or spawning time. As an example, crappies stage along deep slopes for a few weeks until the water temperature is right for them to move to the shallows in order to spawn.

STAR-DRAG KNOB The star-shaped knob on a conventional reel used to tighten or loosen the drag.

STICKBAIT See *jerkbait*.

STINKBAIT A bait made by grinding natural or synthetic materials into a thick paste, or molding the ground paste into nuggets or chunks. Used in catfishing, stinkbaits are made with foul- or strong-smelling materials, such as garlic, animal blood, or rotten fish. They are supposed to attract catfish by slowly melting underwater and creating a scent trail the fish can follow to the bait.

STONEFLY A classification of water-borne insects that consists of over 3,500 species. Stoneflies are found in rivers, streams, ponds, and lakes throughout the U.S. and they are common trout and bass forage. Many fly variations are tied to mimic stoneflies, and, unlike caddis or mayflies, some stoneflies grow quite large.

STREAMER Any fly stripped below the surface to mimic forage that swims, such as baitfish, leeches, or crayfish.

STRIKE INDICATOR See *indicator*.

STRINGER A string or metal chain used to secure fish that will be kept for the table. The stringer can be left in the water while fishing to keep the fish cool and wet. When the trip is over, the stringer allows the angler to drag or carry out the day's catch.

STRIPPING BASKET A shallow rectangular container, similar in shape to a dish-washing tub, worn on a belt at the waist or stomach to hold loose fly line during the cast or retrieve to keep it from getting tangled on the ground or around your feet when wading in still waters.

STRIPPING GUIDE The first and widest guide on a fly rod, designed to allow easier intake of the fly line when stripping a streamer fly or fighting a fish by hand instead of using the reel.

SUCKER A common baitfish species found throughout the U.S. with an underslung mouth that feeds off the bottom using suction. Suckers are most often used live or dead for pike and muskies.

SUSPENDING LURE Any lure designed to maintain its position at a certain depth in the water column without sinking any deeper or rising to the surface.

SWIMBAIT A loose classification of hard and soft lures that usually mimic baitfish, but differ from standard crankbaits and jerkbaits. Many have a hard plastic head with a diving lip, but a soft-plastic paddle-shaped tail that kicks and vibrates during the retrieve. Many anglers use the term to describe a wide variety of soft-plastic shad imitations with molded, internal weights and kicking tails.

SWIVEL A piece of terminal tackle that features two eyelets on posts connected at a central barrel-shaped or cylindrical hub that allows the eyelets to rotate 360 degrees independently of each other. Swivels are most often used to connect the main line to a length of leader that will hold the hook or lure. They reduce line twist by allowing the lure or bait to spin without twisting the main line or leader.

TAILING LOOP When the leader and front section of fly line crashes into rear section of working fly line during a cast, causing knots and tangles and stopping your cast from fully unrolling. Tailing loops occur most often when making casts longer than 50 feet.

TAILWATER A river whose primary source is water released from the bottom of a reservoir. Tailwater rivers start at the base of dams, and since true tailwaters are formed by water released from the bottom of a reservoir instead of the top, they often maintain a consistent temperature year-round.

TANDEM RIG Any rig in fly or conventional fishing that allows the angler to present two baits, lures, or flies at the same time.

TEXAS RIG A method of rigging soft-plastic lures, where a sliding bullet weight is pegged at the node of the soft-plastic, typically rigged weedless style on a wide-gap hook.

THERMOCLINE A abrupt gradient in a large body of still water where layers of water of different temperatures stack on top of one another without mixing. As warmer water is less dense than cold water, the position of the thermocline can change throughout the season, but it will appear on a well-tuned fishfinder or depthfinder as a distinct band in the water column.

TIPPET A length of monofilament or fluorocarbon added to the end of a tapered fly leader to prolong its life by taking away the need to cut down the main leader every time a new fly is tied on. In most cases, the tippet material is the same diameter as the end of the main leader.

TIP-UP A wooden or plastic X-frame with a central post that features a line spool on the bottom of the post, and spring-activated flag on the top of the post. Used in ice fishing, the baited line is lowered into the hole to the desired depth, and then the tip-up is positioned over the hole with the spool end of the post in the water. The line is then connected to the spring-activated flag, which remains bent over until a fish strikes, causing the flag to pop up and alerting the angler to the bite.

TROLLING The act of imparting action to baits or lures by pulling them through the water behind a boat moving under engine or paddle power.

TROLLING MOTOR A small electric motor usually mounted to the bow of the boat that allows an angler to maneuver around fishing spots or into tight areas quietly and efficiently. Many have a foot pedal to allow the angler to keep casting while the boat is moving.

TROTLINE A long fishing line with many shorter lines spaced at uniform intervals attached along its length. Each short line has a hook tied to the end that's baited, and the ends of a trotline are usually held in place by two stakes stuck in bottom of a lake or river.

TUBE A style of soft-plastic lure with a hollow, bullet-shaped body that is shredded into thin strips at the rear to create a tail skirt.

TWITCHBAIT See *jerkbait*

WACKY RIG A style of rigging soft-plastic worms where the hook is passed perpendicularly through the center of the bait's body. This allows the worm to fall horizontally, and sharp twitches of the rod tip produce a fluttering action in which the body quickly flexes into a U shape and straightens again as the lure free falls.

WATER COLUMN Referring to the entire vertical plain of water from the bottom to the surface. If a fish is holding in the middle of the water column, it means it's hovering at a depth roughly half way between the surface and bottom.

WET FLY Any fly that mimics aquatic insects in their larval or emerger stages that is designed to fish below the surface. True wet flies are unweighted, though many flycasters rope nymphs into the wet fly category. Likewise, flies that imitate salmon eggs or worms could also be considered wet flies.

INDEX

ABOUT THE AUTHOR

Joe Cermele started his career in outdoor journalism in 2004, covering fishing tournaments for a local magazine in his home state of New Jersey. In 2005, while attending Rider University, he became an intern at *Salt Water Sportsman* magazine, joining the editorial staff full time that same year after graduation. In 2008, he moved to sister publication *Field & Stream*, where he was named Fishing Editor in 2011. His writing appears monthly in the magazine, he blogs weekly on the magazine's website, and also hosts and produces *Field & Stream's Hook Shots*, an award-winning web-based fishing show with a punk-rock edge. Cermele has fished all over the country and abroad, but when he's not traveling on assignment, you can find him on his boat chasing tuna and striped bass off the Jersey coast, pitching tubes to smallmouth bass on the Delaware River, or flyfishing for trout in New York's Catskill Mountains.

ABOUT THE MAGAZINE

In every issue of *Field & Stream* you'll find a lot of stuff: beautiful artwork and photography, adventure stories, wild game recipes, humor, reviews, commentary, and more. That mix is what makes the magazine so great and what's helped it remain relevant since 1895. But at the heart of every issue are the skills. The tips that explain how to use the right lure for every situation, the tactics that help you catch that trophy bass, the lessons that you'll pass on to your kids about the joy of fishing—those are the stories that readers have come to expect from *Field & Stream*.

You'll find a ton of those skills in *The Total Fishing Manual*, but there's not a book big enough to hold them all in one volume. Besides, whether you're new to fishing or an old pro, there's always more to learn. You can continue to expect *Field & Stream* to teach you those essential skills in every issue. Plus, there's all that other stuff in the magazine, too, which is pretty great. To order a subscription, visit www.fieldandstream.com/subscription.

ABOUT THE WEBSITE

When *Field & Stream* readers aren't hunting or fishing, they kill hours (and hours) on www.fieldandstream.com. And once you visit the site, you'll understand why.

First, if you enjoy the skills and opinions in this book, there's plenty more online—within our extensive archives of stories from the writers featured here as well as our network of 50,000-plus experts who can answer all of your questions about the outdoors.

At fieldandstream.com, you'll get to explore the world's largest online destination for hunters and anglers. Our blogs, written by the leading experts in the outdoors, cover every facet of hunting and fishing and provide constant content that instructs, enlightens, and always entertains. Our collection of adventure videos contains footage that's almost as thrilling to watch as it is to experience for real. And our photo galleries include the best wildlife and outdoor photography you'll find anywhere.

Perhaps best of all is the community you'll find online at fieldandstream.com. It's where you can argue with other readers about the best trout fly or the perfect venison chili recipe. It's where you can share photos of the fish you catch and the game you shoot. It's where you can enter contests to win guns, gear, and other great prizes.

And it's a place where you can spend a lot of time. Which is okay. Just make sure to reserve some hours for the outdoors, too.

FROM THE AUTHOR

I'd like to thank Kevin Toyama, Allister Fein, Conor Buckley, Mariah Bear, and the entire staff at Weldon Owen for—once again—making the process of putting a book together seamless and stress-free. A special thanks goes out to *Field & Stream* Managing Editor Jean McKenna for compiling all the stellar fishing articles from the last few years in the magazine, without which this second edition could not be possible. I'd also like to thank all the exceptional photographers who lent their work to the pages, particularly my good friend Tim Romano. Finally, I owe a great debt of gratitude to all the magazine contributors who, like me, appreciate a great fish story or a great tip and soak them in when they're on assignment to provide such cutting-edge fishing information to our readers. This book could not have come to fruition without them.

CREDITS

All articles by Joe Cermele, with the following exceptions: *Jace Bauserman*: 288; *Will Brantley*: 152, 195, 290; *C.J. Chivers*: 210; *Kirk Deeter*: 55, 61-62, 65, 70, 72-74, 80, 141, 225-227, 230, 236, 241, 245, 257, 267; *David Draper*: 79, 198; *Ben Duchesney*: 163, 190, 192, 311; *Gary Edwards*: 305; *Jimmy Fee*: 29, 244, 285; *Paul Fling*: 142; *Mark Hicks*: 12, 15, 44, 48-49, 115-116, 127, 130, 149-151, 157, 166, 189, 203, 249-251, 253, 255, 266, 287, 289; *Mark Hicks, Steve Price & Don Wirth*: 118, 122-123, 128-129, 132-133, 254, 261, 263, 273; *Steven Hill*: 124; *Dave Hurteau*: 52, 175, 262; *Mark E. Jackson*: 76; *M.D. Johnson*: 20, 23, 30; *Colin Kearns*: 18, 75; *Tom Keer*: 32; *John Larison*: 140; *Ted Leeson*: 136, 144, 219, 229; *Peter B. Mathiesen*: 8, 39; *Keith McCafferty*: 31, 197; *Aaron Melvin*: 300; *John Merwin*: 1, 9, 11, 40-42, 47, 51, 53-54, 59-60, 64, 104, 117, 185, 188, 194, 268, 283; *Mark Modoski*: 13, 21, 87, 121, 146, 183; *T. Edward Nickens*: 34, 38, 57, 99, 138, 184, 191, 242-243; *Curtis Niedermier*: 153; *Steve Price*: 6, 135, 264, 272; *Lawrence Pyne*: 14; *Ross Robertson*: 165, 258, 276; *Jerome B. Robinson*: 3-5, 7, 19, 25, 33, 69, 85, 93, 95, 97-98, 105, 256; *Will Ryan*: 24, 26, 58, 110, 139, 169, 172-173, 186, 234, 240, 274; *Michael R. Shea*: 164; *Tom Tiberio*: 168; *Noel Vick*: 154, 158, 160; *Slaton L. White*: 107, 145; *Don Wirth*: 100-102, 106, 147, 199-201, 232, 235, 270, 278, 286, 292

Photographs courtesy of: *Rick Adair*: 290; *Barry and Cathy Beck*: 291 (4, 5); *Booyah Bait Company*: 123; *Joe Cermele*: Author Intro, TOC 2-3, Tactics Intro (RHP), 2 (A-C, E-H), 14, 26, 36, 81, 89, 90, 120, 132, 134, 137, 148, 149, 157, 159, 171, 175, 179, 180, 199, 203, 208-209, 211, 217, 223, 230, 247, 265, 275, 277, 282, 293, 295, 298, 301, 310, 313; *Philip Colla*: 217 (fish); *Eric Engbretson Underwater Photography*: 35, 84, 88, 94, 109, 131, 161, 174, 182, 221, 228, 232, 245, 249, 253, 261, 267, 279, 287, 302, 304; *Flambeau Outdoors*: 37; *Jay Fleming*: 309; *Cliff Gardner & John Keller*: 9, 10, 59, 78, 113, 122, 130, 135, 262, 273; *Chris Gotz*: 280; *Brian Grossenbacher*: 86, 146, 190, 192, 219; *Todd Huffman*: 1 (w/ exception of curly tail grub); *Humminbird*: 85; *Dave Hurteau*: Foreword; *iStock*: 24, 107, 210, 316; *Alexander Ivanov*: 1 (curly tail grub), 27, 43 (bullet weights), 49, 67-68, 118; *Alberto Knie*: 308, 314; *Johanna Lazaro*: 16 (waxworm); *Bill Lindner*: 87, 183, 188, 260, 291 (2, 3), 292; *Phil McLaughlin*: 173; *Ted Morrison*: 76; *Jens Mortensen*: 75; *Luke Nilsson*: 77, 258; *Northland Fishing Tackle*: 172 (jig-and-worm); *Pradaco Fishing*: 172 (surface plug); *Rapala Fishing Lures*: Cover, 172 (w/exception of jig-and-worm and surface plug); *Travis Rathbone*: Title page, 8 (lure), 12, 79, 114; *Capt. Ross Robertson*: 83, 164; *Tim Romano*: Title spread, Tools Intro, 64, Techniques Intro, 143, Tactics Intro (LHP), 234, 238, 244, 246; *Jeff Rotman/Getty Images*: 210; *Dan Saelinger*: 18 (cables), 19, 44 (sinkers), 54, 57, 61, 104, 176, 184, 207 (creature bait), 211, 315; *Shutterstock*: TOC 1, 2 (D), 3-6, 8 (fisherman), 16 (w/exception of fathead, golden shiner, waxworm), 18 (worm), 23, 24, 31 (notebook), 33-34, 39, 41, 45, 47, 62, 65 (fish), 69-70, 73-74, 79, 80, 92-93, 95, 97, 102, 105-106, 119 (fish), 144 (fish), 152, 161, 162, 168-169, 177, 185, 207 (w/exception of creature bait), 217 (boats), 220, 263, 286, 291 (1), 294, 297, 299, 302, 305-306, 312; *Lawrence Taylor/Lurenet.com*: 314; *Uland Thomas*: 16 (fathead, golden shiner); *Kyle Thompson*: 63; *Umpqua Feather Merchants*: 55, 65 (flies), 144 (flies); *Kirby Wilson*: 317; *Windigo Images/Aaron Stortz*: 281

Illustrations courtesy of: *Conor Buckley*: 7, 29, 32, 76, 91, 99, 111, 115, 117, 124, 129, 136, 142, 145, 154, 158, 167, 202, 227, 246, 254, 264, 269, 279, 300, 303; *Liberum Donum*: 311; *Hayden Foell*: 19, 31, 53, 55, 62, 95, 107, 116, 138, 150-151, 160, 173, 189, 193-194, 204, 213-216, 274, 276, 278, 287, 290, 296, 302; *Kevin Hand*: 240; *Ryan Kirby*: 288; *Jason Lee*: 70, 157, 164, 181, 225; *Dan Marsiglio*: 17, 52, 72, 140-141; *Samuel A. Minick*: 125-126, 155, 235, 248, 266, 291; *Chris Philpot*: 12, 18, 240; *Robert L. Prince*: 28, 58, 75, 128, 178, 186, 272; *Paula Rogers*: 38, 48, 123, 127, 205-206, 208, 226, 268, 283-284; *Steve Sanford*: 108; *Jason Schneider*: 163, 285; *Pete Sucheski*: 9, 21, 184; *Mike Sudal*: 153, 168, 176, 197, 198, 212, 229, 231, 237, 241, 243, 250, 259, 270; *Bryon Thompson*: 11, 51, 178; *Lauren Towner*: 43, 50, 66, 96, 100, 133, 195, 200-201, 217, 236, 239, 251, 253, 255-256, 269, 307

weldon**owen**

PRESIDENT & PUBLISHER Roger Shaw
SVP, SALES & MARKETING Amy Kaneko
FINANCE MANAGER Philip Paulick
ASSOCIATE PUBLISHER Mariah Bear
PROJECT EDITOR Rob James
ASSOCIATE EDITOR Ian Cannon
CREATIVE DIRECTOR Kelly Booth
ART DIRECTOR William Mack
DESIGNER Allister Fein
ILLUSTRATION COORDINATOR Conor Buckley
PRODUCTION DIRECTOR Chris Hemesath
PRODUCTION MANAGER Michelle Duggan

Weldon Owen would also like to thank Amy Bauman,
Laura Harger, Andrew Joron, Katie Schlossberg, and
Marisa Solis for editorial assistance, and Lucas Aldrich
for administrative help.

© 2013 Weldon Owen International
1150 Brickyard Cove Road
Richmond, CA 94801
www.weldonowen.com

Field & Stream is a division of Bonnier

ISBN: 978-1-68188-263-5

Library of Congress Control Number
on file with the publisher.
Originally published in 2013 (ISBN: 978-1-61628-487-9)

13 12 11 10
2024 2023 2022 2021 2020
Printed in China

FIELD & STREAM

EXECUTIVE VICE PRESIDENT Eric Zinczenko
EDITOR-IN-CHIEF Anthony Licata
EXECUTIVE EDITOR Mike Toth
MANAGING EDITOR Jean McKenna
DEPUTY EDITORS Dave Hurteau, Colin Kearns,
Slaton L. White
COPY CHIEF Donna L. Ng
SENIOR EDITOR Joe Cermele
ASSISTANT EDITOR Kristyn Brady
DESIGN DIRECTOR Sean Johnston
PHOTOGRAPHY DIRECTOR John Toolan
DEPUTY ART DIRECTOR Pete Sucheski
ASSOCIATE ART DIRECTORS Kim Gray,
James A. Walsh
PRODUCTION MANAGER Judith Weber
DIGITAL DIRECTOR Nate Matthews
ONLINE CONTENT EDITOR David Maccar
ONLINE PRODUCER Kurt Shulitz
ASSISTANT ONLINE EDITOR Martin Leung

2 Park Avenue
New York, NY 10016
www.fieldandstream.com